ABOLISH THE MONARCHY

www.penguin.co.uk

# Abolish the Monarchy

*Why We Should and How We Will*

GRAHAM SMITH

PENGUIN BOOKS

TRANSWORLD PUBLISHERS
Penguin Random House, One Embassy Gardens,
8 Viaduct Gardens, London sw11 7bw
www.penguin.co.uk

Transworld is part of the Penguin Random House group of companies
whose addresses can be found at global.penguinrandomhouse.com

Penguin
Random House
UK

First published in Great Britain in 2023 by Torva
an imprint of Transworld Publishers
Penguin paperback edition published 2024

A CIP catalogue record for this book
is available from the British Library.

ISBN
9781804992272

Typeset in 10.93/14.25pt Granjon LT Std by Jouve (UK), Milton Keynes.
Printed and bound in Great Britain by Clays Ltd, Elcograf S.p.A.

The authorized representative in the EEA is Penguin Random House Ireland,
Morrison Chambers, 32 Nassau Street, Dublin D02 YH68.

Penguin Random House is committed to a sustainable
future for our business, our readers and our planet. This book
is made from Forest Stewardship Council® certified paper.

For Mum and Dad

# Contents

Preface to the Paperback Edition     xi
Introduction     1

PART ONE: WHAT IS IT GOOD FOR?     7

1. But What About the Tourism?     9
2. Schrödinger's Monarch     35

PART TWO: IF IT'S BROKE, DON'T FIX IT     63

3. Wrong in Principle, Wrong in Practice     65
4. Out of Touch, Out of Time     111
5. A Constitution Fit for a King     153

PART THREE: ABOLISH THE MONARCHY     181

6. The Imagination to Change     183
7. A Democracy We Can Be Proud Of     217

Acknowledgements     249
Index     255

# ABOLISH THE MONARCHY

# Preface to the Paperback Edition

On the morning of Charles's coronation, as I prepared to exercise my right to protest on Trafalgar Square, I was arrested along with seven of my colleagues. I hadn't committed any crime, of course. In fact, I'd been discussing our plans with the police quite amicably for four months. When a detective came to my cell door at around one p.m. that day, I told him what I thought about my unlawful detention. The officer replied, with some sympathy, 'If it makes you feel any better, you're on the news all around the world.'

By that time, the book you are holding had already gone to press. My republican colleagues and I were all too aware that the coronation had the potential to be a PR coup for the royals, securing their future for another generation. Charles could have embraced modernity, made peace with his youngest son and stripped his brother of his remaining titles. He could have insisted on a low-key ceremony, one that recognized the huge social and cultural changes that have shaped this country over the previous seventy years. Instead, in the first few months of 2023, as the sight of yellow 'Not My King' placards became commonplace at Charles's public outings, it was increasingly apparent that change was not on the agenda.

It was clear Charles had no interest in innovation – what he wanted was a coronation like his mother's in 1953 – at an estimated cost of between £100 million and £250 million. Yet we are no longer in the days of grainy black and white images, broadcast on the only television channel available, images that conjured up a link with a bygone age. Instead, Charles was embracing obscure traditions in the era of high-definition TV and social media. From the peculiar costumes to a baffling religious ceremony, all this was presented to a public who were able to respond instantaneously. And indeed they did, with incredulity, ridicule and disinterest.

Here was a very ordinary man from a very ordinary family, one with their hands deep in our pockets during a cost-of-living crisis, demanding the nation doff their collective cap without noticing that we are living in a more democratic age, where deference is rapidly dying out. This stark contrast between the view looking out from the palace, and the world looking in was thrown into sharp relief by the bizarre suggestion that those watching the coronation at home could swear a 'people's oath'.

Truth be told, as awful as it was to be arrested that day – locked up in a police cell for sixteen hours, having never committed a crime – knowing that the world had been told about our arrests did lift my spirits. It was only later that I learned just how widely the story had been reported, and the impact it had on the debate about the monarchy and the right to protest.

It's become increasingly obvious that a lot of people don't care about the monarchy, but they assume everyone else does, because that's how it is portrayed in much of the media. Crucially, they also believe the monarchy is harmless. Yet on the day of the coronation people saw an institution intolerant of dissent, its acolytes apparently happy to put innocent people behind bars, to defend the police action on the grounds of there being 'a time and a place' for protest. The Met police declared the coronation a 'special day' on which they would, in the words of Commissioner Mark Rowley, have a 'low tolerance' of protest. The footage of arrests and police harassment of protesters that poured out from Trafalgar Square and the Mall jarred sharply with the image of a benign, harmless and occasionally amusing relic.

It wasn't just the palpable public outrage at the unlawful arrest of peaceful protesters before we had even begun protesting. Nor was it the sudden stratospheric boost to Republic's profile. Although under-reported, throughout 2023 there was a seismic shift in the fortunes of the republican movement, and public attitudes toward the monarchy.

2023 began with scandal – fresh accusations and revelations from Harry's book *Spare*. It also ended with scandal – further revelations found in newly released documents from the Epstein trial in Florida. The royals stood accused of racism, bullying and indifference to the difficulties faced by Harry and Meghan. Andrew stood accused of the sexual abuse of underage girls both in London and on Epstein's island home. The months between were peppered with tales of royal extravagance, tax avoidance and a massive 45 per cent increase of the Sovereign Grant, rising from £86 million to £125 million while people faced crises in housing, schools, the NHS, and even feeding their families. News that Charles, now the Duke of Lancaster, was taking money from the estates of those who died on his land, to spend on the upkeep of his own homes, soured the public's view of him still further.

The polls vary, but the pattern was clear. Four months after the death of the Queen, most people still fell into two camps: the minority who were excited by the coronation (9 per cent according to a YouGov poll published in April 2023), and the majority who simply weren't interested. Yet most continued to support the retention of the monarchy over abolition, if only because apathy breeds inertia. Yet, by the end of the year, those preferring to keep the monarchy over an elected head of state had fallen below fifty per cent for the first time.

The monarchy may now be in serious trouble. A Savanta poll, asking if people preferred a monarch or an elected head of state, put the royals on 57 per cent in May 2023. By November the same question asked by Savanta and YouGov put them on 52 per cent. By January 2024 Savanta had the monarchy down to 48 per cent, while YouGov put them on 45 per cent. By these polls, at least, the monarchy had lost its claim to popular support, and the question of its future was no longer a settled issue.

Unlike a political party or a listed company, the royals don't have the option of refreshing personnel, or reinventing who they are. Charles and Camilla, William and Kate are all they have, and all they will have for years to come. The institution is resistant to serious reform, and anyway, what reform could they countenance that wouldn't lead to a further erosion of support? Opening up their archives would expose them to fresh scandal; cutting back on spending might give them some respite, but their finances are so out of kilter with modern expectations that it's hard to imagine them foregoing their luxuries. As for their PR, their armoury is empty. 2023 was the year they threw everything at the task of shoring up their support, from costly parades to fawning documentaries shamefully broadcast by the BBC. Yet with all that effort spent, their support continued to decline.

The monarchy is trapped, in a way. They may feel that exposure is how they will win back the support and interest of the public. Yet it appears to have the opposite effect in a more cynical age. Photo opportunities are often derided, involvement with charities often met with charges of hypocrisy or cynical use of good causes for royal PR. The problem is their most sycophantic cheerleaders demand exposure and seem to think hyperbole is the answer. Yet the more shrill and obsequious the headlines, the more people see royalism as something strange and disconnected from the real world the rest of us live in.

At the House of Commons Home Affairs committee two weeks after the coronation, where I was asked to give evidence on the policing of protests, Tim Loughton MP asked me: 'Can you tell me what you and your organization hoped to achieve on the day of the coronation?'

'We wanted to use the opportunity to get our message across,' I replied, 'which is that in a democracy we should have an election instead of a coronation. Instead of being told, "It is going to be Charles", we ought to have a choice about our head of state. We wanted to be very clear in front of the world's cameras that we are not a nation of royalists.'

The arrests certainly amplified that message, against the backdrop of a monarchy rapidly falling out of favour with the public. A year on and a third of the country now prefer an elected head of state. As many as a quarter 'don't know' which they prefer according to the polls, while the monarchy has lost its claim to popular support. All of which tells us one thing: now is the time to talk about the democratic alternative. After all, if monarchy really is the best system, why would they arrest their critics instead of having an honest, robust and informed debate?

# Introduction

In June 2021, I headed to the hallowed halls of the Oxford Union debating society. I was there to debate the future of the monarchy. In this rarefied atmosphere, where countless prime ministers, statesmen and diplomats have supposedly cut their oratorical teeth, I was to debate the simple proposition: 'This House Would Abolish the Monarchy.' Arriving in a world inhabited by people who take their place in society for granted, where black tie is worn as comfortably as a football shirt, I had expected robust opposition. The air of confidence was present, but the debate was unimaginative and often ill-informed. I've had a version of this debate many times before, and the quality here was no better than at any other venue or society I have visited. I found myself hearing the same superficial, implausible and – in some cases – slightly bizarre arguments for retaining this creaking, corrupting institution. The speakers were capable and at times entertaining, although royal commentator and author Anna Pasternak managed to shock the hall into silence with her reimagining of the poem 'First They Came . . .' with the words, 'First they came for the royals, and I did nothing.' Peter Hitchens espoused his unique view as a self-proclaimed monarchist who doesn't like the royals. The most measured voice against the motion was that of Lieutenant General David Leakey, former director general of the European Military Staff and former Black Rod. But even Leakey struggled to say more than, 'It's there, why change?'

I've never heard a good argument for the monarchy, so I shouldn't have been surprised. In twenty years of campaigning for its abolition, I've not once heard an argument that isn't wrong in fact or in principle – sometimes both. Some of the most common points raised by monarchists are often the weakest. Whether it's the claim the monarchy is good for tourism, the notion that it unites the country or the suggestion that it does no harm – it's easy to demonstrate that these simply aren't true.

It isn't just dogmatic defenders of the Crown who resort to feeble arguments against the case for a republic. More thoughtful commentators also repeat these claims. Perhaps monarchists believe the monarchy sells itself, and doesn't require much hard work from its supporters. That looked like a miscalculation when I took part in a debate in Bath in 2012, held a week after the Diamond Jubilee weekend. An audience of more than one hundred people went from passing a vote in favour of the monarchy at the start of the evening to voting overwhelmingly for a republic ninety minutes later.

Roy Hattersley, the former deputy leader of the Labour Party and a committed republican, once said that the problem with monarchy is that it makes normally sensible people do and say silly things. This has been proven to be true time and again, no more so than during major royal celebrations. As the horses trotted out for the equestrian leg of the Platinum Jubilee in June 2022, the presenter Alan Titchmarsh gushed on air that 'our identity, heart and soul is embodied by Her Majesty the Queen', adding that the Queen was in some way comparable to Nelson Mandela.

Writing a couple of days later in the *i* newspaper, liberal commentator Ian Dunt came out for the monarchy in the most preposterous terms, reciting more of those tired old clichés and misrepresenting the republican case ('opponents act like it's some kind of harbinger of fascism'). In his article, Dunt claims that the monarchy is 'working perfectly well' but declined to elaborate on how. This is particularly striking given the secrecy, corruption and abuse of office that is rife – and increasingly made public – within the royal household. The system fails to afford us any choice in head of state that might reflect the huge social and cultural changes that have taken place in Britain over the last seventy years, let alone those which will take place over the next seventy. Dunt frets over the possibility of elections for head of state, insisting that the position 'must not, under any circumstances, be democratic'. Yet while he makes the common error of pointing to other European monarchies as proof that our own is no detriment to progress, he ignores the very successful democratic republics across Europe, in which the head of state is directly or, in the case of Germany, indirectly elected.

As Thomas Paine once said, 'A long habit of not thinking a thing wrong, gives it a superficial appearance of being right.' Perhaps that is the problem here. People assume there must be good reasons why we have a monarchy and so try to flesh out what those reasons might be, not wanting to look too closely at the alternative for fear of realizing long habit has led them astray.

Coming from a point of ignorance makes it much easier for royalists to defend the monarchy with confidence, reciting arguments they believe will knock us republicans out of the contest. They'll tell you the positives of monarchy include the hard work and sense of duty of the royals, their contribution to charity, and a head of state who is above politics, while the institution protects our history, traditions and boosts our economy via tourism. These arguments suggest a lack of seriousness in debating one of our key national institutions. But they also betray a lack of confidence in ourselves and our fellow citizens. Royalist claims highlight a failure of imagination about how much better things could be, if only we ditched an archaic, corrupt and secretive institution that, in the words of Ian Dunt, claims a near-monopoly on our national sense of belonging and identity.

For most people, it isn't a consideration of these arguments that prompts them to tell pollsters that they want to keep the monarchy. Rather it is something closer to indifference, buttressed by three common assumptions: it is profitable; everyone else likes it; and it does no real harm. Again, popular support, as with the support from more informed speakers, comes from that long habit of not thinking a thing wrong. But here's the problem: none of those assumptions about the monarchy are true. It isn't profitable, it does us harm and, while most people – for now – are happy to keep the monarchy, they don't care for it when pressed.

However, the need for a republic is clear. The monarchy is bad for Britain. It stands in opposition to our most cherished values and proudest traditions. As an institution, the royal household falls well short of the standards we should expect from public bodies. Standing at the centre of Britain's ramshackle constitution, the Crown damages our democracy, gets in the way of reform and leaves us without an effective head of state or meaningful checks and balances.

The alternative, far from being the unknown, mythic and terrifying notion imagined by royalists, is simple, democratic and tried and tested across Europe and around the world. It is a parliamentary democracy similar to what we have today, but transformed into a political system that is principled, genuinely democratic throughout, transparent and accountable. It is a system that in places like Ireland, Iceland, Germany and Finland, to name just a few, has provided not only stable and effective government, but also some exceptional and inspirational heads of state. All of these countries have transitioned either from monarchies or authoritarian regimes, quickly establishing constitutions which provide effective institutions that have, for the most part, stood the test of time.

We can learn from our neighbours and allies not only what works, but how that transition can be made. The journey to a parliamentary republic is far simpler for Britain than the huge cultural and political shifts that some countries made during the 1990s, after the collapse of communism. Yet this isn't about importing ideas from abroad. It is about learning from Britain's own political experience and traditions and creating a republic that we all have a stake in.

It is something we can, should and – in my view – will do.

## PART ONE

# WHAT IS IT GOOD FOR?

# I.

# But What About the Tourism?

One sunny day during the hot summer of 2022 I took my two nephews, Alex (fourteen) and Michael (twelve), to visit Parliament, before lunch, and Buckingham Palace in the afternoon. Parliament of course is not a museum, but a working building that, aside from the two chambers, the House of Commons and the House of Lords, caters for more than fourteen hundred parliamentarians, many more advisers and researchers and more than three thousand employees. Even so, the Palace of Westminster makes a good stab at providing an engaging and informative tour, explaining how Parliament works – baffling and archaic as it is – and allowing tourists to walk through both chambers, as well as see all the historic halls and corridors where power has been exercised and great debates held for hundreds of years.* After a quick lunch in the café, and the purchase of Speaker Hoyle's single malt, we made our way down Whitehall, across Horse Guards Parade and through St James's Park to Buckingham Palace, which has been the

---

\* Although, of course, the current Houses of Parliament date back only to the mid-nineteenth century, built after a devastating fire that left just Westminster Hall standing.

symbolic home of the British monarchy for the past two hundred years.*

In stark contrast, Buckingham Palace is surprisingly lacking in real insight into the contemporary monarchy or its history. Walking around, you are invited to bask in the bright dazzle of eighteenth- and nineteenth-century opulence, while being recited one set of numbers after another. Over 1,000 clocks across 775 rooms, including 52 principal bedrooms and 19 state rooms, 100 candles and 43 floral arrangements for a state banquet, more than 50,000 people visiting each year as guests to dinners, investitures and garden parties.

The interior is impressive, the rooms decked out in gold leaf and intricate friezes, each depicting a scene or theme from Britain's history, real and mythical. Yet as we progressed from one room to the next, our audio guides seemed constrained in what they could tell us. There were no unexpected insights into life at the palace, or the history of the institution it had been home to for two centuries.

In one dining room we were treated to the unspectacular revelation that it would be used to entertain guests, whether they be individuals or groups. You might forgive them for not having too much to say about one of the many dining rooms, but perhaps they could offer more than thirty-three seconds of commentary on the Throne Room, or say more about the art collection on display in the Picture Gallery, beyond commenting that the pictures on display – which included works by Rubens, Rembrandt, Canaletto and Parmigianino – were collected over

---

\* The actual headquarters of the House of Windsor is St James's Palace, a short walk back along the Mall, which is why diplomats are appointed to the Court of St James.

the centuries by a succession of kings and queens. I imagine most visitors would take that as read and might like to know more about the pictures they were looking at.* Away from the Picture Gallery, most of the paintings appear to be of former monarchs, their consorts and an assortment of long-forgotten minor royals and elderly aristocrats.

As we were encouraged to make speedy progress through the state rooms, one recurring theme was the impact on the palace interior of John Nash, the eighteenth- and nineteenth-century architect also responsible for Marble Arch, Regent Street and the Royal Pavilion in Brighton. It is perhaps appropriate that Nash was also a theatre designer, as Buckingham Palace certainly gives the impression more of theatrics than substance. Nothing much was said about work done or accomplishments achieved.

Heading towards the exit, we glimpsed the one room where anything of any constitutional or political significance happens. Just off the Bow Room, which leads out into the back garden, is the 1844 Room (named after the year of the state visit of Tsar Nicholas I), where audiences with the King are held, as well as meetings of the Privy Council. Unfortunately, the room is inaccessible. Visitors can only catch a brief glimpse through open doors, while being given a rather sanitized explanation of the Privy Council's function.

As one Tripadvisor review comments, it's nice if you like the Queen! And that's a real shame, because the palace has been witness to two hundred years of history and is the home of an institution that has had an immense impact on Britain's – and

---

* Most of the royal art collection is locked away, but there are more works on display at the Royal Art Collection galleries in London and Edinburgh.

Europe's – story, not to mention the countless societies decimated by slavery and empire. Rather than reflect on this rich and complex history, the monarchs and their lives, or the intrigues and constitutional developments that swirled around them, a visit to the palace will only tell you about the historically irrelevant trivialities of the current monarch's reign – and how many cups and saucers they own. It's an underwhelming experience. You'll probably say, 'Well, he would think that.' But in a sense, I'm the target audience. I'm fascinated with history and, as a campaigning republican, more interested than most in the history of the royal household. But Buckingham Palace makes little effort to share its history with visitors beyond the most superficial details.

Three weeks earlier I had taken Michael and Alex to see the Tower of London. Visit the Tower, a royal palace that hasn't been occupied by the royals for centuries, and you can see the lost potential of Buckingham Palace. It grabs your interest and holds on to it for hours, giving you a detailed and entertaining insight into its many layers of history, from medieval castle to Tudor palace to twentieth-century prison. We enjoyed it so much that we were still there at closing time and missed our chance to walk down the road where we had intended to climb to the top of the Monument.

All this might explain why, according to figures from the Association of Leading Visitor Attractions and from the royal palaces, the Tower of London ranks number eight in the 2019[*] list of top tourist attractions in the UK, while Buckingham Palace ranks just sixty-seventh. Kensington Palace, which is still occupied by a number of royals, ranks seventy-sixth. Windsor

---

[*]  I've used figures from 2019 only because it's the last full pre-pandemic year.

Castle does much better, although at number twenty-two it is still eleven points behind Legoland Windsor. It's hard to avoid the conclusion that it's the history and the monuments that interest tourists, not the royals or the contemporary monarchy.

This is an important distinction that often gets missed: our culture and heritage are good for tourism but the monarchy itself isn't. Not only do the current royals not draw the crowds in the way Henry VIII does, but their need to limit access and carefully manage their image leaves contemporary royal sites lagging far behind their historic counterparts. Buckingham Palace doesn't pull the tourists in as much as it should, which is a shame because it has all the potential to be one of our nation's greatest attractions.

## The Tourism Myth

It is strange that a book about democratic reform should have anything to say about the UK's tourism industry. Stranger, perhaps, that this is the opening topic. Unfortunately, the idea that the monarchy is good for tourism – and for the wider economy – is so pervasive and, for many, so persuasive, that it is the first point that needs to be tackled.

Even in the face of the direst scandal or criticism, the reply still comes back, 'But what about tourism?' The choices and habits of tourists should not inform crucial decisions about our democracy and constitution. But even if they did, the tourism claim is simply not true. There is no evidence that the monarchy makes any difference to the UK's economy or tourism industry.

Despite that, the view that Britain's economy would suffer a significant downturn should the monarchy be abolished is so commonplace that it is repeated ad nauseam. 'Look at the crowds outside Buckingham Palace, look at the jubilee and weddings!' Yet on any given day you'll see the same crowds, often bigger, outside Parliament, on Trafalgar Square and along the South Bank, not to mention the millions of visitors to Bath, Eryri,* Edinburgh Castle or Chester Zoo (which attracts approximately three times as many visitors each year as Buckingham Palace). The numbers filling up the Mall for the Platinum Jubilee may have looked impressive, but they were dwarfed by the million-plus crowds drawn to the capital by London Pride or the Notting Hill Carnival.

VisitBritain, the UK's leading tourism body, didn't help matters when, during the run-up to the 2011 wedding of William and Kate, it put out a statement saying that the event would boost Britain's tourism. This sounded like good news for a country still recovering from the economic shock of the 2008 crash, but sadly – again – it simply wasn't true.

After reading the statement by VisitBritain, I sent them a freedom of information request, asking for any documents or communications relating to the drafting of their press release. What came back was an email from the group's head of research and forecasting, David Edwards, addressed to their press office, in which he flatly contradicted the claim that the wedding would be a boon for tourism. Edwards pointed out that in July 1981, when Charles and Diana married, foreign visits were down 15 per cent on the same period every other year from 1980 to 1985. In his email he added:

---

* Snowdonia. The national park officially adopted its Welsh name in 2022.

If we look at the marriage of Andrew and Sarah in July 1986 we find that across the year as a whole there were 4% fewer visitors to Britain than in 1985, but that in July [1986] there were 8% fewer than in July of 1985 [. . .] While this and the results relating to 1981 are inconclusive, such as it is, the evidence points to royal weddings having a negative impact on inbound tourism.

In their press coverage at the time, Sandie Dawe, then CEO of VisitBritain, also claimed that 'Britain's monarchy generates well over £500m a year directly and indirectly from overseas tourists'. Republic, the campaign group of which I'm CEO, challenged this claim and asked to meet with Dawe and the chair of VisitBritain, Christopher Rodrigues. We were rebuffed until the *Guardian* carried the story about their research department's assessment of previous royal weddings. At that point I was invited, along with a colleague, to sit down with Dawe and Rodrigues to discuss the claims VisitBritain was making. Our problem with the £500 million figure, I explained, was that it was nothing more than the total ticket sales of all heritage sites in the UK with even a passing connection to the monarchy. This included St Paul's Cathedral, one of the most iconic landmarks in the UK. Surely, they weren't suggesting tourists visited St Paul's because the royals held a wedding there three decades earlier?

My point was simple. You can't conclude that these ticket sales for heritage sites are the result of the continued existence of the monarchy. They seemed to readily accept this point and the obvious conclusion drawn from the evidence produced by their own research department – royal weddings don't boost tourism. As the meeting ended, I wanted to raise another, broader point with the heads of VisitBritain: there is no evidence that in the event of the monarchy being abolished tourism revenue would fall. Rodrigues replied quite emphatically that he agreed – no such evidence existed.

Today the refrain 'But what about tourism?' is often the first line of defence. Given the widespread belief in the royal tourism claim, set against the complete lack of evidence to support it, it's worth considering how it came to be so prevalent in the public debate about the monarchy. There was a time that public discussion on abolishing the monarchy was more limited, and what discussion there was tended to focus on monarchy as a constitutional bedrock, rather than any notion that it might generate a profit.* Two critical books on the subject of the monarchy, Kingsley Martin's *The Crown and The Establishment*, published in 1963, and Willie Hamilton's *My Queen and I*, published in 1975, make no mention of tourism. Yet by the 1980s, the notion of the profitable monarchy had become commonplace, with Edgar Wilson, in his 1989 book *The Myth of British Monarchy*, listing the tourism dividend as one of the key myths that needed to be rebutted. Hamilton hints at an early shift in attitudes when he retells the sorry saga of Prince Philip crying poor during a TV interview in the US in 1969. In that broadcast, the prince suggested the royals would be 'in the red' the following year, a comment that triggered a heated debate back home. Three years later, the Heath government was setting the 1972 Civil List, the annual grant paid to the monarch to cover official expenses, prompting more public debate about the cost of the royals to the taxpayer. It was around this time that the link between tourism and royals appears to have emerged.

---

\*    That said, the notion that the monarchy helps international trade goes back much further, but specific claims about tourism appear to be a fairly recent invention.

In late 1977, just two months after the Silver Jubilee, the *Daily Mirror* reported that, 'Tourists have poured an estimated £3,000 million (£3 billion) into Britain in this Jubilee year.' The brief article made no mention of whether there was any connection between the income and the jubilee, but simply allowed readers to draw that conclusion. A year later, former Labour MP and then journalist Woodrow Wyatt, bemoaning critics of another Civil List increase in his *Sunday Mirror* column, asked: 'Why do we earn so much from tourism in Britain?', adding: 'Not because of our lousy climate and worse restaurants. It is because millions of foreigners want to see living history in action. Destroy the Queen and we add several hundreds of millions to our balance of payments deficit.' While sometimes dismissed as eccentric, Wyatt was not a stupid man. Yet he made these claims without any evidence to support them, in order to see off a perceived danger to a monarchy he keenly supported.

Throughout the 1970s and 1980s, Britain faced rising unemployment, recession and deep social divisions. Against this backdrop we were treated to royal spectacles of a jubilee in 1977 and two big royal weddings, Charles and Diana in 1981 and Andrew and Sarah Ferguson in 1986. By the time we reached the 1990s, the scene was set for public outrage at the suggestion, made swiftly and unapologetically by the Secretary of State for National Heritage, Peter Brooke, that the taxpayer would pick up the repair bill after a devastating fire at Windsor Castle. The taxpayer baulked at such a suggestion and a year later Buckingham Palace was opened to tourists for the first time, in the hope of raising funds for the restoration, while the Queen agreed to pay income tax (although how much, we don't know).

A decade later and Buckingham Palace began publishing their accounts annually, rather than every ten years. With changing public attitudes and greater access to the financial records of the monarchy, it was clear that some effort had to be made to excuse the extravagant and wasteful costs of the royal household (which we will explore later on). So, the palace and its cheerleaders insisted that spending tens of millions of pounds on palatial homes for a dozen or so royals was a good investment in UK plc.

It was Roy Hattersley who spotted the way things were headed. Writing in the *Guardian* in 2005, Hattersley pointed out that the basis of monarchy was not cost, but divine right. 'A queen who imagines that she is personally ordained by the Almighty does not bother about the cost of an occasional journey by royal train.' Resorting to suggestions that this was a 'value-for-money monarchy' cheapens the institution in more ways than one, reducing it to a financial transaction in which extravagance is offset by income. With the palace in no mood to cut its costs, royalists instead needed to tell people that it put money in their pocket. Yet, as Hattersley concluded: 'Once the monarchy feels it necessary to justify its existence in prosaic terms, the argument for monarchy collapses.'

With deference on the decline, royalists appear to have seen public anger at royal extravagance as the greater threat. Public profit seemed to them the strongest line of defence against abolition or reform. Without any serious challenge, the assertion began to be repeated so often, and by so many authoritative sources, that it gained the illusion of truth.

Since our meeting, VisitBritain has been a lot more circumspect about their claims. In the run-up to the 2018 wedding of Harry and Meghan, I sent them another freedom of information request, this time asking for any research they had into the question of whether the monarchy boosts visitor numbers. They came back unable to offer any research or data. From an organization dedicated to understanding and promoting inbound tourism, which does endless amounts of research into why people come here, that lack of data is damning.

Unfortunately, the £500 million figure, totally made up, has become lodged in the minds of a great many commentators. It is often trotted out by people who should know better. Yet *even if* we took that figure to be true – which it isn't – it is, in terms of the wider tourist economy, a very small amount indeed.

It's sometimes hard to get our heads around large numbers, and the larger the number the harder it is to understand in concrete terms. So people can be forgiven for thinking that £500 million is a large amount of money to risk losing from our economy. In truth, in the context of the UK's economy, it is almost nothing. Using 2019 statistics, the last full pre-pandemic year, the tourism industry brought £127 billion into the economy. Heritage tourism alone, which includes palaces, castles, old country homes and the like, was responsible for a whopping £20.2 billion. £500 million is just 1.9 per cent of the UK's heritage tourism revenue, 0.3 per cent of all tourism revenue and only 0.01 per cent of our total economy. To put that into perspective, imagine you needed to find £25,000 towards the deposit on a house, and I said I'd help out by giving you £2.50. That's the scale of the impact of the monarchy on the UK's economy, if we believe that £500 million figure. And that's the most optimistic figure that anyone has offered as a measure of the monarchy's impact on tourism, and it's not even true.

## Brand Value

Richard Fitzwilliams, the former editor of the *International Who's Who* and long-standing royal commentator, is one of the most ardent and committed royalists I've debated with. We've clashed a number of times on radio and TV and, while he is charming and eloquent, his defence of the monarchy often resembles a deeply held faith rather than a serious assessment of Britain's constitution. On more than one occasion I have challenged his assertion that the monarchy draws in tourists, but he is not deterred by the evidence. Instead, Fitzwilliams recites the mantra of 'intangible benefits' to the British economy. These benefits cannot be defined, quantified or measured. (Synonyms for 'intangible' offered by the *Collins English Dictionary* include 'abstract', 'elusive', 'vague' and 'unreal'.) Intangible benefits are useful when trying to prove the benefits of the monarchy, because they cannot be seen and must simply be believed.

Unfortunately, these intangibles were cited in a 2012 report published by Brand Finance, a company that specializes in advising businesses wishing to sell their brand to foreign markets. The year of the Diamond Jubilee saw lots of companies jump on the royal bandwagon, including Marmite (Ma'amite), Peppa Pig, T-Mobile and Kingsmill bread, which was briefly rebranded Queensmill, in the belief that to have something to say or a product to sell associated with the monarchy would give you a good chance of getting free advertising through the rolling news coverage. Brand Finance was no exception, and as the newsrooms were lapping up every mention of royalty in the run-up to the jubilee celebrations, the company released its first annual report on the value of the British monarchy.

Brand Finance certainly made some bold claims.* In 2012

---

\* Brand Finance didn't write the report to promote the monarchy, but to promote Brand Finance and, specifically, their 'Coats of Arms Service'. In that, they were very successful, getting a small they decided the monarchy was worth £44 billion to the British economy, which had increased to £67.5 billion by 2017. A closer inspection of their findings reveals that the headline figure is divided into £25.5 billion in tangible assets, real stuff you can identify and quantify, and £42 billion of intangible value. Of the tangible assets, the report includes the Crown Estate, the Duchies of Lancaster and Cornwall, the Royal Collection and the Crown Jewels. Claiming these as part of the value of the monarchy to the economy is difficult, to say the least. All these assets are national property and would remain so, with or without the monarchy. The Crown Estate and the two duchies are, in effect, property companies. That property will still be there once the monarchy is gone and while their value to the economy will ebb and flow with the value of property markets, their value to the taxpayer will increase, as revenue from the two duchies returns to the Treasury. The Royal Collection, which includes art and the Crown Jewels, may have a hypothetical value, but cannot be sold and so its value is only in its historic and cultural significance.

It's worth stressing that Brand Finance does not claim the monarchy generates £25 billion in income, only that the assets nominally held by the monarchy are worth that value. Any claim of income or wealth *generated* by the monarchy must pass the abolition test: in the event of the monarchy being abolished, would this value be lost? Given that these assets belong to the nation and not the Mountbatten-Windsor family, the answer must be no.

On the question of intangible value, the claims of Brand

company in a niche market widespread coverage free of charge thanks to the endless jubilee coverage.

Finance are harder to understand. They say with confidence that the monarchy generated 'an estimated uplift of £1.76 billion to the UK economy'. But there isn't a single source contained within the report to back this up. It breaks down that figure into several areas, including global press coverage, informal endorsements, royal patronage, media industry and the arts, trade and tourism. They also add the surplus income of the Crown Estate and the value to companies of coats of arms and royal warrants.

As we've seen, inclusion of tourism should immediately alert you to the doubtful veracity of the report's findings. On trade, the best Brand Finance can say is that trade delegations join the royals on overseas trips. Business leaders often join government ministers on official visits overseas and are involved in countless other international networks that facilitate Britain's global trade. There isn't any evidence that royal overseas visits influence the investment decisions of global corporations, or that such influence makes any difference to the UK's GDP.

Moreover, the royals have widely advertised their ineptitude when it comes to acting as ambassadors for the nation. In early 2022 Prince William and Kate, and shortly after them Prince Edward and Sophie, conducted tours of the Caribbean realms, to disastrous effect. Prince Andrew – who for ten years was the official UK trade ambassador – was an active hindrance to our trade even before his friendship with Jeffrey Epstein came to light. According to one report, there was disquiet about him 'lunching at Buckingham Palace with a "notorious" member of the former Tunisian regime', while he was also known to be friends with Saif Gaddafi, the son of the former Libyan leader, and Libyan gun smuggler Tarek Kaituni. One *Daily Mail* report quoted a former UK diplomat saying that among diplomatic corps, Andrew was referred to as 'HBH: His Buffoon

Highness', for his crass tone with officials and his unwillingness to follow the Foreign Office brief. So, it's unclear how the report calculates a dividend from royals on tour.

One of Brand Finance's most extraordinary claims is that the royals are responsible for a £50 million boost in media and the arts. The claim appears to rest entirely on the audience figures for *The Crown* on Netflix. To suggest TV ratings are to do with the royals themselves is simply daft. We do not celebrate organized crime for the success of crime drama *Ozark*. The value generated is, of course, thanks to the hard work and creativity of the TV and film industry, not the continuity of the monarchy.

## Royal Patronage and Charities

Benefits from royal patronage of charities and informal endorsements of products are slightly more believable, but there isn't any evidence of an overall gain for the economy. Even if some charities benefit from royal patronage and some brands sell more products because of a fleeting association with Kate Middleton, that is a benefit for those charities and companies, not the economy. It doesn't increase overall spend levels, it just influences preferences for where money is spent or donated. It's hard to measure the benefit to private companies, as the detail of their sales data isn't readily available. As for charities, the picture is a little clearer thanks to a comprehensive study by the research group Giving Evidence. Giving Evidence exists to generate data and intelligence for the charity sector, to aid that sector in making decisions in relation to fundraising and service delivery. In 2019–20 the organization conducted a comprehensive study of royal patronages. The report included detailed and complex data analysis, comparisons between charities supported and not supported by royals, between charities of similar types across different regions and between UK charities and those abroad.

The result of this work was clear. The involvement of royals in UK charities makes almost no difference to charity income.

In late 2020 I was pleased to interview Caroline Fiennes, the founder of Giving Evidence, for Republic's *Abolish the Monarchy* podcast. Fiennes was at pains to stress that she had no axe to grind when it came to the monarchy. One of the main reasons for looking at the question of royal patronages, she explained, was simply that no one else had done it before. In the absence of evidence, it was widely assumed that having a royal patron would be a boon for any charity and so, understandably, a lot of charity trustees would put a lot of effort into trying to get royal approval, endorsement or patronage. While the charity sector's public response to the Giving Evidence report was muted, Fiennes told me that she had numerous charity CEOs thank her for the research, as it armed them with the information needed when faced with persistent demands from trustees that they try to secure a royal patron.

The report so completely eviscerated the idea that royal patronage impacts on charity success that even I was surprised by the strength of its findings. I was also surprised by how many charities claim royal patronage, although the data here is sketchy at best. As many as 1,200 UK charities claim to have a royal patron, although, as Fiennes pointed out, the information provided on the official royal website is both incomplete and out of date.*

---

* Quite a few have more than one royal patron, which is why the figure you might read elsewhere is far higher, as they're double-counting.

The report found that a staggering 74 per cent of these charities had no contact with their patron during the preceding year, while a pattern emerged showing royals were far more likely to support the charities they had a hand in founding than charities they have lent their name to. For example, Prince Charles, as he was then, had carried out ninety-four engagements for the Prince's Trust during the previous five years, but none for Plant Heritage. Giving Evidence also found the charities royals associate themselves with are disproportionately large (with revenue typically thirty times that of the average charity), based in London, the south-east or south-west of England (near the main royal residences) and concentrated on uncontroversial issues, with housing, employment and social services being of least interest to the royal family. Peter Tatchell has often made the point that royals have mostly steered well clear of LGBT charities, while it was noted that until very recently no royal had ever visited a food bank. Many charities the royals support are sports clubs, yacht clubs and golfing associations – charitable in law, but arguably not in spirit.

The Giving Evidence report compared Air Ambulance charities in the UK, contrasting those with royal links to those without, and found no discernible difference in their fundraising capabilities. The report drew comparisons between the UK and other countries without royal families, and found no differences in the giving habits of citizens. The report was quite clear: 'The effect of royal patrons on charities' revenue is small or zero.' Contrast that with the claim by Brand Finance that the monarchy generates an 'uplift' of around £150 million to the charity sector through royal patronage. The truth is that, along with tourism, trade and TV, the royals' impact on charity is so small as to be nothing.

The reply to this is usually to point out charities such as the Prince's Trust or the Duke of Edinburgh's Award, or Prince William's Royal Foundation and its flagship project, the Earthshot Prize (which has since become an independent charity in its own right). The argument goes that it cannot be true that the royals have little impact on charity – just look at these few organizations, the good work they do and the money they raise. I certainly concede that the Prince's Trust and Duke of Edinburgh's Award do a lot of good. But those are independent charities. They have never been the personal projects of Charles or Philip.

I took part in the Duke of Edinburgh's Award scheme myself, visiting St James's Palace to collect the Gold Award in 1994. Philip made a brief appearance, said a few words, asked a girl where she was from, her answer prompting a dismissive remark about Australians, and then vanished into the next room, before the Olympic figure skater Robin Cousins handed out the certificates. I enjoyed the ceremony and was proud of what I had achieved. It is an excellent scheme and one definitely worthy of praise, not least for all the teenagers who complete the various and often arduous challenges and the legion of adults who give up their time to deliver the busy programme of activities. The one person who shouldn't get credit for the Duke of Edinburgh's Award is the Duke of Edinburgh, Prince Philip. This shouldn't be a controversial statement, because it was Prince Philip who said it.

To Philip's credit, he was never worried about being lauded for other people's charity work, including the creation of the Duke of Edinburgh's Award, one of the best known and widely celebrated 'royal charities'. For his ninetieth birthday, the BBC broadcast an interview with Philip, conducted by Fiona Bruce.

Bruce, inevitably, brought up the Duke of Edinburgh's Award, asking if the prince was proud of this particular achievement. Philip's reply was rather less than the interviewer may have wanted: 'I've got no reason to be proud of it. I mean, I think it's satisfying that we've set up a formula that works.' Pressed to clarify, Philip added, 'I don't run it [. . .] I've said it's all fairly second-hand, the whole business. I mean, I eventually got landed with the responsibility, or the credit for it.' Bruce, clearly keen to give Philip credit where credit wasn't due, pointed out that it is named after him, to which Philip replied, 'Well, that was strictly against my better judgement.'

As Philip mentioned during the interview, the Duke of Edinburgh's Award Scheme was the brainchild of Kurt Hahn, founder and headmaster of Gordonstoun School, where Philip – and later Charles, much to his distaste – went to school. Hahn pioneered ideas about education centred on learning leadership and responsibility from a young age. He founded other schools and was also responsible for the Outward Bound scheme. It was Hahn who approached Philip and asked him to be involved, to which Philip replied that he would chair the committee. The man who went on to design, set up and run the award from the start was John Hunt, a British Army officer and explorer. The Duke of Edinburgh's Award scheme recognizes the role of Hahn and Hunt, and Philip was quick to reject responsibility for either coming up with the idea or setting it up, beyond some notional involvement and attending awards ceremonies.

Clearly, when it comes to charities, philanthropically minded citizens are capable of forming, running and funding effective organizations that better the lives of millions. The sector would be no worse off if royal patronage ended tomorrow.

## The 'Hard-working' Royal

Royal association with charity isn't new. Monarchs have been patrons of arts and culture for centuries. In modern times, concern for charitable activity has been more carefully attuned to public opinion. In the words of American historian Frank Prochaska, having lost much of their political power and patronage by the middle of the nineteenth century, 'royalty took greater care to foster its philanthropic associations with the ascendant middle classes'.

These days they are keen to project that same image, of a noble family all too aware of their privilege and wanting to give something back, to offer service to the nation. It is not just that they patronize good causes, but also that they wish to brush off accusations of indolence by pointing to the charity work they do. We can easily see how these myths bind. The concept of royal charity work adds not just to the profitability myth, but also to the myth of the 'hard-working royal'.

We are treated to an annual scorecard of royal engagements, widely shared by the press. For 2021, Princess Anne took the 'hardest-working royal' trophy, with Charles coming in second place. The annual list was first published as a letter to *The Times*, from one of their readers, staunch royalist Tim O'Donovan, in 1981, in which he simply offered an insight into what the royals did. Back then, of course, the Court Circular, which publicly lists royal engagements, could only be read in the newspaper and it took a devoted royalist like O'Donovan to collect the cuttings and compile a league table. Initially the palace weren't all that happy with O'Donovan's lists and asked him to stop, explaining that they were concerned it would lead to news reports of work-shy royals. O'Donovan persuaded them other-wise and, while there has been the occasional criticism of those royals further down the list, on the whole the press dutifully acclaims those at the top of the list as 'hard-working'. In response to the 2021 league table, the *Daily Mail* exclaimed: 'Princess Anne is the year's hardest working royal! Queen's daughter pips Prince Charles to the crown with 387 engagements in 2021 – while Her Majesty, 95, still managed 184.'

There are two big problems with this reporting. What the royals do does not amount to work as most people would under-stand it, and they do far less than those superficially impressive figures might suggest. In 2005, Prince Charles's former press officer, Mark Bolland, admitted as much when he said, 'The Windsors are very good at working three days a week, five months of the year and making it look as if they work hard.'

Edgar Wilson, in *The Myth of British Monarchy*, cites a 1957 quote from a royalist: 'The royal family do not have a very hard life compared with most of their subjects ... The royal family have plenty of time on their hands; thirty-odd public appear-ances in ninety days is hardly a back-breaking programme for a company whose principal *raison d'etre* is the making of public appearances.'

I'm not sure if he means thirty appearances for the whole family, but in the first ninety days of 2022 (excluding his disaster-tour of the Caribbean), William had seventeen engage-ments, including attending a game of rugby.

In July 2022, to highlight this fallacy of the hard-working royal, I trawled through the Court Circular for all the engage-ments carried out by Prince Charles and Prince William for the first half of the year. To say they had a light schedule would be to overestimate their workload. In the past, when I've pointed this out, royalists have replied that the Court Circular doesn't tell the whole story, that the royals are busy behind the scenes. But they never say what that busy work entails, and we never see any discernible results of it. Going through the list of their official duties, it's remarkable to note how much padding it contains. Remember, the Court Circular is supposed to set out the official engagements of the royal family, the things they do in their capacity as royals, on behalf of the nation. And those engagements are always promoted as significant moments in the nation's life. Yet the list includes phone calls and conversations over Zoom, as well as meetings of 'their' charities, and meetings of the executive of the Duchy of Cornwall which, at other times, they are at pains to insist is a private estate. They can't feel all that confident that the list of legitimately public and official engagements will be viewed as particularly impressive if they need to add Prince William's chats with William Hague, former Conservative Party leader and now chair of the Royal Foundation.

Whatever the nature of the work, what's most shocking is how little of it there is. In January 2022, Charles did nothing at all until the 14th of that month, William nothing until the 12th. Charles had a handful of meetings, one on the 19th, three on the 21st plus a phone call with the Greek prime minister that same day. He visited the Holocaust exhibition in Buckingham Palace on the 24th and Didcot and Abingdon a week later. That was it; a smattering of engagements over five days spread out over three weeks in January. Prince William's January diary was similarly empty, with a couple of phone calls, an investiture to hand out gongs and a couple of other brief engagements, all done on six days spread out over three weeks. In February, aside from a brief trip to Dubai, in which he also attended an event for the Earthshot Prize, which is not official business, William's engagements consisted of one investiture, a visit to MI6, a twenty-minute meeting with Ben Wallace, the defence secretary, and the England versus Wales rugby match on the 26th.

The pattern is similar each month, with April being William's laziest (excluding meetings with 'his' charities, which are not official engagements). The only official engagements that month were a visit to the Disasters Emergency Committee in London, an Anzac Day memorial service followed by a charity gala, a meeting two days later and a solitary video call the day after that. From 27 March, when he and Kate arrived back in the UK from their ham-fisted tour of the Caribbean, he did absolutely nothing for four weeks. May was a bit busier, thanks presumably to the jubilee at the start of June, but once that exertion was over, he resumed the normal pattern of occasional engagements separated by long stretches of downtime.

Charles, who at the time was still heir and increasingly a stand-in for the Queen, would be expected to be a lot busier than William, which he was, to a point. But by a 'lot busier' I do not mean busy. At no point does he do a full week, or even a full day. As with William, most of the engagements are at or near one of his three main residences, Clarence House in London, Highgrove in Gloucestershire or Dumfries House in Scotland, about an hour's drive south of Glasgow. As a generous estimate, the average length of an official engagement is an hour, but many are far shorter. If we assume they're each an hour long, then during the whole of 2021 Charles did the equivalent of eleven weeks' full-time work or, to put it another way, an average of four and a half days a month.

In December 2022 the press were again reporting how Princess Anne was 'the year's hardest working royal', with 'an incredible 217 engagements under her belt'. That's no more than 217 hours of attendance, which adds up to about six weeks' full-time work. Kate reportedly had ninety engagements, the full-time equivalent of a little more than two weeks for the whole year.

Even if you are impressed with the hours the royals put in, what they do with those hours never amounts to work as most of us would recognize it. The *OED* defines work as 'activity involving mental or physical effort done in order to achieve a purpose or result'. Normally, in terms of paid, professional work, this comes with obligations, responsibilities, deadlines, not to mention accountability, with the possibility of being sacked or made redundant. The royals, in this sense, don't work per se. They attend. They turn up at events others have organized.

Hard work is something done by teachers, nurses, police officers, even MPs. It's the low-paid shop staff who had to persevere through Covid lockdowns who work hard, people in call centres, builders, carers. For most of us, we do this hard work alongside many other obligations, such as paying rent or a mortgage, getting the kids to school or looking after elderly relatives. We do this without the help of an army of servants. The royal claim to hard work is a lie, and it should be offensive to those who do put in long hours for a tiny fraction of the multi-million-pound funding we give the royal family. For most days of most weeks of most months of the year, the royals pursue their own interests and pastimes. They do not work hard.

Perhaps it doesn't matter if they work hard or not. Perhaps you believe what's important is not what the royals do, but that they are there. But the enthusiasm with which monarchists claim they toil away in the service of the nation suggests we need to believe the royals do something useful beyond 'being royal'. We want to believe theirs is a life of service and sacrifice on behalf of the nation. But it isn't. It is a life of leisure and luxury.

## Principles Over Profit

It is a curious feature of debates about the monarchy that the incidental benefits are so often the first line of defence. The royals, they say, make us all better off. Through tourism, charity and industry, royal association opens the floodgates to billions of pounds of investment and philanthropy. The institution's global reach, amplified by weddings and jubilees, make it an asset this country cannot afford to lose, no matter the criticism, no matter the scandal.

It should alarm true believers to see these incidental, collateral benefits being trumpeted as powerful arguments for the monarchy because it tells us a lot about how little people care about the more substantial purpose of the institution. To defend the institution on the grounds that we would suffer an economic downturn in the event of its abolition is to reduce it to a kind of life raft, to which we cling tight for fear of letting go. But it's an illusion. If we stop and look at what is really driving our economy – for good or ill – we will see that our country stands on its own two feet, sustaining our own culture, tourism and charity sector without help from the royals or the monarchy.

The simple truth is that there would be no financial loss, no economic downturn caused by the abolition of the monarchy. So, if that is a nagging concern when discussing the future of the Crown and the possibility of a British republic, rest assured – your concerns are misplaced. The monarchy, and the royals in particular, are largely irrelevant to our economic fortunes and charitable enterprises, bit parts in a multi-trillion-pound economy, a handful of peacocks attending events in a society in which millions of ordinary people work hard, make sacrifices and champion good causes. As far as these supposed incidental benefits are concerned, the data tells us that the monarchy isn't earning us anything.

There is one final, more profound, point about the claim of a profitable monarchy. As an argument for sustaining an unaccountable, undemocratic institution at the core of Britain's constitution, it is an amoral point of view. It is a view that puts profit above principles and values. It says we should turn a blind eye to all that's wrong with the monarchy because it makes money. That is a position from which you could also argue for trading in narcotics, prostitution and even slavery.

If the best we can say, when judging this national institution, is that it makes money through promoting trade and tourism, perhaps that speaks louder than any other argument that it is time it went. But claims of profit aren't just amoral, they are irrelevant, because the monarchy is *not* a tourist attraction. It is the core institution of our constitution, from which all others derive their political and legal authority. Wouldn't it make more sense to judge such matters according to our principles and values and an assessment of their constitutional effectiveness, rather than on what people enjoy doing on holiday?

As we shall see in the next chapter, that's the last thing royalists really want. They will claim the monarchy serves a unique purpose, that it guards us against tyranny and provides a constitutional bedrock for our much-vaunted democracy. Yet, here too, the royalist claims fall short. Rather, the monarchy serves the few, the rich and the powerful. It is a politicians' monarchy, a consequence of compromises between palace and Parliament. It does not serve or protect the people.

## 2.

## Schrödinger's Monarch

Jacob Rees-Mogg agrees that tourism is irrelevant to the debate. I met him a few years ago – long before Brexit made him a household name – when I was invited to a debate at Bath University. Despite our significant political differences, I found him charming, affable and quite entertaining to listen to. While we were waiting to start, I joked that I hoped we could get through the evening without anyone mentioning the T-word. Rees-Mogg agreed that such arguments miss the point, and that the institution should be defended on its own merits. Here was a true believer. Someone who sees the monarchy in its historical and constitutional context and feels Britain is lucky to have arrived in the twenty-first century with its eighteenth-century institutions still intact. In more recent times, Rees-Mogg has been accused of putting on a show for the public, his demeanour and style projecting an image of the aristocrat of yore that appeals to a nation hooked on costume dramas. I suspect there may be some truth in that but, on this issue, I think the MP for North East Somerset is sincere.

During one parliamentary debate, the late Labour MP Paul Flynn referred to Rees-Mogg as the 'Member who represents the middle ages', for his archaic concerns and ability to rattle off obscure historic references to thirteenth-century chancellors. Rees-Mogg's monarchism, however, is more a product of the late eighteenth century. By that time the concept of a constitutional monarchy had firmly taken hold, with Parliament exercising the real power, although not without considerable influence from the King when he was particularly concerned about an issue such as slavery or the American War of Independence (both of which he seems to have been keen to maintain). The degree to which the monarch could wield power varied a great deal, depending to a large extent on the prime minister of the day, and the support the latter enjoyed in Parliament.

The previous century had seen a civil war and two coups, first when the royalists returned from exile and deposed the government of Richard Cromwell, Oliver's hapless son, and the second when parliamentarians invited a Dutch invasion to topple King James II (this is a gross oversimplification of the turbulent seventeenth century, but then this isn't a history book). The so-called Glorious Revolution flipped the relationship between Parliament and monarch on its head. Whereas before, Parliament was at the service of the King, who would govern the nation often without recourse to MPs, after 1689, the King was there at the pleasure of Parliament. This shift was underscored in 1701, when Parliament passed the Act of Settlement, one of the cornerstones of the contemporary British constitution. As in 1689, Parliament was not prepared to leave the succession to wind its natural course through the direct descendants of the current monarch, not least because of the English obsession with keeping Catholics off the throne. Instead, they determined, in law, that no future monarch could be Roman Catholic or married to a Roman

Catholic, and that they must be heirs and successors of Sophia, Electress of Hanover.*

Sophia would have become the next English queen had she not predeceased Queen Anne. Instead, the Crown went to Sophia's son, George I. George reigned as King of Great Britain and of Ireland for just under thirteen years and died in 1727. It was during his reign that power shifted more decisively to Parliament, with Robert Walpole emerging as the de facto first British prime minister, a role he held for twenty-one years until 1742.

There is an important point here, which is that power shifted to Parliament more by convention and through the political struggles of the day than by a revolution or by parliamentary decision. While many royal powers have since been superseded by statute, successive prime ministers have asserted the authority granted to them by dint of having the support of Parliament, to insist the monarch only exercise Crown powers on the prime minister's say-so. Many of the King's powers were never abolished, they were simply handed over to the government. It created what has been called an embrace of convenience, where the government allows the monarchy to continue, with its pomp and stature intact, while the monarch allows the government to exercise Crown powers that are sweeping in their breadth and reach.

Changing social attitudes and fresh democratic reforms shifted power further from the Lords and monarchy. The

---

* That our constitution, to this day, contains direct reference to a Dutch-born German princess who died in 1714, having never held public office of any kind in what is now the UK, is just one of many extraordinary oddities of Britain's political system. Electress, by the way, is the title given to the wife of an Elector, a king, prince or other state leader within the Holy Roman Empire who had a vote when choosing the next Holy Roman Emperor.

Commons was, by the early part of the twentieth century, unchecked and all-powerful in a nation with no fundamental laws or rights that could not be torn up by an Act of Parliament. The notion that the Commons must have 'supremacy' took hold, and this deeply flawed arrangement began to be promoted as a virtue, with the likes of Jacob Rees-Mogg celebrating the 'mother of parliaments', an institution he believes is the envy of the world. This idea of Britain's parliamentary democracy as the blueprint the world has taken to its heart, of Britain as one of the oldest, most stable democracies in the world, is founded on a bargain that has suited the interests of both the royals and the political classes alike. The reality is somewhat different: a parliament that has stumbled from one reform to the next, begrudgingly moving on the issue of suffrage while slowly centralizing power in the hands of the House of Commons, and then concentrating power further into Downing Street. Simply put, who has power and why in Britain, is a matter of historical contingency. We could do a lot better.

## Defender of the Constitution

The monarchy is a key part of the fantasy of Britain's ancient and noble constitution. It's seen as sitting above the political fray, a font of authority, honour and wisdom. It is supposed to lend an air of dignity and historical inevitability to our flawed democratic system. The more substantial constitutional arguments for the monarchy, those put forward by the likes of Rees-Mogg, rest on this fiction. The argument is simple enough: by formally retaining Crown powers, the King offers some kind of defence against the ambitions or grandiosity of the politicians in Parliament. Central to this view is the assumption that we can only check parliamentary excess with a monarch. Presidents are by default partisan and political, nursing ambitions to interfere or challenge the mandate of the elected government and the supremacy of the Commons, or simply willing to collude with the governing party. In the 1969 BBC documentary, *Royal Family*, which the Queen later banned from further broadcast, but which can be found on YouTube, the narrator solemnly explained that:

> While she is the head of the law, no politician can take over the courts. While she is head of the state, no generals can take over the government. And while she is head of the services, no would-be dictator can turn the army against the people. The strength of the monarchy does not lie in the power it gives the sovereign, but the power it denies to anyone else.

The idea that the monarch sits above politics, providing us with an impartial and apolitical head of state who guards the rights and institutions of the British people, is perhaps the most pernicious myth about the monarchy. Not only is it untrue, but perpetuating this fiction serves only to protect the power of the government of the day, to the detriment of Parliament and the people.

Richard Fitzwilliams never fails to talk about the monarchy as a 'constitutional long-stop', a defence against the venal politician, while former Conservative MP Jacques Arnold was genuinely surprised when, during a debate at the University of Kent in Canterbury in February of 2020, I extolled the virtues of having a president. I explained that such a role in a parliamentary republic would be limited to providing an independent head of state who could guard the constitution. Arnold's response was to claim that that was how he saw the role of the monarch. But the claim that the monarchy's constitutional strength lies in the King's independence and impartiality simply doesn't hold up.

What's curious about these claims is how contradictory they are. On the one hand, the monarch is powerless. A figurehead. A unifier who cannot and will not act in a way contrary to the wishes of the government. On the other, the King holds the power to check the ambitions of politicians. Which is it? It can't be both. Power is not something you can put in a box and lock away, as the BBC's narrator seems to imply. Someone has it, or no one has it. In the UK, power emanates from the Crown, and the Crown's power is arguably limitless, save for the powers explicitly removed from it – or provided somewhere else – by laws passed by Parliament.

As the prime minister's command of Crown powers increased over the two hundred years after Walpole, the chances of the monarch acting as any defence against the ambitions of politicians has evaporated. While reigning monarchs from George I to Edward VII sought to exercise a degree of independence in some matters, such as when the latter 'connived with the Conservative opposition to try to thwart the radical programme of the 1906 Liberal government', to quote former MP Norman Baker, the Queen made it clear she would exercise no power independent of government advice. Not only would she collude with the government, it was seen as her duty to do so.

In recent years, there has, from time to time, been speculation, and occasional calls, that the Queen might step in to resist the demands of the prime minister or resolve a constitutional deadlock. The palace, however, has been at pains to stress that she would not, particularly in the days shortly after the 2010 election, and again during the election of 2015, when expectations of another hung parliament were high.

According to one report in 2010, Buckingham Palace was 'desperate to ensure that the Queen be seen to be thoroughly out of the fray' and that the priority for the 'golden triangle' of advisers – the Cabinet secretary, the Queen's private secretary and the prime minister's principal private secretary – is to 'protect the Queen from political blowback during what can be a delicate moment for the monarch'. Peter Riddell, journalist, author and constitutional authority, told the *Guardian* that one of the two principles guiding the Queen's role is that 'the Queen does not get involved – she is recipient of advice but not an active participant'.

The simple reason for this is that the monarch is not prepared to jeopardize the monarchy. Pushing back against the government would be a major risk, even when there may be a constitutionally legitimate reason for doing so. In recent years, Downing Street has behaved in a manner many might consider unconstitutional. This is a problem. There are no checks and balances that can withstand the authority of the Crown or Parliament, both of which are now largely at the disposal of the prime minister. Assuming a government enjoys a large and acquiescent majority, if the PM wanted to suspend elections, they could suspend elections. If the PM wanted to curtail the independence of the courts, then they could. If the government saw fit to put soldiers on the streets and declare war against the citizenry, there is little anyone but the prime minister's own MPs could do to stop them. The government doesn't even need a large majority. It has the power to act independently of Parliament on the one hand and to control or cajole MPs on the other. It was the Conservative peer, Lord Hailsham, commenting on the ability of the 1974–9 Wilson/Callaghan government to control parliamentary business, who used the term 'elective dictatorship' to criticize that control despite the lack of a sizeable majority. Day to day, the reality is less alarming than all this suggests. But that's not because of any constitutional checks and balances. It's because Britain is largely a peaceful society with a strong democratic and liberal culture. The chances of a government having such slavish backbenchers that they would allow a PM to go to these extremes is remote. But remote is not the same as impossible, while it is not hard to imagine many less extreme measures a government may take that would nevertheless be a cause for concern.

You may argue that this passive, impotent role for the monarch is proper. You may think a monarch should have no discretion whatsoever. But if that's true, the monarch can't exercise power to act as a counterweight or obstacle to the demands of a prime minister. Those unlimited and largely unchecked Crown powers now rest solely in the hands of the prime minister and their Cabinet, constrained only by laws (which they can amend or repeal) and the political realities of the day. The constitution is in dire circumstances, defenceless – and so are we.

## There One Minute, Gone the Next

With Boris Johnson there were certainly concerns that the rule of law may be eroding. Johnson, of course, is an admirer of the monarchy and no doubt fully subscribes to the fantasy of Britain's glorious constitution, so it is an irony that his brief premiership has done the cause of constitutional reform a great favour, throwing into sharp relief the limitations of Britain's constitutional monarchy and the very real dangers that a sitting prime minister could pose.

When Johnson first became prime minister in July 2019, he inherited a minority government, albeit with a majority in practice forged by a £1 billion deal with Northern Ireland's Democratic Unionist Party. That working majority vanished at the height of highly charged parliamentary debates on the government's plans for Brexit, when one Conservative MP defected to the Liberal Democrats and another twenty-one rebelled to support a bill that further delayed the UK's departure from the EU. As Members of Parliament on both sides of the House were organizing to further frustrate his plans to 'get Brexit done', Johnson sent his ministers to visit the Queen and 'request' a prorogation, a suspension of Parliament. The prorogation was unprecedented in recent times, scheduled to last for five weeks and – in the view of critics – intended for the purpose of stopping parliamentary opposition in its tracks. Such a request has the force of an instruction when the monarch is so clearly unwilling or unable to exercise any independent judgement.

The prorogation was granted, and Parliament was suspended on 10 September. Fourteen days later, the Supreme Court ruled the decision to be unlawful because, in the words of Lady Hale, president of the Supreme Court, 'It had the effect of frustrating or preventing the ability of parliament to carry out its constitutional functions without reasonable justification.' It was said, both by those keen to protect the monarchy and those keen to put all the pressure on Johnson, that the monarch had no choice, that she must always act on the advice of the prime minister. And they were right. But the upshot of this is that Britain's head of state is constitutionally bound to take instructions from our head of government, even when instructed to do something unconstitutional. The court's ruling was that the prime minister acted unlawfully in advising the Queen to grant a prorogation, but it said nothing of the Queen's decision to follow that advice. It was also argued that Johnson had effectively lied to the Queen about the constitutionality of the prorogation, without anyone asking why the Queen lacked the judgement – or at least the advisers – that would allow her to spot that lie. This interpretation renders the head of state obsolete and redundant, a puppet on a string.

You might argue that the Supreme Court's judgement offers solace, that the prime minister's powers are, or at least can be, curtailed. But their decision was not without its critics and, anyway, if so minded and in different circumstances, the government could simply change the law and ensure their power to prorogue was absolute.

Fast-forward to July 2022 and Boris Johnson is facing a political and personal fall from grace that threatens to become a different kind of constitutional crisis and which, in the words of Jonathan Sumption, a former Supreme Court judge, narrowly avoids turning into a 'constitutional coup'. The point is quite simple. In a parliamentary democracy like ours, a prime minister owes their job to Parliament, and only indirectly to the voters. If a PM loses the support of Parliament, they no longer have a legitimate constitutional claim to the job. Johnson was attempting to hang on despite that loss of support. As it happened, he was finally persuaded by colleagues, friends and civil servants that there was no route to survival, and he resigned. Had he ignored all that advice it was unclear how he could be dislodged. Only the Queen had the power to sack him directly but, as we've seen, that was never going to happen. In the absence of royal action, it would be theoretically possible for Parliament to pass a law that removed him, but that would have been fraught with difficulty, not least because of the wish of many Tory MPs to be rid of their prime minister but to avoid an immediate election.

For almost two days, from the Tuesday evening when Rishi Sunak and Sajid Javid resigned from government to Johnson's announcement that he was going on the Thursday, there was increasing frustration, anxiety and trepidation about where this would all lead. Countless journalists, MPs and commentators speculated on the constitutional position, and arguments were made by Johnson's more vociferous (and constitutionally illiterate) supporters that it was the prime minister who was the victim of an attempted coup, that Parliament should be ignored and that the three-year-old general election result should be the basis for our democracy.

The day after Johnson went, I had this letter published in the *Guardian* newspaper:

These past few days should serve as a lesson as to why we need an effective, elected head of state. In a parliamentary democracy, the prime minister must have the confidence of parliament, yet Boris Johnson illustrated how it is possible to continue without that confidence.

His resignation was forced by political manoeuvres, not by constitutional checks. During this time, there has been uncertainty, speculation and considerable concern about where this was heading and the damage it could do. Yet despite the biggest political crisis for years threatening to blow up into a constitutional crisis, our head of state has remained silent.

It is extraordinary to see some commentators fret that the monarch might be 'dragged' into this crisis, or that it might cause her some embarrassment. It is the job of the head of state to get involved in these moments of peril, to steady the ship, offer counsel and, if necessary, take steps to protect and enforce the constitution. That's not a job that can or will be done by a monarch.

We are told that the monarch defends our constitution, protects us from the ambitions of a wayward prime minister, yet when there was a very real danger of a prime minister governing without the consent of Parliament, the monarch was nowhere to be seen. Her powers already in the hands of the PM, her role already reduced to the rubber stamp of government; had Johnson been minded, he could have carried on for some time, and caused considerable damage, while Britain's head of state sat on the sidelines, keen to avoid any embarrassment.

In 1935, the physicist Erwin Schrödinger published his famous thought experiment, to attempt to illustrate a 'paradox of quantum superposition', a phrase I don't pretend to understand. With apologies to physicists, the pop-culture summary of this thought experiment is that if you place a cat in a box, then close that box so that you can't see the cat, under certain conditions you must conclude that the cat is both alive and dead at the same time, and that it will only be one or the other when you open the box and look inside (and you won't know which it'll be until you do so). It occurred to me that, as with the feline's condition, we are also uncertain, at any given point, whether we have a head of state or not. The position both exists and doesn't exist, and we can't know which it is until we are required to look.

At the start of June 2022, we could see the Queen very publicly celebrating the jubilee. Yet just four weeks later, as the constitution, at the centre of which lies the Crown, was in crisis, the Queen had vanished. Not a word from the palace. No reassuring comment or useful clarification of the constitutional position offered. One moment we see the monarch, and are told of her great virtues, the next she is nowhere to be seen, as we're told that under no circumstances can the Queen be 'dragged into' doing her job.

Schrödinger's monarch holds on to power to deny it to others. Yet they cannot use it except when told to by the PM. They are at once ever present and never available, an apparition who appears one moment to receive applause, then disappears the next to avoid constitutional responsibility.

Gus O'Donnell, former Cabinet secretary under Tony Blair, suggested that the monarch should be 'above politics – not out of it, but above it', yet the Queen seemed to have risen so far above the fray as to have drifted off into the atmosphere. Rather than the monarch defending the constitution and, by implication, the British people, it has been the responsibility of subjects to defend the monarch not from injustice or tyranny, but from embarrassment. In the UK, embarrassment is, it seems, a central principle of our constitution.

## The Importance of Impartiality

This anxiety about sparing the monarch from embarrassment comes from the idea that to be a check on the powers of the government, the monarch must always be impartial – or at least seen to be impartial. And that's a fair point. Unfortunately, royalists are confusing impartiality with secrecy, silence and mystery. They will argue the Queen remained above the fray, and therefore impartial throughout her reign, but this makes no sense for all sorts of reasons, not least because the monarch is anything but impartial, whether in their constitutional role or personal beliefs.

By dint of their office, the monarch will choose to side with the government on all matters every time. Even at times of political crisis or when there's uncertainty over who has the confidence of the Commons. Even when the government is in breach of the constitution. Not knowing much about what the Queen thought, or what she did behind closed doors, meant we couldn't really know whether she was impartial or not, on whose advice she acted or on what basis she decided to act.

Royalists will say we can't possibly have someone whose views we know, or who has been a politician, because they can't be impartial. But that's not how impartiality works. Everyone has opinions and everyone has a political leaning one way or another – that's just the way we are. Those opinions may not be strong and political leanings may not be formalized in open support for a political party, but only the most ill-informed, uninterested and uninquisitive person can go through life without forming an opinion on issues that affect this country.

We can assume, then, that the Queen had views and opinions about a whole range of matters. It's fair to conclude that, broadly speaking, she was a conservative person who held views that are typical of people of her background. Yet, for all those assumptions, we don't know what she thought about any particular issue. How did she feel about taxes or public spending? What was her view on prison reform or sentencing? What about immigration? We have no idea if she held strong views on anything other than monarchy, church, Commonwealth and horses. And that's a problem if we want to believe that the Queen was impartial, because impartiality in the real world means making decisions without allowing yourself to be influenced by your own views or interests.[*] How can we judge someone on whether they successfully committed to impartiality if we don't know what their views or interests are?

This fallacy isn't argued anywhere else in the UK. Judges must be impartial and are expected to execute their duties without fear or favour. Yet they are not barred from office if they have previously made political statements, or in the case of Cherie Booth, been openly political and married to the prime minister. The chair of the BBC is required to be impartial, and by knowing if they have a political bias, we can judge whether that bias is affecting their decisions in that role. MPs cannot be impartial as such, because they're elected on a partisan basis. However, they must declare their personal and financial interests so we can judge whether those interests have swayed their votes. The Speaker of the Commons is also elected on a party ticket, to later be ceremonially dragged to the chair and stripped of any further political allegiance, in the expectation that he or she will remain neutral in the course of parliamentary debates. When doubts are raised about the Speaker's neutrality, as they were with John Bercow during the rancorous 2017–19 parliament, judgements can be made about his conduct precisely because he was previously on record as an MP and partisan politician and because, even after his appointment as Speaker, he was not surrounded by secrecy. In other words, the impartial execution of one's duty must be seen to be done, not just believed to be done.

It has been speculated that the Queen was not particularly

---

[*]  The question of interests is different to that of opinions and I'll come back to the secrecy surrounding the royals' financial and other interests later in the book.

inquisitive and did not hold any strong views on government policy. The same cannot be said of either King Charles or Prince William. While Charles has lobbied government ministers secretly in the past, they have both made their views clear on a number of issues, including on the environment, homelessness and health care. So, if you believe in this royal fantasy of the impartial monarch, we don't have that now the Queen is gone and Charles is on the throne. Charles's efforts at influencing public policy are particularly egregious, with almost daily missives being fired off to numerous Cabinet ministers. Yet if he continues that lifelong habit now he is King, there would be little we could do to stop him.

When the *Guardian* fought a ten-year battle to uncover just a fraction of the letters Charles had written, the then Attorney General, Dominic Grieve, inadvertently gave the game away. In overruling a tribunal decision to order the release of a batch of Charles's letters dating back to 2004 and 2005, Grieve said:

> Much of the correspondence does indeed reflect the Prince of Wales's most deeply held personal views and beliefs. The letters in this case are in many cases particularly frank [ . . . ] They also contain remarks about public affairs which would in my view, if revealed, have had a material effect upon the willingness of the government to engage in correspondence with the Prince of Wales, and would potentially have undermined his position of political neutrality.

In short, Grieve was arguing that it is better to keep Charles's views secret and pretend that he is impartial, than to release the letters and prove that he is not. The Attorney General was making it quite clear that the impartiality of the royals is a fiction, that it is only necessary to maintain the appearance of impartiality, not to insist on it in practice.

## The Long Reign

The impartiality of the hereditary head of state is combined with their longevity. Together – according to the monarchist – this provides a source of continuity and stability that republics can only dream of. The notion of continuity is often expressed in terms of the Queen's long reign. Politicians and presidents come and go, but the Queen was a constant source of national focus and unity.

This is nonsense. Firstly, the royalist is citing the circumstances we have found ourselves in until recently, with a long-living and long-reigning monarch, as evidence of a wider universal point. Moreover, the benefits of a long-reigning monarch could only have been felt since a time when her reign could reasonably be called 'long'. One of the common points made here is that the Queen had fifteen prime ministers, each of whom could benefit from the wisdom of her years and the years of her experience. Yet this raises the obvious question of what benefit the seventy-seven-year-old Winston Churchill may have found in having a twenty-five-year-old monarch who had hitherto enjoyed no formal education and had little experience of the outside world. What advice or wisdom could Anthony Eden draw on five years later when confronted with the geopolitical realities of the Suez Crisis? It wasn't until Margaret Thatcher's election in 1979 that the prime minister was a contemporary of the Queen. Yet, whatever your thoughts are on Thatcher, she was an accomplished, highly educated politician with significant parliamentary and political experience. The notion that Thatcher – or any prime minister – would have benefitted more from a monarch than she might have from an elected head of state, one who had had an education and a career, as well as a degree of genuine independence, simply isn't credible – except to say that a prime minister would find it far easier to exercise unchecked power in the presence of the Queen.

Setting aside the fallacy of the philosopher queen, Elizabeth Windsor was monarch for seventy years for three simple reasons: her uncle was forced to abdicate, her father died at a relatively young age and she lived a long life. If her uncle hadn't been a Nazi sympathizer who, thanks to a relationship with an American divorcee, gave the government an easy pretext to push him out, the Queen was unlikely to have ever been monarch. If her father had lived for as long as his wife, the Queen Mother, Elizabeth would have ascended to the throne in the late 1990s. If the Queen had lived only for as long as her father she would have died after a thirty-year reign, or if her father had lived longer, she may never have reigned at all. Her longevity was chance – it was not a part of the monarchy's design.

One final point to make about the impartiality of the monarch is that the office of monarch and the existence of the monarchy is itself deeply political and fundamentally conservative in nature. It instils a conservative ethos into our constitution. It serves to block reforms that step too far from that received wisdom that our constitution is the envy of the world and a source of strength, stability and continuity. Yet a constitution ought to be neutral on the question of its own design and merits, instead serving to provide only a framework within which power can be exercised and constrained, allowing at all times free, fair and frank debate about future reforms of the system if required.

## Just Look at Norway

Interestingly, this fiction of the monarch as a bedrock of stability, defender of the nation and source of wisdom isn't limited to Britain's own constitution. It is often cited as a universal idea – that monarchies prevent dictatorships and defend democracy, delivering the fairest and freest societies in the world.

Winston Churchill is often quoted as making the baseless claim that Germany would have avoided Hitler had they not got rid of the Kaiser. The journalist Peter Hitchens argued, in that Oxford Union debate in 2021, that the power of the monarchy is to be a focus for awe, adulation and deference, a lightning rod that redirects highly charged feelings of nationalism and nostalgia away from the figure of a populist political leader.

Unfortunately, Churchill and Hitchens have both conveniently ignored the role of Europe's royal houses in plunging the Continent into the crises that toppled governments and sowed the seeds of extremism and despotism. They also forget that the Kaiser, who lived another twenty-two years after being ousted in the German revolution of 1918, would lobby Hitler from his exile in the Netherlands, seeking an arrangement that would put his family back on the throne while leaving the Nazis in power. To give Wilhelm some credit, he was no admirer of the Führer or his monstrous regime, but he was willing to set aside differences if it meant restoration of the monarchy.

That was a sentiment shared by the king of Italy, who accommodated Mussolini's fascists for twenty years (appointing Il Duce against the wishes of the elected prime minister), until it was clear which way the war was going. The Greek King George II allowed a heavily rigged plebiscite to restore the monarchy in 1935, only to embrace the authoritarian rule of Ioannis Metaxas from 1936 until Germany invaded in 1941. George's nephew, King Constantine II, was equally hopeless in the face of the military coup of 1967, after which the junta abolished the monarchy. Once democracy was restored, a fresh referendum resulted in the understandable decision to remain a republic.

Monarchies in Thailand and Cambodia have spectacularly failed to defend nascent democracies, too often colluding with those who seize power, while in Eswatini, formerly Swaziland, the constitutional monarch took absolute power for himself in 1974 and he, and then later his son and heir, have held on to it ever since, albeit with some very modest reforms.

The actor, presenter and writer Stephen Fry is well known for his atheism and love of science, so it's understandable that people might label him a rationalist and might, perhaps, be surprised to hear that he is a royalist. What's most surprising is that his defence of monarchy rests on some quite implausible reasoning. On more than one occasion on the BBC panel show *QI*, Fry has reminded Alan Davies that 'correlation does not equal causation'. Yet he forgets his own rejoinder when he comes to discuss the apparent strengths of the monarchy. Speaking on *The Rubin Report*, a show hosted by American conservative commentator Dave Rubin, in 2016, Fry makes a bold stab at defending Britain's attachment to the monarchy. Denying that he is a rationalist, he says he is instead an empiricist and keen on the notion of 'clear thinking'. He then goes on to argue that: 'Countries that have kings and queens, which are rationally stupid, weird ideas, are empirically freer and more socially just than countries that don't [. . .] Look at social justice, happiness, freedom and equality in the world and you're

thinking Sweden, Denmark, Norway, Benelux countries ...
and Britain.'

This is a common argument, one repeated by almost every
monarchist I've argued with. Ian Dunt wrote in his jubilee article that: 'Some of the most egalitarian and social democratic
countries have a royal family, including Denmark, the Netherlands, Norway and Sweden. Some of the most unequal, like
the United States, do not. Nor, for that matter, do countries like
Russia or China.'*

This is a riposte to a presumed key republican argument:
that monarchy 'entrenches social hierarchy'. The suggestion
here is that this position is 'parochial', disproven when you look
at other countries around Europe. Yet both Dunt and Fry
miss the glaring holes in this claim. They ignore the countless
progressive, free and prosperous republics in Europe and elsewhere, including Iceland, Ireland, Finland, Germany, Portugal,
the Baltic states and Switzerland. They also assume that what
counts for Denmark and Norway counts for the UK. Despite
Fry's hesitant appending of Britain to his list, the UK does not
rank in the top ten of any indices of the most free, fair, prosperous, democratic or equal nations. Correlation does not equal
causation. Countries with monarchies are not free or stable or
prosperous because they have monarchies, but it is reasonable to
assume that monarchies are more likely to survive in the modern era if their countries are freer, fairer and more prosperous,

---

* I won't get into the daft comparison with Russia or China
  here, other than to say that this discussion is about mature
  democracies, not dictatorships. I could just as easily respond
  with 'What about monarchies like Saudi Arabia?', but that
  would hardly enhance the debate.

because there is less pressure or demand for significant constitutional reform.

It's worth taking a closer look at these various rankings and indices that Fry is referring to, but before we do let's add one small caveat. The distinction being drawn is between those countries that have a monarch on the throne, acting as head of state, and those who do not. Falling in between are the Commonwealth realms. It is difficult to argue that Australia or Canada gain any benefit from being a monarchy when, as far as the everyday governing of their countries is concerned, they are quasi-, de facto republics. The monarchy has almost no political or economic impact on these nations, while they each have a quasi-head of state in the person of the governor general. Whether we include them or not, the global rankings of countries do not prove what Fry or others think they prove. The evidence doesn't support the argument that because these other countries have monarchies, and they are progressive, free and democratic, the British monarchy makes Britain progressive, free or fair.

If we start by looking at the 2021 United Nations Human Development Index and just take the top ten democracies (Hong Kong makes it into the top ten, as democracy and human rights aren't part of the measure), then they are, in descending order: Switzerland, Norway, Iceland, Australia, Denmark, Sweden, Ireland, Germany, the Netherlands and Finland. Five out of ten are republics and Australia is one of the five monarchies. The UK does not make the grade (we're number eighteen, or seventeen if we only count full democracies). *The Economist*'s Democracy Index looks at how democratic each nation is, and whether their democracies are judged to have improved or deteriorated. Their top ten, in descending order, are Norway,

New Zealand, Finland, Sweden, Iceland, Denmark, Ireland, Taiwan, Switzerland and Australia. Again, the UK doesn't make the grade (ranking number eighteen) and again the top ten is split evenly between monarchies and republics, including quasi-republics Australia and New Zealand. The Human Freedom Index has Switzerland at the top, followed by New Zealand, Denmark, Estonia, Ireland, Finland, Canada, Australia, Sweden and Luxembourg. Four out of ten are republics, but again with two quasi-republics in the list. Again, the UK fails the grade. The UK fails to get into the top ten of the Corruption Index and doesn't appear in the top twenty of the Gender Equality Index or Political Stability Index.

All we can really conclude from these global rankings is that having a monarchy makes no discernible difference to the freedom, prosperity or equality of nations. That is, however, a general conclusion on the correlation between monarchies or republics and measures of other attributes of nations. These correlations do not and cannot answer the question of whether in the UK the British monarchy has an impact on the country's political freedoms, the quality of our democracy, social mobility or anything else. What we can conclude, with some certainty, is that when a monarchist says that we only have to look at places like Norway, Denmark or the Netherlands to see that the monarchy produces freer and fairer societies, they are wrong.

## A Patriotic Attachment to Our Past

In arguing for the monarchy on grounds of stability and the longevity of the impartial monarch, royalists will usually move seamlessly to exclaim that these benefits are buttressed by tradition and history that predate the Queen's reign by many hundreds of years and which, together, form the essence of what Britain is today. To abolish the monarchy is to put everything at risk, to throw away valuable traditions, forget our glorious history and to tear at the fabric of what it means to be British.

More than once I have heard royalists say that the monarchy *is* Britain, or even that the Queen *is* Britain.* Through our devotion, the monarch unites us, and so to oppose the monarchy is to stand apart from everyone else. It is to be unpatriotic, or at the very least ill-informed and reckless.

The notion of patriotism can divide opinion. It has so often been bound up with nationalism and xenophobia. The view that patriotism, in the words of Oscar Wilde, is the 'virtue of the vicious', is common, as it is so often a pretext for either excluding 'outsiders' or shouting down critics. The American author Mark Twain said, on the other hand, that his patriotism is loyalty to his country, not to its institutions, nor its office holders. And America, like France, Ireland or any other democratic republic, serves to remind us that patriotism – of the kind that focuses on nation and community, rather than on institutions – does not need kings or queens.

I'll come back later to the issue of public support for the monarchy, but for now it's worth noting that the unity the monarchy offers the country is a mirage. Across the UK a sizeable – and growing – number of people oppose the institution. A much larger number are simply uninterested, with only a small minority – between 15 and 25 per cent – interested in

---

* I've yet to hear it expressed in such terms for Charles, but give it time.

major royal celebrations. The truth is that the United Kingdom of Great Britain and Northern Ireland is not all that united, at least politically, whereas where we find common ground has little to do with institutions of state. The UK is still grappling with the fallout from more than thirty years of political violence in Northern Ireland, violence in which the Crown played a symbolic role, and it's quite possible – perhaps inevitable – that the UK will cease to exist in its current form with the reunification of Ireland. Support for Scotland breaking away as an independent country continues to hover around 50 per cent, while Scottish support for the monarchy has collapsed. Across the four nations of the UK we are divided in all manner of ways, whether by inequality of wealth, race or politics. Yet we still find commonality and unity through sport, culture, language and shared national experiences, good and bad. What unity and disunity there is doesn't come from the monarchy, an institution only 14 per cent celebrated even when given an extra bank holiday to do so. Unity comes from shared values. It comes from our everyday lives and our common concerns. We have a shared culture that exists far beyond the gates of Buckingham Palace.

Besides, to argue for the monarchy on the basis of tradition is, like tourism, an amoral position. Traditions are many and varied, some good, some bad, some trivial, some profound. Something cannot be considered good simply because it has been labelled a tradition. Tradition means 'giving votes to the most obscure of all classes, our ancestors', to quote G. K. Chesterton. It is 'the democracy of the dead'. If a tradition is harmless, if it represents a link back to our past, helps us understand our history, then it can be useful, important even. But if a tradition is promoted as a means of obstructing change or cementing certain people in positions of power or status, then it is not a tradition worth keeping – it is one we must reject.

Interestingly, a great many traditions linked with the monarchy are relatively new, designed to shore up public support, project a more acceptable image or ingratiate royals with the political classes. The Changing of the Guard we know and recognize today dates back to 1837. The House of Windsor is an invention of wartime necessity when George V wished to distance himself from his cousin, Kaiser Wilhelm II. A large part of the honours system, often seen as an ancient tradition dating back to times of gallant knights in shining armour, is of the same vintage. OBEs, CBEs and MBEs, along with many (although not all) of the knighthoods handed to compliant backbench MPs, party donors and civil servants, date back to 1917. These are not natural extensions of our culture, the origins of which are lost in time. They are consciously constructed symbols and ceremonies designed to protect the status quo. To some extent the same is true of coronations. While these ceremonies have been held for centuries, the details have varied considerably, including the cost, size and opulence. In 1830, William IV wasn't all that keen on having a coronation at all, something he shared with his European cousins. Sweden's monarchs haven't had coronations since 1873, Denmark's since 1849, while the Dutch monarch has never been crowned as such, but instead has an inauguration ceremony at a joint sitting of Parliament. There is no constitutional or legal reason for King Charles to have had a coronation: he had it because he wanted to.

It makes no sense to say that we are somehow bound by the decisions taken by Queen Victoria or George V, or any other long-dead monarch or prime minister, not least because these monarchs and politicians felt no compunction to be bound by their ancestors. When they reshaped the coronation ceremony, stripped away the King's power, invented honours designed to appear ancient while being younger than the invention of powered flight, they were reshaping our traditions, ditching some and inventing new ones. There is no reason we cannot continue in that tradition of change.

While some traditions may be lost – if we choose to lose them – our history is going nowhere. We may forget details, we may re-evaluate how we interpret events that have shaped our nation, but no matter what we do with Britain's contemporary constitution, our history will always be with us. In a republic, the palaces, castles and museums will remain standing. Windsor Castle and Buckingham Palace can join the pantheon of historic buildings that includes Hampton Court, Blenheim Palace and the numerous castles you'll find scattered across the length and breadth of the country. History books will still be written, perhaps more freely, with greater access to archived material. However, the most fundamental point about history is that it must continually be made, each generation forging their own path, leaving their own imprint on the society we leave behind. History can be a useful guide. But it should not be a prison from which we can't escape. It is neither sensible nor patriotic to latch on to institutions designed by men two or three hundred years ago and declare them sacrosanct, or to limit our ambitions or growth in the name of protecting those institutions or traditions. For those concerned about history, rather than fret about the history made by past generations, perhaps think about the history we are making for future generations. What would be more historic than Britain standing up collectively and deciding, through the ballot box, to abolish the monarchy and embrace the values of democracy and equality? Imagine how that history will be remembered and celebrated in the decades and centuries that follow.

In these chapters, my aim has been to dismantle positive claims about the monarchy made by ardent royalists and casual observers alike. These defences have been repeated so often and are believed so widely, that it can be surprising to see that they either aren't true or don't make sense. It is telling that most of the modern benefits ascribed to the monarchy are incidental. Yet whether it's tourism, charity or global appeal, the figures don't add up.

When pressed, royalists will turn to the supposedly substantive benefits of a hereditary head of state – the importance of an independent, impartial monarch, the unity and stability the institution provides us, and so on. Yet these too are fallacies, not supported by either evidence or experience. Increasingly, the failures of our constitution are exposing the fallacy of the monarch as a guardian of democracy.

For many people who defend the monarchy, I suspect, their support is more an act of faith, or a habit so ingrained that they cannot see anything wrong. So often, when I see a royalist's arguments challenged, they eventually resort to the last line of defence: it works. This is often backed up with the notion that this issue isn't important enough to warrant anyone's time and attention. To quote Ian Dunt: 'The truth is, it's just not that big a deal. It works fine, people generally like it and we've plenty of other things to worry about.'

'If it ain't broke, don't fix it.' The problem is that the monarchy, which lies at the very heart of our constitution, is broken beyond repair and that should be cause for concern.

## PART TWO

# IF IT'S BROKE, DON'T FIX IT

# 3.

# Wrong in Principle, Wrong in Practice

In the world of consumer technology, there are innovators and early adopters. Those people who are at the front of the queue outside the Apple store at 5 a.m. on the day of a new product launch, or who signed up to streaming services when they began to come online more than a decade ago. At the other end of the scale are the 'laggards', those who stubbornly stick with their Nokia phone or refuse to give up their VHS film collection. I imagine the innovators struggle to understand why anyone would want to hang on to technology that has been superseded more than once over the past twenty years. Having known people who fit squarely into the laggard camp, I imagine the explanation is simply, 'it works'. If all you want from a phone is to make and receive calls, send and receive text messages, why bother with an iPhone that offers dozens of features you would never use? Why abandon a film collection you've lovingly built up, only to buy all those films again from Amazon, Apple or Paramount, if your old VHS tapes or DVDs still work?

When it comes to personal technology, 'it works' is a perfectly reasonable response to suggestions you move with the times. But that response doesn't stand up when we're discussing national institutions or the nation's constitution. When it comes to the monarchy, 'it works' falls at every hurdle. Works for whom? Does it work as well as it could? Are there better ways of doing things? Is this an ethical, principled way to organize our constitution?

That last question is particularly pertinent, because 'it works' can be a defence of any number of laws, constitutions and institutions that nonetheless operate in an unethical or unprincipled way. The Chinese government, to take a stark example, can be said to 'work'. In terms of keeping China running, making laws, enforcing them, collecting taxes, maintaining infrastructure and developing their economy, the Chinese government works as well as most. But it would be immoral for most liberal, democratic-minded people to actively support the continuation of a brutal dictatorship that, while 'working' for many, does so at huge cost to millions. Political prisoners, torture, widespread use of the death penalty, not to mention petty corruption, police intimidation and the lack of democratic freedoms, all impact on people's lives with devastating consequences. It would therefore be reasonable, and the ethical position, to argue that a different way needs to be found to govern China, one that works without the dreadful human cost.

I am not suggesting a moral equivalence between the Chinese regime and the British monarchy. I am, however, arguing that to dismiss arguments against the monarchy with 'it works' is unethical. It ignores those important questions. People come out with this argument, however, not because they are unethical but because they will say the monarchy does no harm. As I mentioned at the beginning, the three common misconceptions that act as a defence of the monarchy in the face of an otherwise indifferent public are that it is profitable, it is popular and it is harmless. The first section dealt with the 'profitable' part. The third will get on to polling and popularity. In this section, I will explain why the monarchy is *not* harmless. Beyond the material and political impact of the institution, monarchy undermines our principles. It forces us to compromise our values. It stands four-square against British ideals such as equality, democracy and the rule of law.

From time to time I get emails from supporters of Republic, saying that we shouldn't need to comment on the cost of the monarchy or the latest gaffe from a senior royal, that our cause is one of principle. On principle alone the monarchy is wrong and should be abolished. I agree with the sentiment, although that principle means something in practice. Highlighting real and tangible failings of the monarchy serves to make the principled point.

However, in an ideal world the principled argument should be enough. Time and again I have heard people concede that, okay, if we were starting from scratch, we wouldn't invent the monarchy. But it's here and why bother doing anything about it? Or they say, 'Yes, I know it's not democratic, that it's wrong in principle, but . . .' There should be no 'but' at the end of that sentence. If the monarchy is wrong in principle, if it's undemocratic, then it should be abolished.

British people overwhelmingly support democracy. In 2020, the More in Common think tank conducted a study of attitudes to democracy in Germany, France, Poland, the US and the UK. The study showed that despite widespread dissatisfaction with the outcomes of British democracy, democratic values continued to enjoy high levels of support. To quote the report: 'Eighty-seven percent also believe that democracies generally lead to fairer societies, and seven in ten believe democracies lead to more orderly and peaceful societies.'

The vast majority of us agree that the government must obey the law and respect due process. Political opponents have every right to express their view. We rank 'fair elections, the rule of law, and equal rights for everyone' as the most important features of British democracy. Interestingly, the British people are quite aware that while democracy is a good thing, British democracy is deeply flawed. The More in Common report found that 60 per cent believe the UK's political system is 'rigged to serve the rich and powerful' and complain of the lack of accountability of leading politicians, while more than 80 per cent believe politicians don't care what they think. Most striking is that three-quarters of people believe they are 'looked down on' by politicians, government and the wider 'establishment'. In other words, while the British people are committed to the values of democracy, we are increasingly unhappy with our variant of it. Our institutions do not live up to our values. Yet at least Parliament, government and local authorities can claim some democratic legitimacy, something that cannot be said of the monarchy. It is an institution that admits, by its existence, that it looks down on the rest of us. It regards members of the royal family as a cut above the rest. It implies they deserve honour and privileges regardless of merit, solely because of rank and bloodlines.

Quite often people will respond to this principled criticism of the monarchy by arguing that not every position in a democracy needs to be elected, which is true. But being democratic and having elected positions are not the same thing, although there is of course a requirement that the most important political positions are accountable directly to the people. The courts are part of Britain's democracy and very few people argue for elected judges. The same is true of the Civil Service and any number of state agencies and their governing bodies. The difference is that all these institutions are governed by a clear set of laws. They are ultimately accountable to Parliament, and they perform a function of democracy. On a point of principle, all of these institutions of state rest on the notion that we are political equals, equal in law and rights, laws and rights that are determined by the democratic process.

That is not true of the monarchy.

The monarchy rests on an entirely different set of values. Values that are the antithesis of those held by the British public. It is an institution that historically believed the monarch is anointed by God, an idea developed by Roman emperors and, later, by early medieval rulers such as Charlemagne and Otto the Great. The threat of eternal damnation, as well as more immediate punishment by beheading or being burnt at the stake, was an effective means of keeping subjects at bay. It suited the Roman Catholic Church, too. It maintained the Church's power and relevance through regal imposition of Catholic teaching. After the English Reformation, when Henry VIII broke with the Church, the monarch's relationship with God was made more explicit. Henry embraced the concept of the divine right of kings, while using charges of heresy to deal with some of his more intractable opponents. This religious and feudal language helps to give an appearance of legitimacy drawn from ancient roots. But the story of monarchy is, in essence, a history of a spiritually opportunistic, violent dictatorship.

There is endless fascination with the Tudor monarchs, and for good reason. After centuries of conflict between rival houses, the Tudors brought greater stability and security to England. The long reign of Elizabeth I is seen as a 'golden age', not just for the monarchy but for the country at large. Yet it is still the case that Elizabeth was a vicious despot, even by the standards of the day, and certainly by the standards of twenty-first-century Britain. Even after the dictator was defanged in favour of Parliament, the fiction of divine right was maintained until modern times. Queen Elizabeth's coronation in 1953 saw her take an oath to serve Church and God.

The point here isn't so much the religiosity of the monarchy, although in an increasingly atheist – or at least non-Christian – society that issue needs to be addressed. The problem is that this claim to divinity justifies elitism, snobbery and exceptionalism. It underpins a fundamentally anti-democratic system, one that sees inequality as a natural order rather than something to be addressed. Of course, the monarchy has, to some extent, evolved over the years. It now plays down the very values that underpin its existence. But that poses a problem, because if we don't believe in the values of divine right and a natural class order, what possible justification is there for ignoring the values we do believe in, and maintaining an institution that stands against equality, democracy and the rule of law?

It is arguable that by keeping the monarchy and the House of Lords, we dilute our commitment to democratic principles. Maintaining them means making intellectual room for fundamentally undemocratic – even anti-democratic – institutions. We see this when people sound aghast at the thought of electing a head of state, or when commentators argue for an appointed upper house. So often the conversation is about how we cannot trust the British people, who will inevitably – we are told – make daft decisions, choosing washed-up celebrities or famous footballers as head of state or electing career politicians to the upper house, which would otherwise be filled with the great and good, those who offer wisdom and expertise. In most other countries it would be unthinkable to suggest that a house of Parliament should be appointed by party leaders, or that the role of head of state should be the preserve of one family. Yet here it is taken for granted. It is turned into a virtue. I imagine if you told an American that their elected Senate should be replaced by party appointees, hereditary landowners and Anglican bishops they'd think you were mad. In the UK we're told of both the Lords and the monarchy: 'It works.'

If, like most people in the UK, you believe in democracy, equality and the rule of law, then it is unprincipled and wrong to support the continuation of the monarchy. This isn't just because principles have some theoretical value. Principles also have very real meaning in terms of how we are governed and the society we live in. There's a reason we put great store in political equality, the right to speak in opposition to those in power and the need for accountability to the electorate. Because without those things we suffer oppression, arbitrary and unjust rule and a general suppression of our rights. Principles don't just exist in the world of the theoretical, they matter in our day-to-day lives. To undermine our principles is a problem. As if to prove a point, it is notable how quick the police were to arrest even the most harmless protester in the days after the Queen's death, suggesting that, when it comes to the monarchy, free speech is cancelled out by deference. Symon Hill was arrested for simply shouting, 'Who elected him?' as he walked past the Oxford accession ceremony. Barrister Paul Powlesland tweeted on the Monday after the King's accession: 'Just went to Parliament Square & held up a blank piece of paper. Officer came & asked for my details. He confirmed that if I wrote "Not My King" on it, he would arrest me under the Public Order Act because someone might be offended.'

The frequent cries of shame from commentators and MPs when free speech is perceived to be under threat were conspicuous by their absence when, three months later, Hill was charged with 'using threatening or abusive words, or disorderly behaviour'. It is shocking that no one was willing to defend free speech in the face of royal deference. Shocking too that King Charles has made no effort to speak up in defence of our values when they are under threat in his name. It is only thanks to the good sense of someone at the Crown Prosecution Service that the charges were later dropped.

Of course, the monarch has long since lost the power to inflict tyranny on the people, and it's been centuries since a king or queen has committed crimes against the population at large. Yet the principles matter in the wider context, because if we compromise them in one area of public life, we compromise them in all. Either we are democrats or we're not. Either we enjoy the freedom to oppose those in power or we don't.

If we are democrats, what are we doing with a hereditary monarchy founded on medieval values of divine right and natural-born inequality?

Principles matter, not least because they underscore the standards of behaviour we set for ourselves. Those standards must necessarily differ depending on the principles we believe in and the philosophical basis for someone being in a particular position or public office. Public anger about MPs' expenses and, more recently, the serial breaches of Covid rules by Prime Minister Boris Johnson and his staff at Number 10 – in what became known as Partygate – stemmed from our shared democratic values. Similarly, public anger at a string of political scandals, notably the 'cash for questions' affair, did considerable damage to the Major government in the 1990s, which led to the Nolan Report and the adoption of the Seven Principles of Public Life, also known as the Nolan Principles. These principles are selflessness, integrity, objectivity, accountability, openness, honesty and leadership. While systems of accountability in Parliament and government remain fairly weak, these standards nevertheless apply. They apply to all public bodies and at every level of government, from Whitehall to the town hall. Except one: the monarchy. The Nolan Principles are hard to disagree with. They feel instinctively right because they come from those shared values of democracy and equality. Yet not only are these principles not routinely and systematically applied to the royal household in any meaningful way, there is also plenty of reason to believe that the monarchy fails – and fails badly – on every single one of them.

## Royal Expenses

Quite often, when discussing the abolition of the monarchy, an early retort is that republicans are wrong to complain about the cost, that the monarchy either costs the taxpayer very little or nothing at all, and anyway republics are just as expensive. This notion of the cost-effective monarchy is nonsense, as we'll see, but it's important to note that the cost of the monarchy is not why republicans want it abolished. Yes, heads of state in parliamentary republics tend to be a lot cheaper, but even if this wasn't the case, I would still call for the monarchy's abolition. It isn't the price tag that's the problem, it's what that price tag represents.

In 2009, after considerable effort from journalist and campaigner Heather Brooke, parliamentary expenses were becoming a serious issue for the government, MPs and the Speaker, Michael

Martin. Brooke's freedom of information request for details of MPs' expenses was making headway in court, while parliamentary authorities continued to challenge every ruling in favour of disclosure. Then the matter was dramatically taken out of their hands when a copy of several years' worth of data was leaked to the *Telegraph*, which promptly published the information over a number of days in May and June that year. The scandal rocked the political classes, with countless MPs facing accusations of wrongdoing. There were resignations, while others lost their seats or decided not to contest the next election. Six MPs and two Lords faced criminal prosecution resulting in jail time. Speaker Martin was a casualty of the affair, having come down on the wrong side of the debate in defending official secrecy over expenses. He reacted to the scandal by seeking police action for the leak, rather than concerning himself with the abuses of parliamentary expenses. The public outrage was palpable, directed not just at those who had broken the law, but also at those who had technically followed the rules but nevertheless breached the trust of the electorate. Curiously, it was both the largest and smallest claims that exercised public opinion, where claims for biscuits or a trouser press were ridiculed by a public who were, on average, paid far less than an MP's salary, while claims for £10,000 or more to redecorate second homes were met with genuine anger.

The claims that attracted most attention ranged between £5,000 and £15,000, although some were higher. The amount of money wasn't the issue; what caused the anger was the sense of double standards and dishonesty. Public anger was projected, sustained and amplified by the press and those MPs who hadn't abused the system, along with campaigners and commentators. Eventually, the entire process governing MPs' expenses changed.

Yet when a member of the royal family is found to have spent not thousands but *millions* of pounds of public money on second, third and fourth homes, these same people remain silent.

Each year the royal household publishes their accounts. They claim core costs are somewhere around £40 million, while another £40 million a year is currently being spent on refurbishment of Buckingham Palace. The situation is confused slightly by the way the Sovereign Grant works, with the size of the grant and the amount the palace has spent in any given year being two different things. That's because when the grant isn't used in full, the royal household holds on to the remainder and builds up a surplus, so in 2022 it was reported that the Grant was £86.3 million while the palace spent over £100 million. The truth is that neither of these figures gives an accurate picture of the financial cost of the monarchy to the British taxpayer, which Republic has estimated to be in excess of £345 million a year, enough public money to pay for approximately thirteen thousand new nurses or teachers.

Royalists tell me that this is a drop in the ocean compared to the size of the national budget, a reversal of their excitement over the claimed £500 million raised through tourism. Yet while £500 million is a tiny proportion of our national income, and £345 million a fraction of our national expenditure, the comparison misses the point. When we look at the income, there is a false claim that adds up to an amount that makes no discernible difference to the country. When we look at the expenditure, however, we must ask ourselves not whether it's a 'drop in the ocean' but whether public money is being spent effectively or ethically, and what else it might be spent on.

One of the strangest claims about the royals is their frugality.

On countless occasions it has been suggested that the Queen was 'frugal', with the *Mirror* reporting, a day after her state funeral, how the monarch would use a single-bar heater in her room at Balmoral, or go around switching lights off to save on energy bills. The claim has been inherited by Charles, with the *Telegraph* quoting a 'source' saying that the new King is 'by nature a pretty frugal person'. It's difficult to conclude that someone is frugal when they live in half a dozen palatial homes, travel between those homes by helicopter and rely on a staff of five hundred.

That conservative estimate of £345 million a year is the result of the royal family spending tens of millions of pounds of public money on their own travel, accommodation, bloated security arrangements and unaccountable official costs, while at the same time leaving other public bodies picking up the tab for royal engagements. It also includes the revenue of the two duchies, Lancaster and Cornwall, which, rather than being private estates as claimed by the royals, are Crown property, originating from the same place as the Crown Estate, and which should be sending their profits to the Treasury.

A significant part of the total is an estimated £100 million for royal security. It's an estimate because the government and palace refuse to release data on how much security costs. Republic discovered this some time ago when we submitted a freedom of information request to the Home Office, asking for the figures. The matter went as far as tribunal, where the government continued to argue that revealing the cost of royal security – without any of the detail – would itself pose a security risk. If they confirmed that £100 million figure, they argued, a would-be terrorist could use that to determine weaknesses in royal protection and so a royal life would be in danger. Such an argument is spurious at best.

I won't dwell on the question of security for too long because security is required for a British head of state, as it is for the British head of government, the prime minister. However, it's worth noting that only a handful of government ministers are afforded protection, including the prime minister, defence secretary and Northern Ireland secretary. From the Chancellor down, other ministers can be seen walking about Westminster or catching trains with their staff without any police protection at all. Tragically we know MPs can be at risk, as we've seen with the murders in 2016 and 2021 of Jo Cox, Labour MP for Batley and Spen, and David Amess, Conservative MP for Southend West. Yet with the royals, the security provided extends well beyond the most senior members of the family.

In 2010 it was reported that Paul Stephenson, then head of the Metropolitan Police, was increasingly frustrated at having to provide round-the-clock protection for junior members of the royal family, including Prince Andrew's two daughters, Eugenie and Beatrice. One report suggested Andrew had lobbied hard to retain the security as it was seen as a sign of their status within the royal pecking order. This is a point that's been raised a number of times by Norman Baker, who said in ... *And What Do You Do?* that 'the level [of protection] afforded did not seem to be based on any rational assessment', quoting the former head of the Royal Protection Squad, Dai Davies, as saying, 'I don't know of any real threat to any minor royal over twenty-five years.'

In a recent twist, Prince Harry has been in court, suing the British government for the right to pay the Metropolitan Police to provide him and his wife the same kind of protection he enjoyed before he moved to the States. Lawyers for the government pointed out that Princess Anne doesn't receive round-the-clock protection, arguing that, likewise, it is unnecessary for Harry and Meghan. Here the police are free to apply their professional judgement on the risks posed to the Sussexes and their view is that protection is unnecessary, although this assessment is disputed. Yet minor royals whom most of us have never heard of continue to receive police protection at great expense to the taxpayer. It is reasonable to assume, given their high profile and the significant levels of bile directed at Meghan Markle, that if any risk exists it is greater for her and her husband than it might be for Princess Eugenie.

The estimate of £100 million for royal security comes from various newspaper reports over the years, where journalists have quoted sources from within the Metropolitan Police speaking off the record. That estimate is old and it's likely to now be much higher, which means that the taxpayer spends more on royal security than it does on the entire official budget of the monarchy, the Sovereign Grant. It's easy to see why, when we count up the twenty-plus homes occupied by 'working' royals, all of which require police protection, whether the royal is in residence or not. The monarch alone has Windsor Castle, Balmoral, Sandringham, Buckingham Palace, Clarence House and Highgrove. Then there's the security provided en route between houses and to and from private and official engagements.

In 2009, Andrew's youngest daughter, Eugenie, spent a gap year travelling in South-east Asia. The Metropolitan Police were required to ensure a protection detail was always with her and her friends. Of course, a police officer based in London doesn't want to spend six to twelve months away from home, so instead two officers were flown to Thailand and Cambodia and back every two weeks to rotate the detail and limit the officers' time away, leaving the taxpayer to pick up the cost of regular business flights between Heathrow and Bangkok.

In 2002, my dad was volunteering at Bluebell Railway in Sussex. Bluebell is an extraordinary example of the many steam railways lovingly restored and operated by charities up and down the country, all of whom rely heavily on volunteers to work as drivers, ticket collectors and station staff. That year they invited Princess Alexandra to visit as part of the Golden Jubilee. Despite most people having never heard of the Queen's cousin and few but the most ardent of royalists being able to pick her out in a line-up, there was a sizeable police operation before her arrival, including sniffer dogs, searching drains and sealing the historic postbox. It was the sort of operation you might have expected for a visit by a prime minister, not a junior royal for whom it was assessed there was little to no risk.

You may think that having a royal visit your home town would be a good thing, drawing attention to the local community, businesses, schools and charities. We know from the Giving Evidence report that the impact of royals on charitable giving is limited, but the impact on local communities can be substantial, although not in the way imagined by royalists. A conservative estimate based on two dozen freedom of information requests submitted by Republic in 2015 puts the annual collective cost to local councils of royal visits at around £22.2 million. The figures are difficult to collate as budgets aren't always neatly allocated to a visit by Charles, William or Anne, but my guess is that the true total is substantially higher.

In 2012, to kick off her jubilee tour, the Queen visited Leicester, a visit billed as signalling a recognition of Britain's growing multi-culturalism. A virtue was also made of the royal entourage taking a scheduled train, rather than the royal train – although they did fly back to London by helicopter. The Queen was there for four hours, a trip that took in lunch, a church service and a visit to the De Montfort University. For that brief glimpse of our head of state, the good people of Leicester paid more than £180,000, money spent by the local council, Leicestershire Police and the university, where she couldn't have stayed for more than thirty minutes. This at a time when George Osborne's budgets were stripping millions of pounds of funding from every government department and local authority.

In 2007, the Queen's three-hour visit to Romsey in Hampshire had a far more serious impact on the local community. The town council ended up with a bill of almost £60,000 for the privilege of hosting the monarch, which almost wiped out their reserves and which represented more than a third of the council's annual budget, leaving them to seek financial assistance from the local borough council. Those costs included £5,000 to install new toilets at the insistence of the palace, as well as risk assessments, hiring stewards and erecting crowd barriers, all costs you might expect the palace to cover.

You may think this is small change, and I agree that this kind of money pales into insignificance compared to the multi-billion-pound budgets of most local authorities. But at a time of cuts, tens of thousands of pounds spent on a three- or four-hour visit from the Queen is money not spent on saving local jobs or services. None of these costs show up in the royal accounts, yet they are part of the cost of running the monarchy, an institution happy to let local people stump up the bill rather than add to their own budget.

Royalists often tell us that rather than costing the country a small fortune, the monarchy pays for itself, because the cost is more than offset by the revenue of the Crown Estate, surrendered by the Royal Family to the Treasury in exchange for the Sovereign Grant. There is a fair bit of confusion about the relationship between the Crown Estate and the Sovereign Grant, with reports often suggesting the grant comes from the Estate, when in fact the whole grant is funded by the government. Any increases to the grant are calculated with reference to Crown Estate revenue, with the grant being at least equal to 25 per cent of its profits. But the money doesn't come from the Crown Estate. If profits fell to zero, the grant would remain unchanged. There is no sense in this arrangement, which was set up by George Osborne partly to relieve the government of having to deal with the issue of royal funding.

Royalists will also dispute the inclusion of the profits from the duchies of Lancaster and Cornwall in the cost of the monarchy, as these are also assumed to be private property. Time and again they are referred to by the press and by the royals themselves as private estates. Yet while the two duchies are treated as private enterprises by the monarch, who receives the profits from the Duchy of Lancaster, and the heir, who is handed effective ownership of the Duchy of Cornwall, these estates are public property. They are provided, by Parliament, to the monarch and heir as a means of providing an independent source of income for the two most senior royals. If Parliament no longer felt obliged to provide that income, the revenues from the two duchies would revert to the Treasury.

Given how often these questions of land ownership are misunderstood or misrepresented, it's worth pausing here to take a look at royal land in general, and the duchies in particular. The Crown Estate is an organization established by Parliament to manage Crown lands – a huge land portfolio – for the purposes of raising revenue for the government. It is governed by the Crown Estate Act 1961, which establishes how it is managed. The land the Crown Estate manages belongs to the Crown (the clue is in the name). Not all Crown land or property is part of the Crown Estate, or even most of it – the Crown also runs prisons, commissions warships and dispenses justice through Crown courts. Of course, the language of monarchy often confuses the institutions of state with the people who occupy the palace. The Crown Estate website will tell you that the Crown Estate is *not* the King's personal, private property but that he owns the land 'in the right of the Crown'. This jargon means the monarch has no personal claim to the land, and that it is the state ('Crown') that owns it. We own it.

The land is there to raise revenue to fund the running of the government. When Charles I was executed, the lands were not kept in a personal capacity by the fleeing heir or his grieving family. When James II was deposed by the Glorious Revolution, the Crown remained intact, passing to the newly appointed William of Orange. A century later and George III 'surrendered' various hereditary revenues, including rents from Crown lands. This was not a personal surrender of private property, but a rearrangement of funding sources between two parts of the state. Much has been made by royalists of the fact that each new monarch is asked to renew this exchange of Crown land revenue for a grant, but that is pure theatre. When Charles agreed to 'surrender' the Crown Estate's revenue upon his accession to the throne in September 2022, he was doing the only thing he could do. He had no discretion in the matter. He was simply confirming an arrangement agreed by Parliament.

A paper written in 1901 by civil servant George Percival Best establishes quite clearly that the Crown Estate and duchy lands are public, not private property. The paper sets out the stages in which the lands were surrendered, adding that 'the process is not yet complete, the revenues of the Duchies of Lancaster and Cornwall [. . .] having been excepted from the surrenders hitherto made'. In other words, the duchies are eligible for surrender, but haven't yet been surrendered. Spencer Walpole, historian and MP who was descended from two British prime ministers and whose own father was a former Home Secretary, argued the same point, as did Regius Professor of Modern History at the University of Oxford, Edward Freeman, who said the surrender of Crown revenues was 'a custom as strong as law'. It was not an act of generosity on the part of the monarch, but a necessary restoration of revenues to the public. Even among these nineteenth-century establishment figures, Crown revenues were clearly in the gift of the state.

If you take a look at the websites of the two duchies or the principal royals, they will claim personal possession of these 'private' estates. The implication is that the public has no right to ask questions or demand the surrender of these estates. This is patently false. As early as 1461, at the start of Edward IV's reign, the Duchy of Lancaster was incorporated into Crown lands, the revenues being added to those the Crown already received for the purposes of government. It was, from that moment, only the King's property by virtue of his being King. Any dispute over the historic claims to this land were certainly settled at the time of the Glorious Revolution, when William III acquired the rights and revenues of the Crown in his 'body politic', or official capacity. Since 1701 and the Act of Settlement, the monarch has explicitly had official claim to these lands and revenues only by virtue of that parliamentary Act which makes them monarch. As for the Duchy of Cornwall, its status is clearer, having been created under the authority of Parliament in 1337 and therefore still under its authority today.

If you're still doubtful of the state ownership of the duchies, consider for a moment the stark differences between private estates and royal ones. As a private property owner, you are entitled to complete freedom over its disposal and the use of any revenue that may come from it, governed only by the laws that govern us all. The Duchies of Cornwall and Lancaster, on the other hand, are governed by statute specifically drafted for the purpose, with limitations placed on the disposal of capital assets and a requirement that they both present their accounts to Parliament each year, while each duchy grants its duke various historic and legal privileges not available to the rest of us, enhanced by their claim to enjoy Crown immunity and therefore enjoy exemptions from a great many laws, or sanctions for breaking laws (more on that later). None of that can be said of private estates – even the great landed estates of the Dukes of Bedford and Westminster. The only explanation for why the duchies are governed by statute is that they are not private property – they are rightfully the state's.

There are two important points to draw from all this. Firstly, the Crown is a state institution, which means when we make the transition to a republic, the state can freely transfer all the Crown's assets to some new form of state ownership, whether through Parliament, government or continuing as a quasi-independent body like the Crown Estate. The revenue Crown properties provide to the Treasury now would continue once the Crown was abolished. In other words, it's not the monarchy making money for the country through the Crown Estate, because that money is ours whether the monarchy survives or not.

Secondly, the Duchies of Lancaster and Cornwall have the same history as the Crown land managed by the Crown Estate. They are part and parcel of the land that was used to generate an income for the King when the King was responsible for government. Although Charles claims that the Duchy of Lancaster is his private property – having spent decades claiming the Duchy of Cornwall was his – it is public property. Effectively, as a country we pay Charles a private income in excess of £22 million a year. William, too, now that he's Duke of Cornwall. By some estimates, that's roughly six times the total combined salary of all democratic heads of state in Europe. It is reasonable to conclude that the King and his eldest son are being dishonest in their claim to that income.

The duchies are, for all practical purposes, property companies. While their history stretches back hundreds of years, the contemporary organizations are not areas clearly marked on a map, but vehicles for land ownership and business that have property scattered across England. The Duchy of Cornwall owns more land in Devon than in Cornwall, as well as swathes of real estate across the West Country and in London, including the Oval cricket ground. The total area of land owned by the duchy is approximately the size of Leeds, population 800,000. It is, in essence, a corporation, a company headed by a prince who acts as chairman of the board and sole shareholder, receiving all the profits as personal income.

While prince, Charles paid income tax – voluntarily – on his personal income derived from the Duchy of Cornwall, but the duchy refuses to pay corporation tax. They argued that to do so would be to tax Charles twice. Yet every business owner in the country must pay corporation tax on their company's profits before paying themselves an income, on which they must also pay income tax. When challenged on this unique tax-avoidance scheme, as they were in 2013, when the House of Commons Public Accounts Committee investigated the wider issue of corporation tax, the duchy quickly switched from one defence to another. One minute they argued that Charles shouldn't face a double tax bill, then they claimed that there was no distinction between the duke and the duchy, as if his commercial enterprises were no more than private, incidental projects that just happened to make millions of pounds' profit. If that didn't work, they argued that the duchy wasn't a corporation, as Charles's private secretary, William Nye, did when he told the House of Commons Public Accounts Committee in 2013, 'It's a set of properties that belong to the Duke of Cornwall, the fact that it's a large set of properties and it's worth a lot of money doesn't per se make it a corporation.' They also added, for good measure, that the duchy's legal status was equivalent to a trust or charity, ignoring the fact that trusts and charities that trade can also be liable for corporation tax. Corporation tax is payable by everyone who is making a profit through the sale of goods or services, except for very limited exceptions, such as when profits are being spent directly on charitable purposes, which is not the case with the duchy.

At the time, Republic submitted evidence to the committee in which we detailed the various excuses emanating from the duchy, pointing out why each one was wrong and how some were contradictory. These points were put to Nye by committee member Austin Mitchell. Mitchell appeared to lose patience, saying to Nye: 'You are really dodging around, aren't you? For tax purposes it's not a corporation but for every other purpose it is a corporation. Wouldn't it be better if it was just taxed as a corporation instead of some kind of medieval anomaly which happens to have moved into the business era which we are now in?'

Again, this isn't just about the money being thrown at the royals. But £44 million being handed to Charles and William from the two duchies can make a big difference to public services. In June 2021, the government cut £40 million from a fund to help people on Universal Credit cover shortfalls in rent or to pay deposits on new tenancies, with critics of the cut arguing that it would lead to more people ending up on the streets. While it should be obvious to everyone that spending money on preventing homelessness is a far better use of public money than giving two millionaires personal incomes of £22 million or more, the fact that this arrangement persists to this day speaks volumes about the monarchy, the royals and attitudes towards both from government. William likes to claim a deep and personal concern with the issue of homelessness, yet neither he nor his father pays their fair share of tax, let alone surrender an income that is wholly unjustified. On the contrary, the history of the royals has been one of defending their interests at every turn, always seeking ways to improve their financial position regardless of any concerns there might be about the state of the nation's finances, or the plight of the poorest in our society.

## Tax Avoidance

Royal exemptions from tax are often presented as part of the mix of archaic and ancient rules and precedents that come with having a monarchy. But that isn't the case. There was a time when the monarch and other members of the family did pay taxes, although of course many taxes we pay these days were not around for much of the monarchy's history. Income tax was introduced in 1842 (although income taxes had been raised to fund Britain's war with Napoleonic France, these taxes were subsequently repealed). Queen Victoria paid income tax through to the end of her reign in 1901. Her immediate successor, Edward VII, insisted on an exemption from income tax but was rebuffed by the government. It was his eldest surviving son, George V, who was able to persuade prime minister Lloyd George that he should be exempted from the tax, although as Norman Baker puts it, this was part of a 'grubby deal [. . .] to win royal support for the creation of a large number of Liberal peers to force the radical People's Budget through parliament'. In other words, the King's price for allowing the elected government to introduce a progressive budget was his exemption from income tax. Baker also makes the observation that, while personal taxes for most people in the UK rose sharply from the Great Depression to the end of the Second World War, taxes for the royals dropped or were stopped altogether.

Just how much income tax revenue has been lost is hard to say, but it is likely to be in excess of a billion pounds over the intervening decades. Inheritance tax losses could well be as high. When the Queen died, her estate was estimated to be worth at least £650 million, which at a rate of 40 per cent above the threshold would put the tax bill at around a quarter of a billion pounds. That's a quarter of a billion pounds not being spent on public services.

In 1993, in response to the outrage caused by promises of public money being spent on the restoration of Windsor Castle after the devastating fire the year before, the Queen agreed with the Major government that she would start to pay income tax. However, she did not agree to be bound by the laws the rest of us are bound by, but did agree to make voluntary tax payments, presumably at a rate of her choosing. The government refuses to say what rate that is, so it's possible the new King will be paying the statutory rate or contributing just 1 per cent – or even just £1 – of his considerable income to the Treasury. We have no way of knowing. What we do know is that the Queen's agreement to pay income tax was in exchange for the government agreeing to release her of her obligation to pay inheritance tax when her mother died. The avoidance of inheritance tax enjoyed by monarchs was previously limited to the inheritance by one monarch from their immediate predecessor. So, when the Queen inherited her father's wealth she paid no tax on it. The agreement never included the inheritance from the other parent or anyone else, until John Major decided that on this occasion it would.

The Queen's inheritance of her mother's estate in 2002 was worth an estimated £50–70 million, which means the Queen avoided a tax bill of £20 million. It is understood that the entire estate went to the Queen, rather than being left to various members of the family, as they would not avoid the inheritance tax. The Queen then shared out that inheritance as gifts to her family, and so acted as a one-woman tax-avoidance scheme for her children and grandchildren. The Queen and her family could have chosen not to do this. They did not have to press for multi-million-pound tax exemptions. They could have chosen to pay taxes the rest of us are obliged to, and they could tell the government that they wouldn't object to the law being amended to put upon them the same tax obligations as everyone else. But they don't. They choose to avoid tax at every turn.

The Nolan Principles, which were introduced around the same time the Queen was negotiating her huge tax break, put the onus on public servants to behave in an ethical and dignified manner, to conduct themselves in accordance with the highest standards. Those standards, once more, of selflessness, integrity, objectivity, accountability, openness, honesty and leadership were founded on universal principles that ought to apply to everyone. In this matter, the palace remains immune. Were King Charles to abide by those high standards, surely he would accept his moral obligation to pay taxes at the same rate as everyone else. Would he not have the integrity to refuse such colossal financial benefits? Would you not expect a head of state to step back and objectively assess these arrangements as unfair, unethical and inappropriate? Surely a monarch who upholds the highest standards would accept the need for transparency and accountability, and as their income tax is paid voluntarily, they would make clear what their income is and how much tax is being paid? In 2021, HM Revenue and Customs estimated that tax avoidance cost the Treasury £35 billion each year. Shouldn't a head of state show leadership on matters of public interest, such as the need for all of us to pay our fair share of tax? Rather than abiding by the Nolan Principle of honesty, Charles and the royal household seek to obfuscate, misdirect and confuse in their efforts to justify the avoidance of inheritance and corporation taxes and leave people guessing what the monarch pays in income tax.

It's not just tax avoidance the royals make excuses for, but day-to-day use of public money for their private lifestyles. Helicopters are their preferred mode of transport for short- to medium-distance travel, while private or RAF jets are used for longer journeys. On some occasions, of course, they travel across the UK by royal train. The royal train has at least eight coaches for the purposes of ferrying one or two royals to an engagement, perhaps with a handful of staff along for the ride. I'm sure the train has changed in some respects over the intervening decades, but the 1969 BBC documentary *Royal Family* described the coaches containing 'three working rooms, three dining rooms, five bathrooms, three kitchens, as well as Prince Philip's room and the Queen's room'. When the palace press office excuses use of the royal train, they forget to mention that it lives in Milton Keynes, adding hundreds of miles of travel for the train, if not for the royal family.

When challenged, they will tell you that plane, train and helicopter travel is sometimes unavoidable, as with Charles's trip to Cambridge by helicopter in January 2020, when his spokesperson explained that decisions 'are made based on what is possible within the constraints of time, distance and security. In order for him to undertake as many engagements as he does across the UK and around the world he sometimes has to fly.' The irony seemed lost on the prince, given that on that occasion Charles was travelling from Highgrove in Gloucestershire to the Whittle Laboratory in Cambridge, to lecture scientists on the need to reduce aircraft emissions. As is common with Charles's diary of engagements, despite the impression the spokesperson wanted to give, he wasn't dashing from one thing to another on the same day. This was the first official outing for three days, and it would be a week until the next engagement. Quite why time, distance and security demanded he produce an estimated 2.5 tonnes of carbon emissions (roughly equivalent to two cars regularly driven for a whole year) at a cost of £12,000 rather than drive the three hours by car is a mystery. This is typical of Charles's travel arrangements. In September 2021 he attended the premiere of the last Daniel Craig Bond film, *No Time to Die*. It was later revealed that his attendance cost the taxpayer

£32,000, the cost of a charter flight. His previous official engagement had been in Scotland, seven days earlier, and he was back in Scotland three days later with no other engagements between.

Then there are the two dozen palatial homes occupied by the royals. Each requires round-the-clock security, as I mentioned above. Some of these homes are private property, such as Sandringham and Balmoral. Most are either on Crown Estate land or are otherwise state property, such as Buckingham Palace and the homes contained within Kensington Palace and St James's Palace. Most 'working royals' have at least one home that is subsidized and guarded at public expense, including the Queen's various cousins such as the Duke and Duchess of Kent, Prince and Princess Michael of Kent and the Duke and Duchess of Gloucester. The more senior royals enjoy the opportunity to move between half a dozen homes dotted around the UK.

It's worth stepping back and considering that none of this luxury or wealth is inevitable. We do not, as a nation, owe the Mountbatten-Windsor family this opulent lifestyle. By contrast, we offer the prime minister a flat above Number 10 and Chequers, a large Tudor pile out in the Buckinghamshire countryside. These are both working buildings, used for the official business of the head of government. What possible reason is there not to provide the head of state – and only the head of state – with an official residence in London, a single country residence and a salary pegged to that of the prime minister? There is a curious discrepancy between what we're willing to provide for our elected government and what we're willing to let the royals get away with.

## Lobbying and Secrecy

In 1993, the Queen gave a speech in which she said it was right that every institution is open to scrutiny. Yet then, as now, the monarchy was a secretive institution that went out of its way to guard its interests.

Until relatively recently, their efforts to maintain complete secrecy were largely untroubled by journalists, campaigners or the law. And it wasn't just the monarchy. The UK was, in the words of journalist Heather Brooke (of MPs' expenses fame), a 'secret state'. Then, in 2005, the Freedom of Information Act came into force.

The FOIA established the principle that citizens have the right to know what our public servants are doing. The Act covers wide swathes of public life, including all government departments, police forces, schools and even the BBC. This means you, or anyone, can write to a public body and request a copy of recorded information they might hold. By law you are entitled to a reply, and to receive the information you've asked for, within a certain timeframe. Of course, there are a number of exemptions to the Act, such as personal data, law enforcement, national security and, in the case of the BBC, journalism. However, in most cases, you can challenge an exemption on the grounds that there is a public interest that outweighs other concerns. It is not perfect, but the FOIA has been one of the most significant constitutional changes in recent decades. Yet there is one glaring gap in the long list of public authorities compelled to comply with the Act: the monarchy.

The monarchy isn't recognized by the Act as a public authority. So, where you can compel your local police force to divulge employee numbers and their annual budget for salaries and training, you cannot insist on any disclosure from our head of state or the institution of monarchy. The palace claims to answer requests in the spirit of the Act, but a quick look at the website whatdotheyknow.com, a platform for submitting and tracking FOI requests, shows a large number of questions to the royal household go unanswered.

The problem goes further, however, as all documents and communications that pass between the royal household and public bodies that are subject to the Act are also exempted from disclosure. So where you can request correspondence between the Home Secretary and the head of the Football Association, for instance, you cannot expect disclosure of correspondence between that same government minister and the King, or Prince William. Or Andrew. For five years, from 2005 to 2010, this exemption was subject to the public interest test, meaning that if you could successfully argue there was a public interest in disclosure that carried more weight than the royal exemption, the correspondence or documents must be released. It was under this exemption that the *Guardian* fought a ten-year legal battle for release of just a small sample of Prince Charles's letters, a battle they won in 2015.

Unfortunately that's not a battle that can be repeated. Aside from the huge expense and bloody-minded determination of government and palace to challenge the disclosure (the government alone spent £400,000 on defending their position), the law was changed in 2010 to remove the public interest test, making the exemption absolute. It's worth considering what that means in principle as well as in practice, because removing that test not only means it is now legally impossible to pursue disclosure of royal documents under the FOIA, it also means the secrecy of the royals is given greater importance than the public inter-est. So even if it were clearly in the interests of the country for the public to be aware, for example, of direct and unbearable pressure being placed on the government by the King, the law says the King's demand for secrecy is more important. It's shocking that this amendment was ever proposed, and that it was, shamefully, supported by all the major parties at the time.

We can be sure that this 2010 amendment was the result of intense lobbying by the palace, clearly concerned by the deluge of FOI requests that would, inevitably, eventually lead to damning disclosures. It is no coincidence that in 2012 the SNP government in Holyrood, where there is a separate but very similar FOIA, sought to introduce an identical amendment. Thankfully the Scottish information commissioner Rosemary Agnew, and others, were more vocal in their criticism of the proposed change and it was eventually dropped. Agnew said of the proposed change: 'I have some reservations about the abso-lute exemption of the Royal Family. It is a general principle of freedom of information laws around the world that absolute exemptions should be relatively rare,' adding that this exemp-tion would be 'particularly wide in scope, applying as it would to all information relating to communications'. It raises the question, then, as to why the government in Westminster was so ready to push the amendment through.

The introduction of the FOIA threw a spotlight on Britain's culture of official secrecy and with it the extra layers of protec-tion demanded by the royals. But those demands go back a lot further than 2005. When Prince Philip died in 2021, there was a fair amount of surprise that his will would not be published, as happens with everyone else's will. The palace applied to a judge to have the will sealed and the judge, Sir Andrew McFarlane, the president of the Family Division of the High Court, dutifully complied. The application and hearing were also conducted in secret, with no opportunity to hear, let alone challenge, the arguments for sealing the will. This was a point challenged by the *Guardian*, which subsequently took the matter to court. The sealing of the will itself couldn't be challenged unless the secrecy of the process was deemed by the court to constitute a 'serious interference with the principle of open justice'. The *Guardian*'s case was rejected and the decision, made in complete secrecy, was upheld. The excuse, according to McFarlane, was that the will must be sealed to 'enhance the protection afforded to the private lives of this unique group of individuals, in order to protect the dignity and standing of the public role of the sovereign and other close members of her family'.

As with Dominic Grieve's argument for concealing Charles's letters, the notion that dignity somehow relies on hiding behind official secrecy is as absurd as it is dishonest. There is nothing dignified about keeping matters secret that by law the rest of us must disclose. Dignity is achieved by behaving in a dignified manner, and if a person can be honestly judged to be dignified then that cannot be undermined or threatened by openness and transparency.

This was another lie put out by the palace and – to their shame – upheld by appeal judges Geoffrey Vos, Master of the Rolls, and Victoria Sharp, president of the Queen's Bench Division, who ruled that publicity surrounding the will would 'compromise the need to preserve the dignity of the Queen and her family's privacy'. Yet the publication of wills is there to ensure estates are correctly handled and to prevent fraud. To say that there is no public interest in ensuring these same safeguards are applied to our head of state – as McFarlane claimed – is fanciful. It is notable, too, that since the Queen's death Philip's will remains sealed and will do for ninety years, as if that dignity is also inherited, or must continue to be protected even in death.

McFarlane might at least claim precedent, given this habit dates back to the early years of the twentieth century, although no further. In attempting to defend the indefensible, the appeal judges made this Orwellian statement: 'It is true that the law applies equally to the Royal Family, but that does not mean that the law produces the same outcomes in all situations.' They added that openness would risk a 'media storm', although they did not elaborate on why that would be the case. If the family's financial affairs were above board and in good order, why would it matter? In ruling in favour of sealing the will, McFarlane suggested that 'because of the constitutional position of the Sovereign, it is appropriate to have a special practice in relation to royal wills', again dressing up corrupt practices or faux traditions as something hard-wired into the make-up of the monarchy. There must be a reason, we are left to assume, but as the reason is lost in the mists of time and woven into the fabric of the monarchy, it's best to leave things as they are. Yet, as has been more widely reported in recent years, up until 1911 royal wills were published like everybody else's.

The monarch's will has been sealed by law since 1862, but this only covered the monarch, not the rest of the family. As David McClure explained in his excellent book *Royal Legacy*, the reason for lobbying for the sealing of other royal wills was quite simple – to cover up scandal and save the royals from embarrassment. Edward VII, who reigned from 1901 until his death in 1910, had a string of affairs before and during his time on the throne. One of the women he had a long-standing relationship with was Ellen Constance, a minor aristocrat by marriage who also had an affair with Prince Francis of Teck, great-grandson of George III and brother-in-law of Edward's successor, George V. Francis died the same year as Edward, aged forty. On inspection of her brother's will, George's wife, Queen Mary, discovered that the Cambridge Emeralds, a collection of jewellery acquired by Princess Augusta of Cambridge, had been left to Constance. The potential for scandal and embarrassment was acute, had the public discovered that not only had the late King had numerous affairs, but that one of the women involved was also involved with the new Queen's recently deceased brother. Rather than face the scandal, they covered it up by applying to the courts to seal the will of Prince Francis and ensure these sordid details never saw the light of day. The judge – as now – was only too happy to oblige.

The locking away of historic documents extends far beyond the sealing of wills. In the UK, as in most advanced democracies, government records are, after some time, released to the National Archives, where they will be catalogued and stored indefinitely, open to inspection by anyone who wishes to trawl through minutes, letters, reports and various other documents and communications emanating from the halls of power. As well as being a rich source of original material for historians and researchers, this industrial-scale archiving of everything put on paper by MPs, ministers and civil servants serves a deeper democratic need. Those archives mean we can, over time, gain a better understanding of how government works, how major events or policies have unfolded, allowing us to learn from those experiences.

It is these same records that are now subject to the Freedom of Information Act, so that even if no one thinks to request disclosure at the time, classified and sensitive documents will eventually see the light of day. Unless, of course, those documents are kept by our head of state or his predecessors. Whereas our head of government, the prime minister, and their ministers can expect their decisions, letters and now emails to eventually be published, possibly within their lifetime, our head of state is protected by a simple sleight of hand. Rather than heading to the National Archives in Kew, palace documents are locked away in the 'family archive' in Windsor Castle. The archive will hold on to every document and record, whether it is personal, such as letters between mother and son, or official, such as letters between monarch and prime minister. The archives do not provide a catalogue, as is usual, so you must know what documents exist before asking for them, rather than being able to trawl the records to see what's there. These archives are beyond any legal requirements of the Freedom of Information Act or Public Records Act and for the most part they are jealously guarded from prying eyes.

Interestingly, this level of secrecy doesn't always work in their favour, as Philip Murphy, professor of British and Commonwealth studies argued in 2015, shortly after images were leaked showing the Queen Mother and the future Queen Elizabeth performing the Nazi salute in the 1930s. Murphy, who has previously studied the British security services, said: 'The majority of books about the contemporary monarchy bear a striking resemblance to the intelligence literature of the 1980s. Like the pre-1990s intelligence community, the Palace places entirely unreasonable restrictions on the work of professional scholars. It prohibits all but a small handful of "authorised" writers from viewing papers in the Royal Archives relating to the current reign.'

His argument is that such secrecy leads to speculation against which the royals struggle to respond decisively because they are loath to disclose anything at all, even to dispel accusations of Nazi sympathies from the Queen Mother. On balance, however, the palace has probably judged that allowing a few toxic rumours to persist is preferable – for them – to opening the doors and revealing decades of secrets.

Through exemptions from the FOIA and the squirrelling away of official documents into the private archives, the royal household keeps tight control of information, so much so that they have been compared unfavourably to MI5 (which has an understandable need for secrecy). Historian Alexandra von Tunzelmann said in a 2016 letter in *The Times*: 'I had to fight to be allowed to publish even the tiny amount of tangential detail [the Royal Archives] allowed me to see. Since then, I have left the British royal family well alone and focused on the history of more open and accountable organisations, such as the CIA.'

Of course, it's impossible to keep tabs on every document and letter that passes through the offices of state, so from time to time there are opportunities to at least identify what is being withheld from the public. Where there are cracks in their wall of secrecy, no effort is spared to stop papers seeing the light of day. Historian and biographer Andrew Lownie was forced to spend more than £400,000 in his efforts to have the papers of Lord Mountbatten released into the public domain. Mountbatten was a cousin of the Queen and Philip and, until his untimely death at the hands of the IRA in 1979, a close confidant of Prince Charles. The University of Southampton spent £4.5 million to secure custody of Mountbatten's papers, yet when Lownie requested to see them while researching his latest biography, he was refused permission. Most of the papers were eventually released, but Lownie still faces a huge legal bill for his trouble.

In early 2023, Index on Censorship, which campaigns for freedom of expression, released a report on royal secrecy with the blunt observation that 'the royal family rewrites history to its own advantage without compunction'. In researching the report, Index surveyed two dozen historians, writers and journalists, all but one admitting that their work was 'hampered by the refusal of the archives to grant access to key materials'. One author had to abandon a biography on Prince George, the younger brother of King George VI, who died in a plane crash during the war, because the palace simply refused to allow any access to the archives. The author asked to remain anonymous in the report because he feared falling out of favour with palace officials, giving us some idea of the manner in which our head of state seeks to control access to material, much of which are official state records.

The monarchy is wrapped up in layer upon layer of secrecy, guarded not just by the royals but by the government, too. In researching his PhD thesis, Dr John Kirkhope pursued freedom of information requests relating to the Duchy of Cornwall, which you will recall Charles has always insisted is a private estate. When I interviewed Kirkhope for *The Man Who Shouldn't Be King*, a documentary Republic was making, he retold how he attended an information tribunal to find himself up against a small army of government lawyers and civil servants, as well as representatives of the duchy, all there to protect Charles from unwanted scrutiny.

As with the case of Philip's will, the palace and government don't just wish to keep decisions secret, they want to keep details of the decision-making process secret, too. Kirkhope later took an interest in the process of seeking royal consent for bills passing through Parliament, and in doing so requested Civil Service guidance for managing this arcane rule. He was refused and it took some effort and perseverance to finally overcome Cabinet Office intransigence. Likewise, one of Republic's volunteers spent three years chasing the same Cabinet Office for a copy of the Precedent Book, to be rebuffed at every stage. Eventually the information commissioner came down on the side of disclosure and Whitehall relented. Both the royal consent rule and the disclosure of the Precedent Book raise more serious questions about how secrecy, access and leverage all come together to empower and embolden a royal household always determined to get its way.

## Access and Consent

The royal consent rule John Kirkhope was interested in is as simple as it is outrageous. It stipulates that any legislation going through Parliament that affects the private and personal interests of the monarch or immediate heir must receive their consent before it can complete its passage through Parliament. To be clear, this is not Royal Assent, the process whereby a bill is finally passed and becomes law. This is something quite different.

The Precedent Book mentioned above is essentially the handbook for the Cabinet. It cites precedent to explain how the Cabinet operates, from ministerial appointments and conflicts of interest to seating arrangements at Cabinet meetings. It's about as dry as it sounds and contains very little that could be construed as sensitive or controversial. When it was eventually released to us in 2015, chapter eleven, which deals with communication between Cabinet and palace, had been redacted in full. Not only can we not see communication with the palace, we are also forbidden from seeing the guidelines on how that communication is managed. Secondly, a single line in chapter four reveals that all Cabinet papers were shared with Prince Charles and now, presumably, Prince William. The book says, 'The documents of the cabinet and ministerial committees are issued primarily to the sovereign, the Prince of Wales, and ministers.' Not all Cabinet ministers and certainly not all other government ministers receive *all* Cabinet papers. A year earlier, the government had published updated guidance on the handling of sensitive information, which states, 'The "need to know" principle applies wherever sensitive information is collected, stored, processed or shared within government and when dealing with external public and private sector organisations, and international partners.'

The revelation of the extent of Charles's access made the front pages of the *Guardian* and *Daily Mail*, and prompted forty-eight hours of media interviews in which I repeatedly challenged royal commentators on why Charles could possibly need this level of access. While Charles's aides and supporters tried to explain his unrivalled access to Cabinet papers by saying this was part of his constitutional role, the *Guardian* pointed out that at the same time the palace stated on their own website, 'There is no established constitutional role for the heir to the throne.' Even if there were such a role, quite why he must be routinely sent every minute, report and policy proposal that passes through Cabinet – greater access than actual members of Cabinet – is a mystery.

This all fits together quite neatly: senior royals, who have no qualms about using their access to ministers to lobby government, also have full and early access to what ministers are discussing before any decisions or policies are made public. With their communications protected under the absolute exemptions of the Freedom of Information Act, the King and heir are free to use that information to see off any unwanted changes to the law that would affect them, or to lobby for policy changes in line with their own agendas. To information and access we can add leverage, provided by the aforementioned royal consent rule. The rule means that if a new law is going through Parliament, and that law affects the private interests of either Charles or William, they must be asked to consent before it can complete the parliamentary process. This is not a formality: if either royal sits on their hands and simply declines to consent, without even replying or offering any objection, the law cannot pass. This gives the royals considerable opportunity to make the lives of government ministers quite difficult, were they not to get their way.

You might be thinking that there can't be that many laws that affect the private interests of these two men, but it's worth remembering that they are both landowners, employers, investors and businessmen. Laws concerning employment rights, tax, investments, land management, environmental protection and new infrastructure projects have all required royal consent. Republic had a brief look at determining how many such requests for consent have been made and quickly found a few hundred. The *Guardian* has taken a much deeper look at the issue and has found more than a thousand such laws. A great many have been tailored to exempt the Queen, and now King, and the Prince of Wales, from burdens and obligations the rest of us are bound by. Whether they request exemptions or give consent without comment, the breadth of laws that the monarch and heir can personally vet before our MPs can finish debating them is extraordinary and, given they're such a wealthy family with so many financial and personal interests, it should be a concern that they can intervene on the drafting of new legislation concerning wealth and financial regulation. As the *Guardian* reported in 2021: 'In 2014, for example, the Queen and the heir to the throne screened the inheritance and trustees' powers bill. Two years earlier she vetted the trusts (capital and income) bill.'

One revelation from the *Guardian* was the pressure the Queen put on the Heath government in 1973 to insert a change to a proposed new law, one designed to 'bring transparency to company shareholdings', to guard the monarch from financial scrutiny. But perhaps the most shocking revelation was the palace's insistence on being exempted from new race discrimination laws introduced by then home secretary (and future prime minister) James Callaghan in the late 1960s. The palace stated in a memo to civil servants, in reference to the employment of 'clerical and other office posts', that it 'was not, in fact, the practice to appoint coloured immigrants or foreigners'. They were granted an exemption from the law, and have been ever since, meaning anyone employed by the royal household to this day is not protected against racial discrimination.

It's not just private interests the royals will lobby to jealously protect. We know from the *Guardian* case in which they pursued publication of Charles's 'spider memos' that he writes to government ministers almost every week, pressing for certain policies, from funding of homeopathy on the NHS to military procurement. It is hard to gauge the impact this lobbying has had over the years, which is part of the problem. We simply don't know what he is saying to whom and what impact it's having. And, of course, if a minister is not forthcoming with support for one of his pet ideas, we have no idea whether Charles exploits his position and the leverage afforded him through the royal consent rule to put pressure on the government. It's unlikely a government would tolerate such pressure on high-profile matters of policy, but on lower-order issues it's quite possible action might be taken for the sake of a quiet life and to avoid an embarrassing clash with the palace. Governments have certainly been keen to avoid getting into difficulties with the palace in the past, as memos relating to the new law on shareholdings indicate.

We can assume, and in some cases know, that the royals have exploited these arrangements to win hugely beneficial, or simply unconscionable, legal exemptions for themselves. The question I keep asking myself – to which I have no firm answer beyond suspicions – is whether they also use their privileged position to help their friends and business contacts. It was a question I returned to in June 2022, when the *Sunday Times* revealed that Prince Charles had received €3 million in cash from Sheikh Hamad bin Jassim bin Jaber Al Thani, the former prime minister of Qatar, reportedly a donation to the Prince of Wales's Charitable Fund. Why was the sheikh making a sizeable donation to one of Charles's more obscure charities? Did he want something in return? And did he get it? The meetings in which the cash was handed over in suitcases and Fortnum & Mason carrier bags were private and only Hamad and Charles were in the room, so it's impossible to know what promises were made. Of course, I have no evidence of any promises made and Clarence House denied any wrongdoing, but it is an obvious cause for concern that such people have direct and private access to someone who in turn can exert pressure on the government, in secret and beyond any chance of scrutiny. If Charles did promise something in return for the donation, we will never know.

## A Corrupt Institution

Walter Bagehot, in his 1867 book *The English Constitution*, argued that the monarchy was the 'dignified' part of the British constitution, which was 'to be reverenced', adding, 'and if you begin to poke about it you cannot reverence it . . . Its mystery is its life. We must not let in daylight upon magic.' It is a way of thinking that persists to this day, an acknowledgement that the monarchy rests on fiction, sleight of hand and official secrecy. But in recent years, enough light has been let in to reveal a grubby institution that fails across the board against the high standards of the Nolan Principles.

Our head of state, who holds the highest office in the country, ought to be held to the highest standards. Failings must be scrutinized and reported on, not swept under the carpet or hidden behind closed doors. Being a hereditary monarchy, the same must also apply to the extended family, at least to those who claim public roles, hold honorary titles in our military or are waiting in the wings, ready to accede to the throne upon the monarch's death. Yet, the monarchy is protected by official acquiescence, secrecy and an army of apologists who will excuse the royals of misdemeanours that would cost a politician their job.

Were we to apply the same level of scrutiny and criticism to the monarchy as we do to Parliament, with access to all the information we need and a stringent and robust approach to dissecting and examining the institution, it would be difficult to conclude the institution is not corrupt. That's not to say it is criminal in its behaviour. But if corruption is the abuse of public office for personal gain, if it is to fall short of those high standards of the Nolan Principles, then how can we conclude that the monarchy is anything but?

If the monarchy met those standards, if the royals acted in a selfless manner, with integrity and objectivity, would they avoid taxes the rest of us have to pay? Would they use public money for private purposes? Would they claim gargantuan incomes from duchies they do not own? If the King was committed to accountability, openness and honesty, would he not sign up to the Freedom of Information Act, reject the secrecy of sealed wills and insist the monarchy and his family are bound by the same laws as the rest of us? If he offered leadership, would he not speak to these values and principles, demonstrate a keen awareness of the failures of the institution and seek to rectify them?

To say 'it works' in defence of the monarchy is to ignore these significant failures of leadership, honesty and integrity. To those who might answer, 'Well, of course, but it can be reformed, it doesn't have to be abolished,' I would only say, 'Please try.' These failures aren't an accident of history, they are the result of deliberate choices made by the Mountbatten-Windsor family and their predecessors. Were we to end royal secrecy, it would almost certainly bring the whole edifice down. Were decades of records subjected to scrutiny for the first time, we would have a clear picture of dishonesty, self-serving lobbying and misuse of public funds.

There are those who argue that all is not lost, that the monarchy can be reformed or 'modernized'. The ambition of more cautious observers is to aim for what is often called a 'bicycling monarchy', a reference to the occasional report of a Dutch royal cycling around Amsterdam rather than travelling by motorcade. Yet this is a fallacy, as I have learnt since meeting Magnus Simonsson, the founder of Republikanska föreningen (the Swedish Republican Association) and other republican campaigners from around Europe, who gathered in Stockholm in 2010 for the inaugural conference of the Alliance of European Republican Movements (AERM). Earlier that year a biography of Sweden's King Carl XVI Gustaf, *The Reluctant Monarch* by Thomas Sjöberg, caused a storm with a string of damning accusations, including attending sex parties with strippers, some of which were hosted by notorious crime bosses. Bram van Montfoort of Republiek, the Dutch campaign, has calculated the cost of their monarchy to be in excess of €300 million a year, while the Spanish monarchy has been beset by scandal that led to the abdication and self-imposed exile of King Juan Carlos. In short, the lessons we have taken from our European allies is that there really is no such thing as a bicycling monarchy, of the kind some people suggest we move to. Yes, on a personal level, European royals appear more personable and approachable, and quite a few have careers away from their limited royal duties. But the criticisms levelled at the British monarchy apply as well to every monarchy in Europe – it's just that we don't hear about them beyond the occasional tale of a Dutch royal cycling through Amsterdam.

Monarchies are inherently corrupt and corrupting. By their nature they must exist on fantasy and make-believe because warts-and-all truth demands accountability that hereditary public office cannot provide. The Dutch and Swedish monarchies might be on a different scale, but the criticisms are the same. It is the institution that is primarily at fault. As we saw with the MPs' expenses scandal, institutions that offer people access to power and privilege without accountability or scrutiny invite abuse and corruption. Yet, with a hereditary monarchy, we cannot separate the individuals from the institution. The royals are responsible for the monarchy's failures and, as we shall see, without the protection of official secrecy and deference, it is obvious that they are not suited to public office.

# 4.

## Out of Touch, Out of Time

Many republicans have argued that the royals themselves do not warrant discussion, that what's at stake are our democratic values and the quality of our constitution. Royalists, on the other hand, bristle at the slightest hint of criticism of a royal. With the notable exception of Prince Harry, royals will always be forgiven mistakes or alleged wrongdoing and royalists will quickly return to their view that the Mountbatten-Windsors are paragons of virtue, committed to public service and who, in the words of my local MP, represent the best of us. Even Andrew is sometimes excused his alleged offences, his involvement in the Falklands War often being enough reason to absolve him of wrongdoing.

To republicans, this mindset is clearly wrong, yet many will say it's a mistake to talk about the failings or moral shortcomings of Andrew, William or Charles. The monarchy would be wrong even if these people were saintly, virtuous and singularly cut out for the roles they play in public life. To criticize the royals, the argument goes, is to undermine the republican position, as royalists can simply reply, 'So you'd be happy with the monarchy if it were a different family, one you could support and respect?' From there the discussion becomes royalists versus anti-royal, rather than monarchy versus republic.

Yet, this misses a few crucial points.

The first is that we don't, and cannot, have different royals waiting in the wings. It's a hereditary monarchy firmly anchored to one family. In other words, the family and the monarchy are inseparable. A more substantial point is that the royals and royalists continually promote the family as virtuous people, individuals committed selflessly to public service, who support worthy causes such as the environment, homelessness and mental health. Their virtue and sacrifice is sold as a central reason for keeping the monarchy, and so it is reasonable to rebut and challenge these claims. It is also reasonable to challenge the individual members of the family simply because they hold public office and so should be scrutinized. Just as with any other public servant, we must throw a spotlight on genuine wrongdoing, corruption, hypocrisy or simple failures of judgement.

The royalist argues that the royal family are heroes of our age. They also argue that the system of hereditary monarchy gives us noble and wise men and women. It is reasonable to point out that this is not only a fallacy, but that the opposite is true. There are endless examples of the royal family acting ignobly and unwisely – just like anybody else.

Not only does hereditary power give us people we would be unlikely to elect if given the choice, it also has a significant impact on the character, values and conduct of those who grow up being told they are different from the rest of us.

## 1 Per Cent of the 1 Per Cent

Before I get on to the many and varied reasons members of the Mountbatten-Windsor family are not suited to public office, it is worth raising some issues that are out of their hands. Whether they are honest to a fault or serial liars, frugal or profligate with public funds, they have always represented and will always represent a vanishingly small and very peculiar minority of the British population. Of course, they do and always will represent just one family, but it is a family that even by the standards of modern millionaires is odd and unrepresentative.

Being born into the royal family puts you into a catalogue of tiny socio-economic groups. William, for instance, is comfortably in the top 1 per cent of wealthiest people in the country, and has leapt up the rankings as of September 2022, when he was given the Duchy of Cornwall and its £22 million-a-year income. Although his private, personal beliefs are largely unknown, he is a practising Christian. He has to be. He has a public role as the future head of the Church, regardless of his personal feelings. He attends Church of England services, something fewer than 2 per cent of the country's population does beyond weddings and christenings. Being privately educated puts him into a slightly larger bracket of 7 per cent of Britain's population, while his ownership of vast estates and palatial homes (whether his private property or state property treated as his own) and his love of shooting wildlife for sport also place him within tiny minorities that most of the public cannot possibly relate to.

As well as representing some of the most elite minorities, the royals' stranglehold on these most senior public roles excludes those minorities least represented and often most marginalized from public life, not to mention the significant majorities who have no prospect of serving as head of state.

Prince George could easily live to the age of one hundred and, with health care continually improving and wealth being a key indicator of life expectancy, it wouldn't be too surprising if he reached 110 or higher. That would mean that for the next one hundred years we will have just three white, Anglo-Saxon, Protestant men as head of state, all from one family. While it's possible George will later identify as gay,* statistically it's more likely he'll be heterosexual and obliged to follow the usual pattern of marriage and the provision of heirs and spares. The only chance of another queen ascending to the throne over the next century is if George either dies before his sister, having not had children, or dies much younger than his great-grandmother or grandfather, leaving a daughter of his own, if she's the eldest child. The chances of a monarch who is Black or Asian are more or less zero. The monarchy is, of course, also the exclusive preserve of the upper classes and, occasionally through marriage, the rich middle classes who are prepared to conform to the upper classes' values and habits.

Royalists argue that this provides stability and consistency, a bedrock upon which Britain's traditional values rest undisturbed by the ebb and flow of cultural change. That is, at best,

---

\* In the past it is likely that gay monarchs have simply hidden their sexuality and followed the traditional pattern of marriage and family, albeit with male company discreetly pursued within their narrow social circles. While there has been speculation about the sexuality of royals, none has been openly recognised or accepted as LGBTQ+, even now. I would hope, even with the royals, that if George is gay they would allow him to be open and honest about his identity. Assuming the monarchy survives that long, that would raise the prospect of either the Crown passing, upon his death, to his sister or sister's eldest child, or to a child of George's who was either the product of adoption or surrogacy – although that would require a change in the law, as at present the Crown can only pass to the child of a husband and wife, a point clarified by the government in 2013 during the passage of the Succession to the Crown Act.

a mirage. Hereditary lineage simply ensures the office of head of state remains beyond the reach of anybody who might better represent the nation. It has been commented on and celebrated that Rishi Sunak is Britain's first British-Asian prime minister, and one of very few world leaders who has a recent immigrant family history. The turmoil within the Conservative government over the past few years has seen a succession of Black and Asian ministers in all the great offices of state, including Sajid Javid, Rishi Sunak, Nadhim Zahawi and Kwasi Kwarteng as Chancellor, Sajid Javid, Priti Patel and Suella Braverman as Home Secretary and James Cleverly at the Foreign Office. While largely derided for her failed time in office, Liz Truss's arrival at Downing Street was nevertheless a significant sign of progress in that she was the country's third female prime minister, the second in three years. The Conservative Party certainly made the point that they were the only party to have had three female and one British-Asian leader. Regardless of their politics, this diversity at the top of government has rightly been welcomed across the political spectrum. The profile of LGBTQ+ politicians has risen over recent years, too. Whereas in 1998 the *Sun* ran the headline, 'Are we being run by a gay mafia?' with reference to closeted ministers in the Blair government, LGBT ministerial appointments today are largely met without comment. While class diversity in Parliament has gone backwards since the 1970s, it is still an issue that politicians and commentators often argue needs to be addressed.

Diversity isn't celebrated for diversity's sake, but because it indicates a breaking down of barriers that have often stood in the way of the working class, women, people with disabilities, marginalized ethnic groups and gay, lesbian, bisexual or trans people. It marks a receding tide of prejudice and so is celebrated as a sign of progress. With the monarchy, such opportunities simply don't exist. Every one of our country's citizens is excluded from the top job, except the one next in line.

Royalists often respond by saying that one monarch can never represent every group, race or religion, and so it's better they represent none, thereby representing all. But that isn't the point. Rather than have the same head of state for the last seventy years, or three men from the same family for the next one hundred, over that 170-year period we could have elected two dozen heads of state, each election representing a chance to break with past prejudices, reflect our nation's changing values and choose leaders from a variety of different backgrounds. If you're not convinced, you only have to look to our European neighbours and the elections of Vigdís Finnbogadóttir in Iceland in 1980, the first woman in the world elected as head of state, or the 1993 election of Mary Robinson and seven years later of Mary McAleese in Ireland, the country's first and second women elected president and the first time in the world there has been a democratic succession of heads of state from one woman to another. McAleese was also the first Irish president from Northern Ireland.

Democracy offers an expression of national sentiment and public attitudes, whereas monarchy locks us out, the citizen a mere spectator, an irrelevance to an institution that represents nothing but itself and the most conservative values – values shared by few. To discuss the people who occupy the monarchy is to challenge the notion they can or do represent us.

Challenging and criticizing the royals also challenges sycophancy and deference, reminding us that they are not above criticism. And there are plenty of criticisms to make.

## The Petulant Princes

Dominic Grieve strikes me as a fairly mild-mannered man, the sort of unflappable Home Counties lawyer who wouldn't get easily flustered or resort to intemperate language. Yet, from the 2019 Conservative leadership campaign through to the end of Boris Johnson's premiership, Grieve regularly called into question Johnson's character, calling him, among other things, a four-year-old and a pathological liar. Much has been made of Johnson's character by a wide range of critics from across the political spectrum, whether it's questions of honesty, integrity or laziness, or claims that he needs to be liked and to entertain those around him, to the detriment of good judgement. It was, ultimately, a judgement on his character that led to his downfall in the summer of 2022. His successor, Liz Truss, was quickly judged to be in over her head and not cut out for the role of PM. Although her policies proved terminal for her short-lived time in office, her character was under the microscope and conclusions were quickly drawn that Truss was unable to revive her own or her party's fortunes.

Character matters. Whether in politics or our private lives, we are concerned about those who lack honesty, integrity, good sense or some degree of humility or self-awareness. It is the character, as much as the actions, of Charles, William and other royals that raises serious questions, both about their suitability for public office and about the substantial faults in the whole notion of hereditary monarchy.

As a rule of thumb, I have always believed the royals should be treated the same way we treat politicians and other public figures: without deference, fear or favour, and with considerable scepticism about their motives and actions. If we take such an approach, any benign or generous view of the King soon evaporates. We discover a vain, prickly and thin-skinned man who will not tolerate criticism. And that matters, because character affects judgement and poor judgement leads to poor decisions and questionable behaviour. Just ask Dominic Grieve.

Charles has been raised surrounded by sycophants, believing the circumstances of his birth make him uniquely gifted with the talents required to serve as monarch. If someone disagrees with him or challenges him, don't expect a reasonable or rational reply, or an engaging exchange of views. This was evident when, according to an anecdote retold by Richard Dawkins, an eminent scientist at the University of Oxford met the then prince after Charles had made a speech on a variety of scientific matters. During his speech, Charles espoused his esoteric and eccentric views of the world. The scientist, assuming as you might that the prince was open to discussing the ideas he had set out in a speech, politely suggested when introduced to Charles that he didn't agree with something he had said. He was about to continue when Charles simply turned and walked off, not saying another word. The flunky accompanying the prince leaned in and said, 'One does not disagree with His Royal Highness,' before he too walked off, no doubt leaving the scientist perplexed.

It's a trivial incident. But it nonetheless highlights an attitude that brooks no criticism. It was this same attitude that played out more devastatingly in 2005, when Professor Edzard Ernst publicly questioned Charles's views on alternative medicine. Ernst had been a collaborator on a report that had been commissioned by Prince Charles, which looked at whether alternative medicine was a cost-effective option for the NHS. A newspaper obtained a copy of the draft and spoke to Ernst for comment, which he readily gave. By this time Ernst had asked for his name to be removed from the report because it was, he said, 'complete misleading rubbish', adding that it was 'outrageous and deeply flawed. It is based on such poor science, it's just hair-raising. The Prince ... also seems to have overstepped his constitutional role.' Following the report in *The Times*, Michael Peat, Prince Charles's private secretary, wrote to the vice chancellor of the University of Exeter, complaining that Ernst had committed a serious breach of confidentiality.

I had the opportunity, in 2016, to interview Professor Ernst for Republic's documentary. Ernst was quite clear that in his view the subsequent protracted disciplinary action taken against him by the University of Exeter, where he was professor of complementary medicine, and the defunding of his department, came about because of pressure from Clarence House.

It's a poor reflection on Charles that, as a man with a very ordinary level of educational achievement, he believes himself to possess greater talents and wisdom than accomplished scientists and scholars – so much so that he feels free to ignore, admonish or undermine those who disagree. Charles is a product of the strange world into which he was born, a family cosseted and fawned over, constantly told that they are uniquely talented and wise. Charles clearly believes in the natural order that has him placed at the top, that this chance of fate makes him uniquely suited to high office. He said as much in a handwritten note, which was revealed as part of a 2004 employment tribunal brought by one of his former staff, Elaine Day, in which he complained about Day's concerns about lack of promotion opportunities, saying:

What is wrong with people nowadays? Why do they all seem to think they are qualified to do things far above their capabilities? [. . .] This is all to do with the learning culture in schools. It is a consequence of a child-centred education system which tells people they can become pop stars, high court judges or brilliant TV presenters or *infinitely more competent heads of state* without ever putting in the necessary work or having the natural ability [my italics].

He added: 'It is a result of social utopianism which believes humanity can be genetically engineered to contradict the lessons of history.' In the context of Charles's position, the meaning is clear: the plebs should know their place and let those born to greatness and who are afforded an elite education occupy the higher ranks and offices of state. The accusation of snobbery is hardly going to surprise anyone, but in other quarters it does rile most people for whom such daft, outdated and offensive comments are unwelcome in public life. For Charles, however, this kind of snobbery is no more than an expression of a natural order that he readily accepts and celebrates. His deep sense of entitlement and the expectation that everyone treat him differently is something that is either largely ignored, excused or laughed off, but it is perhaps something we should take more seriously. It is an indication of the kind of man he is.

His own personal behaviour is indicative of someone who has grown up expecting everything to be done for him, the most spoilt of spoilt children. It has long been reported that he has a fierce temper, which flares up at the most trivial moments. One biographer, Christopher Anderson, recently reported that Charles 'tore a sink off the wall' after becoming frustrated that he had dropped a cufflink down the plughole. More alarmingly, he said Charles once was 'desperate' for fresh air and so threw a chair through a window . . . of someone else's home. Whether or not his temper is quite that bad, we all had some insight into his character on the two occasions he lost patience with pens during the days after his mother's death, first at the Accession Council and later when signing a visitors' book at Hillsborough Castle in Northern Ireland. He has been accused of being rude to his staff, too, whether because a shirt hasn't been laid out quite to his satisfaction or because they failed to use the word 'sir' often enough during a conversation – something apparently Diana teased him for. This petulance was neatly illustrated by an anecdote shared by former royal butler Paul Burrell, who told the story of when Charles had accidentally knocked a letter from his mother into the wastepaper bin next to his desk. Rather than bend down and pick it out, he called Burrell into the office and had him retrieve it. This is a man unable to do the simplest things for himself, and if someone did them in a way that displeased him, whether ironing his shoelaces or squeezing out his toothpaste, 'everybody is scolded'.

The brittle temper appears to have been inherited by William, who has also been accused of an abrasive attitude towards staff who 'are insufficiently deferential, or catch him in a bad mood', according to Damian Thompson, conservative and religious commentator and associate editor at the *Spectator*. Royal commentator and journalist Rob Jobson, writing in 2017, suggested William is 'petulant, capricious, even hostile', and displays 'an over-confidence which some say is bordering on arrogance'.

Again, you may say these are trivial matters, but we do not tolerate such petulant behaviour from MPs and ministers. In other circumstances, such bouts of anger and physical violence – albeit directed at objects rather than people – and rudeness directed at staff are cited as signs of a bullying culture in the workplace. Dominic Raab, the justice secretary and former foreign secretary, is just one of a number of politicians who have been accused of bullying for less serious outbursts, yet with Charles it is largely overlooked or excused.

While a lot of these insights into the character and behaviour of senior royals come from former valets and unnamed sources, it all chimes with what Prince Harry has said in his book, *Spare*. He caused a sensation with the revelation that his brother had physically assaulted him during one heated argument. His account is one of a family of delicate egos who concern themselves with petty squabbles and trivial rivalries.

## Political Princes

It's not just their private behaviour that raises questions about their suitability for high office. Both Charles and William appear all too willing to wade into highly politicized issues such as education, health care, homelessness and the environment. Their interventions are often ignored or dismissed, but all too often they are taken seriously, despite being wholly unqualified to lecture anyone on such matters. Some welcome their apparent commitment to the environment, with plenty of politicians, commentators and some seasoned environmentalists questioning the government's decision not to send Charles to COP27 in November 2022. Charles has also been applauded for speaking up in defence of human rights, as he did at the start of 2022 when he praised those standing up for their rights in Afghanistan, Syria and Myanmar, as he has done before in the case of Christians in the Middle East and the plight of Tibetans.

But all of this is deeply problematic, because the environment and how we tackle climate change – even among those who rightly accept climate change as caused by human activity – is a politically charged issue, as is the delivery of effective health care and education. And while no one should find it difficult to support human rights in places like Afghanistan, Charles ignores the crimes of those countries whose leaders he counts among his friends. It is his hypocrisy, and that of William, that is the biggest concern, because their interventions can influence public debate in a way that skews the conversation away from very serious questions. How do we have a serious debate about the corruption and human rights abuses in places such as Qatar, Saudi Arabia and Bahrain, when the royal families of these nations are all good friends of Charles and his family? Sports commentator and former footballer Gary Neville made the point during the World Cup in Qatar in late 2022, when he was facing criticism for his involvement in the tournament. Answering his critics by pointing to the hypocrisy of others, he said: 'If Prince William doesn't want to come to this tournament but he's okay with his father taking charitable donations [from the Qataris], that's fine.' Charles, undeterred by recent accusations of receiving €3 million in cash, stuffed into suitcases and carrier bags, from a Qatari politician a few months earlier, then brokered a £4.5 million donation from Qatar to the Prince's Foundation, accepting money from people who have no qualms about persecuting women and LGBTQ+ people.

These aren't isolated incidents. Charles, and his family, have been close to Middle Eastern royals for decades. The news site Declassified UK recently reported that in the ten years since the 2011 Arab Spring, the royals met with Middle Eastern dictators on average once a fortnight – a total of 217 occasions.

Charles had ninety-five meetings, with Bahrain being the most favoured state for such engagements. Royalists will say it's all on the request of the British government, and often it will be. But there's a reason the British government asks the royals to represent them to these Middle Eastern despots while making little diplomatic use of them elsewhere. The royals are friends with the men who run these regimes.

It's notable that Charles has criticized human rights abuses in Syria and Iraq, but not in Saudi Arabia, Qatar, Bahrain or Jordan. It makes me wonder whether, had the current Syrian dictator's father and predecessor Hafez al-Assad had the foresight to make himself king, would Charles have cosied up to him too?

Royal hypocrisy on the environment is perhaps more problematic. The major polluters, those who produce the most $CO_2$ and therefore contribute most to climate change, are the rich. Globally that means the rich nations are far more culpable than poorer ones. It's not just the carbon emissions produced within our own countries, it's the emissions produced in places like China, where goods are manufactured for export to the West. More locally it is the richest individuals who produce far more carbon emissions than the average person. Charles and William are typical of millionaires and billionaires who routinely fly around by helicopter, occupy several large, energy-sapping homes and go abroad on private jets. Helicopter is the transport of choice for senior royals. When not travelling by helicopter, it's usually by private or RAF jet. The palace claims Charles is 'allergic' to flying by helicopter, but the evidence suggests otherwise. They also come out with the same old excuses, saying in 2022 in response to reports of Charles's high use of private flights: 'You only get to use the helicopter if every other option has failed,' while failing to explain why it would be so difficult to make short journeys by car.

In November 2021, Charles was to fly to Barbados to attend the ceremony marking the country's transition to a republic. The RAF Voyager aircraft (a plane as large as a typical Boeing 737) was based in Brize Norton in Oxfordshire, while Charles was staying in Sandringham, Norfolk. Rather than make the trip down to Brize Norton by car, Charles had the RAF fly this enormous aircraft in the wrong direction, to pick him up in Norfolk, before turning around and flying back, over Oxfordshire and on to Barbados, pumping tonnes more $CO_2$ into the skies above England.

When Charles lectures the public on the need to make changes to our lifestyles, he is drawing the focus away from those most culpable. There have recently been calls from environmental campaigners for a ban on private jets, with Extinction Rebellion protesting at Farnborough and Luton airports in November 2022, while similar protests took place around Europe. While such a move would likely lead to significant cuts in carbon emissions, it's not a move that Charles is ever likely to champion. It's hard to estimate his carbon footprint, but with the regular flights and a dozen large homes all requiring round-the-clock heating and lighting, whether he's there or not, it is safe to say that it is enormous. When gently questioned about this by a BBC reporter in the run-up to COP26 in 2021, he became rather defensive, and his response was telling. Saying he 'cannot do it [tackle climate change] single-handedly', he suggested he is 'trying to reduce as much as possible. I've got electric cars, it's been difficult.' He then added, in a moment of breathtaking lack of self-awareness: 'I haven't eaten meat and fish on two days a week and I don't eat dairy products on one day a week. If more did that, you would reduce a lot of the pressure.'

Rather than give up his multitude of homes or his predilection for private travel, he would prefer if everyone else adjust their diets. He also claims to offset carbon emissions, rather than reduce them, which itself is a problem. Carbon offsetting – a scheme in which you can put money into projects that would help reduce carbon in the atmosphere, rather than reduce your own emissions – is controversial and highly questionable as a means of tackling climate change. As Greenpeace points out on their website, offsetting doesn't reduce carbon emissions, and it doesn't even do what it claims – offset those emissions that are generated. There simply isn't the capacity to, for example, plant enough trees for them to absorb $CO_2$ at anything like the rate carbon is pumped into the atmosphere. In seeking to influence the climate change debate, Charles turns the attention away from the issues that will have an impact on him and shifts the focus on to everybody else.

William too has waded into the environmental debate, making speeches in which he has suggested the greatest threat to African wildlife is population growth, a claim that has been debunked and which attracted – along with his other interventions – accusations of ignorance, racism and white-saviour syndrome. Visiting Kenya in 2018, he was roundly criticized for promoting the 'damaging message' that it was Black Africans who were the danger to wildlife and that it needed Westerners to come to their rescue. Quoted in the *Guardian*, Dr Mordecai Ogada, director of Conservation Solutions Afrika, said in response to William's visit: 'Conservation even now, nearly 55 years after Kenya got independence, is still the one arena where Prince William can waltz into Kenya and tell us he wants us to do this, that or the other.' He added that 'the vilification of local people provides justification for human rights abuses, such as the indiscriminate shooting of poachers'. While poaching is a problem, and the survival of African wildlife a concern, it is typically the poorest Africans who are drawn into poaching in service of demand driven by rich Westerners. William's attitude towards Africa was illustrated in Harry's book *Spare*. The two brothers were arguing about their charitable activities when William shouted, 'Africa is my thing, you can't have it.' That news may have surprised many Africans, but as Nels Abbey said in the *Guardian*: 'Africa is still seen as a colonial plaything for British princes engaged in their own personal scramble, rather than a vast and complex continent that is home to the most diverse population on Earth.'

Meanwhile, Prince William continues to enjoy shooting wildlife on the Balmoral estate and elsewhere, including in Spain where, in 2014, he was widely criticized for shooting wild boar. The prince regularly shoots pheasant and grouse and in 2020 was again criticized, this time for taking seven-year-old George with him.

William expects plaudits for the Earthshot Prize, supposedly aimed at achieving a major breakthrough in tackling climate change by 2030. Its name is inspired by John F. Kennedy's 'moonshot' ambition of putting a man on the moon before the end of the 1960s. Earthshot offers five £1 million prizes, which means over a decade £50 million will be offered to a range of projects around the world. That's all very laudable, but it is a drop in the ocean when it comes to the billions of dollars being spent on tackling climate change, both in terms of mitigation and adaptation of environments to allow communities to be more resilient in the face of environmental challenges. While such a scheme can provide much-needed funding to some projects in the short term, it is not the grand solution promoted by the palace and royal cheerleaders, yet it serves to promote the questionable notion that William is an environmental champion, rather than part of the problem as one of the largest private producers of $CO_2$ in the country.

In 2022, the Earthshot Prize award ceremony was held in Boston. Dozens of celebrities and Hollywood stars descended on the city, many travelling thousands of miles to be there. The five prizewinners were not there, but instead joined the royals and celebrities via video link, apparently for the noble reason of avoiding taking flights that would have created more $CO_2$ emissions.

## Royal Ambassadors

William's cack-handed efforts at lecturing the people of Africa on population and wildlife raise questions about his ability to do something we're told the royals are good at: act as ambassadors. This ambassadorial role is a common feature of UK reporting on the Commonwealth, which rather than receiving serious political coverage, is treated as an adjunct of royal reporting. Philip Murphy, director of the Institute of Commonwealth Studies and professor of British and Commonwealth history at the University of London, said in his 2021 book, *The Empire's New Clothes*,* 'The Queen's involvement in its events

---

\* The book is well titled and is well worth reading if you're interested in a more detailed, under-the-bonnet look at the Commonwealth. Murphy shows the Commonwealth to be a largely empty vessel, full of promise but limited in impact, its

is now virtually the only thing about the organisation that media outlets consider newsworthy.' In recent years you could swap 'The Queen' for 'Prince Charles', although that level of interest is not quite the same. Perhaps now Charles is King, any visits to Commonwealth countries will attract a similar level of attention, although possibly not for the reasons he might hope.

It is not just here in the UK that the Commonwealth is misrepresented thanks to the royals. Speaking on Republic's *Abolish the Monarchy* podcast, Lewis Holden, chair of New Zealand Republic, said, 'The Commonwealth of Nations as an organization does a whole heap of good things we hardly ever hear about, and part of the reason for that is it just gets crowded out by the royals . . . it's promoted as if it's something to do with the royals.'

A royal correspondent with one of Britain's main broadcasters told me not so long ago how colleagues in his office thought the transition of Barbados to a republic, and debates about other Caribbean countries following their lead, meant the Commonwealth itself was falling apart. One of those colleagues was even surprised to learn that the Queen was not the Queen of India, a country that famously became a republic more than seventy years ago. Another correspondent remarked that people in the UK don't appreciate how popular the royals are in Commonwealth countries, although he could only cite his own experience as evidence of this, as someone in the circus tent looking out. The reality is somewhat different.

It is revealing that the royal family has used the Commonwealth to its own advantage, to project a sense of purpose

---

stated values hopelessly compromised by the actions of member states and the recent admission of Gabon and Togo.

that it doesn't have by insisting on a central role within the organization. Yet the King, and the Queen before him, has no formal function within the Commonwealth and no responsibility for it. The royalist will tell you that the Queen and her father were responsible for creating and leading the Commonwealth, and in doing so have forged a strong bond between these countries and their peoples, a bond that would be lost if the monarchy were abolished. In one episode of the Netflix documentary *Harry & Meghan*, the writer and broadcaster Afua Hirsch gave a reasonable assessment of the Commonwealth's origins and the continued inequality of wealth and power between its members, referring to the body as 'Empire 2.0', a term previously used by government officials in relation to efforts to exploit Commonwealth trade relations post-Brexit. Royal commentators recoiled in horror at what was reportedly perceived as an attack on the Queen's 'greatest legacy'. This mythology was clearly believed by the Queen when she gave a speech to the 2018 Commonwealth Heads of Government Meeting (CHOGM) in which she publicly put heads of government on the spot, took credit for the Commonwealth and pushed her son to be the organization's nominal head at some point in the future. In her speech she said: 'It is my sincere wish that the Commonwealth will continue to offer stability and continuity for future generations, and will decide that one day the Prince of Wales will carry on the important work started by my father in 1949.'

The heads of government duly obliged, declaring that the future King would indeed be the next titular head of the Commonwealth. The Queen's plea almost perfectly summed up the royalist mythology of the unifying British Crown under the benign flag of the Commonwealth of Nations. That mythology places the monarchy at the heart of the Commonwealth and claims it as the brainchild of George VI, rather than the real-politik result of a disintegrating empire in a rapidly changing world. It assures us that this great royal project has bequeathed to Commonwealth countries stability and continuity, when in truth so many of its members have been struck by the plagues of political violence, oppression and coups, not to mention chronic poverty, the causes of which often trace back to empire.

The modern Commonwealth was born out of its imperial predecessor, which until the London Declaration of 1949 required all its members to retain the British monarch as head of state. Ireland formally became a republic that year and left the Commonwealth, never to return. India promptly declared its wish to ditch the monarchy, which in turn pushed Britain to agree to reform the Commonwealth into a free association of independent nations. Other countries soon followed their lead in becoming republics.

While the number of republics within the Commonwealth has steadily grown over the intervening years, the organization has also been letting other countries join who have never had any association with the British Empire or Crown. Mozambique, a former Portuguese colony, joined in 1995, Rwanda in 2009 and Togo and Gabon in 2022.

Today, just under 6 per cent of Commonwealth citizens have the King as their head of state. Malaysia, Lesotho, Eswatini and Tonga have their own monarchies, which leaves more than 92 per cent of the Commonwealth's population living in republics, democratic or otherwise. Of the fifty-six member states, just fifteen are Commonwealth realms, meaning they have the King as head of state. That's just 26 per cent of the organiza-tion's membership. Of those, Jamaica, the Bahamas, Belize, St

Lucia, Grenada, St Kitts and Nevis, Antigua and Barbuda, St Vincent and the Grenadines and Australia are all showing signs of wanting to become republics and most (possibly all) will do so before the decade is out. That would leave Canada, where polls are showing a collapse of support for the monarchy over the past few years; New Zealand, who would at least be galvanized into a debate on the subject by Australia's move away from the Crown; Papua New Guinea, Solomon Islands and Tuvalu. And us.

It is in the context of this modern and changing Commonwealth that the royals best advertise their inadequacies and temperament. There has been a marked shift in attitudes across the Commonwealth in recent years, particularly in the Caribbean. With the heightened awareness of colonial and racial injustice and the Black Lives Matter movement helping to refocus minds on the horrors of the transatlantic slave trade, many Caribbean citizens have had enough of the British Crown. Calls for reparations are now very real and aren't going away, while the appalling treatment of the Windrush generation by the British government has only added fuel to the anger and resentment many feel towards the monarchy, an institution that for so long lay at the heart of Britain's role in slavery and which rejoiced in empire. Add to that the significant damage done to the monarchy's reputation abroad by the farcical handling of Prince Harry and Meghan Markle's departure and the subsequent accusations of racism and indifference to issues of mental health, and we can see why the shine is quickly wearing off the royal brand. And it isn't just younger generations who are rejecting the Crown, as some of the most vocal proponents of Caribbean republicanism are seasoned campaigners and senior politicians.

In an apparent effort to ward off this tide of rejection, the royals thought it would be a good idea to conduct two tours of the region, first by Prince William and Kate, and then by Prince Edward (the Queen's youngest son) and his wife Sophie. Before William and Kate had arrived at their first stop in Belize, villagers were protesting against their visit, which was swiftly cancelled. William made no attempt to address their grievances. A trip to Jamaica treated us to photos of the royal couple being greeted by Jamaican children through a wire fence, which, if we are to be charitable to the couple, was not quite what it seemed once cameras panned back to capture the whole scene. That said, the power of the images and the re-action to them spoke volumes about the strength of feeling about white English royals patronizing Jamaicans with their jubilee-year tour. The couple didn't help themselves when they chose to inspect local troops while standing in the back of a Land Rover, with William dressed in a white military uniform, neatly conjuring up images of the country's colonial past. None of this compared to the excruciating sight of Andrew Holness, the Jamaican prime minister, standing in front of the cameras tell-ing William to his face that they planned to ditch the monarchy, with the royal couple standing there like a couple of students brought into the headmaster's office for a dressing-down.

You might have thought that Edward and Sophie's tour to Grenada, St Lucia, St Vincent and the Grenadines and Anti-gua and Barbuda would have been called off, or perhaps moderated. But on they blundered, headlong into more excru-ciating embarrassment. First, their visit to Grenada was cancelled at the last minute, in an echo of the cancellation of William and Kate's first stop on their tour. As Edward arrived in the region, the Antigua and Barbuda Reparations Support

Commission published an open letter, addressed to the royal family, in which they dismissed the empty rhetoric they'd heard from William a few weeks earlier, saying:

> It has become common for members of the Royal Family and representatives of the government of Britain to come to this region and lament that slavery was an 'appalling atrocity', that it was 'abhorrent', that 'it should not have happened' . . . We hear the phony sanctimony of those who came before you that these crimes are a 'stain on your history'.

Edward and Sophie held a painfully embarrassing meeting with Gaston Browne, prime minister of Antigua and Barbuda. On being asked by Browne – again, in front of reporters – to take a message back to the UK government concerning the issue of reparations, all Edward could do was laugh awkwardly and say that he had not been taking notes, so couldn't comment on what Browne had been saying.

These tours showed the royals to be inept, tone-deaf and mostly concerned with promoting their own image, an image barely moderated from seventy years earlier. The only time they showed an interest in local communities was in the context of carefully organized cultural events. At no point, beyond statements of 'phony sanctimony', did they show any interest in the grievances their visits threw into the spotlight.

William was reportedly furious with staff and advisers after the Jamaican debacle, shifting the blame to others rather than asking himself why someone supposedly equipped with a lifetime of training couldn't have seen the obvious pitfalls, responded more graciously and eloquently when put on the spot and adapted more quickly to the unfolding litany of errors.

## Racism and the Royals

In May 2018, just days before the wedding of Harry and Meghan, there remained lots of speculation on how well the newest member of the royal family would fit in or, more accurately, be accepted by the royal family. Piers Morgan, speaking on the US documentary *Meghan Markle: An American Princess*, said, 'Meghan's marrying into a family that, to put it mildly, has a dodgy track record on race.' Yet, for the most part, the marriage was trumpeted as a sign the monarchy was modernizing. Fast-forward three years and Harry and Meghan have since left the country, deciding instead to live the celebrity lifestyle in California and, as if to underline their celebrity status, they agreed to an interview with the queen of American chat shows, Oprah Winfrey. A week before the interview was aired, it was obvious the couple had more to say about their experiences with the royal household than polite anecdotes about official engagements and cups of tea with the Queen. Harry and Meghan made it very clear that they were made to feel unwelcome and that, at least in some quarters, despite Harry's later denial of accusations of racism, there were racist undertones to the way they were treated. To say the result was explosive is an understatement. The impact of the interview continues to reverberate to this day, amplified by the subsequent release of the Netflix series and autobiography.

In the States, the reaction was almost entirely one of shock, on the one hand, and instinctive support for Meghan Markle on the other. In the UK, things were quite different. The palace had begun briefing against Meghan Markle the week before, leaking accusations against her by staff of bullying. Some commentators in the British press denounced the accusations of racism or complained that the couple had the temerity to raise such issues in public. They stood accused of choosing 'division, destruction and to hurt people', suggesting the interview looked 'vengeful, self-absorbed and attention-seeking' and was 'a disgraceful betrayal'.

What surprised me most of all was the astonishment, confected or not, at the suggestion that any royal might be racist. Piers Morgan, who called Harry and Meghan's allegations 'vile, destructive, self-serving nonsense', added, 'I have met the royals many times and I don't believe they are racist at all.' Yet the family has a long history of racism, while the institution itself is built on racist ideas of bloodline and superiority. In other words, as Morgan had said three years earlier, the family has a dodgy track record on race. Quite a few royals have at some point at least raised eyebrows, if not sparked anger, on the issue of race, including, it should be said, Prince Harry. Princess Michael of Kent caused outrage in New York in 2004 when, in the upmarket restaurant Da Silvano, she berated a table of diners for causing too much noise and told them, 'You need to go back to the colonies.' In 2017, she caused further offence by wearing a blackamoor brooch to a lunch where she would meet Meghan for the first time. The brooch depicts black men and women as slaves.

In late November 2022, Susan Hussey, lady-in-waiting to the late Queen and godmother to William, was accused of racist behaviour towards a guest at a reception at Buckingham Palace. Speaking to Ngozi Fulani, the founder of one of the charities invited to the palace, Hussey repeatedly asked, 'Where are you from?' When she couldn't get anything other than the obvious answer that Fulani was British, she pressed on, saying to her shocked guest, 'No, but where do you really come from, where do your people come from?', to which Fulani replied, 'My people, lady, what is this?' Hussey, determined to pursue the point, said: 'Oh, I can see I am going to have a challenge getting you to say where you're from. When did you first come here?' Hussey is hardly a household name, but she was a close confidante to the Queen and typical of the class of people who occupy the various peculiar jobs and offices within the household. Such behaviour in other public bodies, in the wider context of a history of racism, would normally prompt some kind of inquiry, but none has been announced at the time of writing.

Hussey stepped down from her role and, as former BBC royal correspondent Peter Hunt said on LBC, the palace on this occasion moved with speed, in the manner of a corporation concerned about a falling share price. Clearly, they knew how damaging the incident was, but as is often the case, they sought to use the 'bad apple' defence, rather than acknowledge that there is a wider problem with the culture within the household. Royalists heaped accusation upon accusation on Fulani in an effort to discredit Hussey's accuser, including public attacks on her domestic abuse charity that led to harassment of staff. It's not gone unnoticed that King Charles did nothing to defend the charity or Fulani.

The incident with Susan Hussey reminded me of a similar case involving Charles when, in 2018, he was visiting the Commonwealth People's Forum, where writer Anita Sethi was due to speak. On meeting Sethi, Charles asked where she was from, to which she replied: 'Manchester.' Charles's response was to say, 'Well, you don't look like it,' before laughing and walking off, leaving Sethi feeling 'stunned' and 'angry'. Understandably. The reaction to the Hussey case, which attracted far greater attention, perhaps in light of the Harry and Meghan accusations, has raised serious questions not just about the palace but about people's understanding of racism and willingness to acknowledge it for what it is. The public response has been marred by a row between those who accept that this kind of behaviour is racist and a significant number who try to excuse it. Commentators diminishing 'where are you from?' as a simple question that should be met with a simple answer fail to consider why, when people like Hussey meet white guests, their question is usually 'and what do you do?' Yet, as Dr Shola Mos-Shogbamimu said in an interview on Sky News, Black and Asian people 'understand what racial micro-aggression is'. What Hussey was doing, by interrogating Fulani, as much as Charles was doing when dismissing the possibility that Sethi might be from Manchester, is telling these women that they are not British. To quote Mos-Shogbamimu again, 'racism does not require intent for the act to be racist', so any defence of Hussey, Charles or other royals on the grounds that they aren't racist doesn't alter the fact they have said racist things.

Prince Philip was renowned for being rude and dismissive towards people when on public engagements, often resorting to racist comments such as when he met British students in China in 1986 and remarked, 'If you stay here much longer you'll all be slitty-eyed,' and later, in 2002, when he asked indigenous Australians, 'Do you still throw spears at each other?' To their shame, the BBC and other news journalists have often downplayed these offences, suggesting instead the prince 'isn't afraid to speak his mind' or that they are at best 'gaffes'.

The Queen Mother was one of the worst offenders, known to

be particularly offensive and unpleasant in the company of confidants and foreign dignitaries alike. Speaking at the Hay Festival in 2017, Roy Strong, diarist and former director of the National Portrait Gallery and the Victoria and Albert Museum, revealed that the Queen Mother made racist comments that, in his view, were 'too awful' to include in his books. In a conversation about Africa, she apparently said to Strong, 'Beware the blackamoors.' William Shawcross, the authorized biographer of the Queen Mother, said, 'She entered a reception with the Japanese Prince with the words "Nip on! Nip on",' while Woodrow Wyatt, a friend of the royals, said she 'had some reservations about Jews'. One of her staff was reportedly told by the Queen Mother that 'the Africans just don't know how to govern themselves . . . what a pity we're not still looking after them'.

The Black Lives Matter movement has heightened awareness of historic and institutional racism and injustice that remains largely unaddressed. The pulling down of statues and loud demands for reparations have focused more attention on those alive today who continue to benefit from empire and slavery. Some institutions, such as the Church of England, have sought to understand and make amends for their past. Others, including the royals, have not. Yet it is the royal family that, historically, has more to reconcile than most. They were at the heart of empire and the transatlantic slave trade for more than four hundred years and continue to profit from both.

From Elizabeth I onwards, the royals have been implicated in slavery. Right up until its abolition in 1807, every monarch was in favour of, and invested in, this appalling criminal enterprise. King William IV, while still prince, stood in the House of Lords and defended slavery, arguing against those who were fighting for its abolition. It's been argued, as a way of excusing their crimes and prejudices, that the royals are a product of their generation. But then, as now, the royals were at odds with others of their generation who had more enlightened views on liberty and justice. Just as William fought his contemporaries to protect his own investments in slavery, so later generations of royals were well behind the social progress being fought for in the UK and abroad. As I mentioned previously, during the late 1960s and early 1970s, the Queen insisted the palace was excused from race discrimination laws. When this was revealed by the *Guardian* in 2021, some commentators dismissed it as typical of the attitudes of the time, even going so far as to say racism was commonplace, as if to excuse the royals their own behaviour, on the grounds that others were just as bad. Perhaps that's true, but this ignores the very obvious fact that a majority of MPs at the time supported these new laws, and that many people in the UK and elsewhere – both younger and older than the Queen and Philip – were in the vanguard of the fight against racism.

While presidents John F. Kennedy, nine years older than the Queen, and Lyndon B. Johnson, eighteen years her senior, were campaigning on the issue of civil rights in the US, the royals were excluding Black and Asian people from employment at the palace. While activists, politicians and church leaders of all ages campaigned against South Africa's apartheid regime, the Queen Mother was praising the country's president P. W. Botha, an appalling man who inflicted untold misery upon the majority population.

Similar excuses have been made for Philip, suggesting that his views and comments were typical of his generation. This denies any responsibility he might be expected to have for showing leadership and setting a higher standard, whilst offending the many people of Philip's age (and older) who would be as appalled at his behaviour as your average millennial. The same argument was made to defend Susan Hussey, with 'She's 83' trending on Twitter as people tried to suggest that she couldn't have known her comments were offensive because of her age, begging the question: what is the cut-off point at which racism is to be excused? Eighty? Seventy? Hussey was in her forties during the 1980s, when millions of people were fighting apartheid, and rather than the sheltered old lady some presented her as, was a senior member of palace staff who had spent sixty years working at the heart of the royal household. She was hardly insulated from public life or the changing nature of Britain. How could she not have been aware of these kinds of issues and better in tune with how to speak to people with kindness and respect?

The behaviour of people like Charles, William and Susan Hussey cannot be excused, not least because of their claims to occupy positions of leadership and influence, from where we might expect them to set higher standards. You might, however, dismiss the views and behaviour of those royals who are no longer alive as irrelevant to the contemporary monarchy. Nevertheless, there remain calls for the royals to make a more sincere apology – and reparations – for the family's historical crimes. These calls are difficult to argue against for two important reasons. Firstly, the monarchy and its supporters make a great deal out of the family's history and their regal ancestors. History, bloodline and how these things supposedly connect us to a glorious past are central tenets of the pro-monarchy argument. It is hard to suggest the royals can bask in the reflected glory of their ancestors while remaining immune to criticisms of those same ancestors who inflicted empire and slavery upon generations of Africans. How can they justify their position through inheritance while denying any responsibility for those who went before them? Of course, a more sensible response would be to say they are not responsible for the crimes of their forefathers. But if that's the case, they must also say that the status and privileges of their forefathers are no justification for continuing to inherit royal titles and the position of head of state. They can't accept the 'good' while denying a connection to the truly awful.

The problem the royals have, however, is that it wasn't just the titles and positions they inherited. As I've said, up until Victoria, British monarchs were personally invested in slavery, including William IV, who retained the wealth he'd accumulated from slavery when prince, plus that of his predecessors, long after slavery was abolished. While these kings would often spend their fortunes and end their reigns in debt, it remains the case that what fortunes they had, not least the vast estates and property, have subsequently been inherited down the line, meaning that a significant portion of the estimated £650 million Charles inherited from the Queen originated from the slave trade. That's money made off the backs of Africans transported to North America and the Caribbean, communities who over subsequent centuries have been plagued by poverty and further indignities such as segregation and institutional racism. To quote Afua Hirsch: 'The roots of that poverty are based on the extraction of their wealth elsewhere. Those in Britain who extracted that wealth continue to be intergenerationally wealthy. Those from whom it was extracted continue to be intergenerationally poor. It's a very clear economic relationship.'

It would seem to me that a full-throated, sincere apology for their family's crimes and a substantial payment of reparations from that vast, untaxed hereditary fortune would be a more meaningful response to Caribbean protests than empty words of sorrow.

## Not People We Would Vote For

On more occasions than I can recall, when discussing this issue on air, as we get on to the democratic alternative to the monarchy and who our head of state might be in a republic, I am asked if I would object to Charles or William standing for election as president. My answer is always the same: no, of course not. A republic is about equality of citizenship, a country in which we enjoy equal political rights, and those rights must, of course, extend to Charles, William and the rest of the family. The question is often followed by the assertion that, of course, if either Charles or William did stand for election they would win by a landslide. I don't think they would. I believe they would struggle to compete against an open field of candidates and in a fair contest free of deference and sycophancy. And this is the point of this chapter – that with the monarchy we have had foisted upon us people we would never elect if given the choice. That point alone should sink the monarchy.

The royals must instinctively know this, hence the secrecy, the pretence and the insistence we mustn't let the daylight in on the magic. Or, to put it another way, don't let the truth disrupt the carefully spun image of a dutiful family, virtuous, hard-working and sharing the values and concerns of the rest of us. In truth they are a family who have inherited public office but have never really earned much at all, whose upbringing has left them ill-equipped to live by the high standards we should expect of our head of state.

I haven't said much about Prince Andrew so far, not least because there's not a lot to say that hasn't been said a thousand times already. But Andrew is a product of the same upbringing as Charles, William and the others. As with William and Charles, Andrew is said to have a quick temper, to be rude and obnoxious towards staff and have a heightened sense of entitlement. The difference between him and his brother isn't simply that he stands accused of serious sexual offences – the royals appeared to be willing to turn a blind eye to that for years. His bigger problem, as far as the palace is concerned, is that he mishandled the situation so badly that there was a real risk of the light breaking through and revealing many more unpleasant truths – truths that risked causing fatal damage to the monarchy. His actions reflect not just on him, but on the whole institution.

To understand why the affair reflects on the whole family, particularly Charles and William, it's worth noting how reluctant they were to act on the allegations of sexual abuse. Andrew's relationship with Jeffrey Epstein first came to light in 2011, after Virginia Giuffre spoke out publicly for the first time, having previously sued Epstein in anonymity. While it was agreed Andrew would step down from a government role as trade ambassador, it was later reported that he was continuing to represent the country on trade missions and international events, including the World Economic Forum at Davos. The palace took no steps to reprimand Andrew or diminish his public role, beyond cosmetic changes. It was in 2014, following the admission of evidence to a Florida court, that Giuffre made direct accusations against Andrew, yet still the palace did nothing. He failed to cooperate with the US authorities despite having said he would, and still the palace took no action. The palace did act in late 2019, not because of fresh revelations but because he had agreed to a disastrous interview on the BBC's *Newsnight* programme. Even then the palace did as little as possible, saying he was 'stepping back' from public duties but would retain his titles, honours and patronages. By 2021, Giuffre was pursuing the matter in the civil courts and the case was becoming a serious threat to the monarchy. Andrew's lawyers adopted the appalling tactic of publicly attacking Giuffre, before suddenly folding and agreeing to pay an undisclosed sum in damages, subsequently reported to be £12 million, the money being provided by the Queen and Prince Charles.

It wasn't until January 2022 that the Queen took more drastic action, stripping Andrew of most of his honorary titles and patronages, all except the positions of Duke of York, Earl of Inverness (much to the irritation of local residents of those cities) and vice admiral of the Royal Navy. By this time most of the country had made up their mind that the allegations were to be believed, a suspicion compounded by Andrew's claim he had never met Giuffre despite a photo that was in circulation proving otherwise. It should be noted, of course, that he has never been convicted or successfully sued in relation to this matter, and that he maintains his innocence, but for a lot of observers it wasn't just the initial accusations that mattered, but his attempts to avoid court that made his position untenable.

The decision to finally strip Andrew of most of his titles came twenty-four hours after a letter was sent to the Queen, signed by 150 ex-services personnel, demanding action be taken. It was a letter I drafted and circulated to the signatories who had come forward expressing their concern at Andrew's continued association with Britain's armed forces. These men and women who had served their country were quite clear Andrew must go, saying in the letter:

> . . . were this any other senior military officer it is inconceivable that he would still be in post [. . .] We are therefore asking that you take immediate steps to strip Prince Andrew of all his military ranks and titles and, if necessary, that he be dishonourably discharged [. . .] These steps could have been taken at any time in the past eleven years. Please do not leave it any longer.

King Charles has since faced his own accusations of law-breaking. In September 2021, the *Sunday Times* reported that Michael Fawcett, by then working as chief executive of the Prince's Foundation, had written to Mahfouz Marei Mubarak bin Mahfouz, a Saudi billionaire, offering to secure a knighthood and to assist with an application for British citizenship in return for £1.5 million in donations to another of Charles's charities, which in turn helped with the cost of renovating the Castle of Mey, and Dumfries House where Charles usually resides when in Scotland. The letter said:

> In light of the ongoing and most recent generosity of His Excellency Sheikh Mahfouz Marei Mubarak bin Mahfouz, I am happy to confirm to you, in confidence, that we are willing and happy to support and contribute to the application for citizenship. I can further confirm we are willing to make an application to increase His Excellency's honour from Honorary CBE to that of KBE in accordance with Her Majesty's Honours Committee.

He added: 'Both of these applications will be made in response to the most recent and anticipated support of the Trust.' The exchange of honours for cash or any other kind of consideration is a criminal offence, one senior political figures were investigated for in 2006 and 2007, following accusations party donors were being offered peerages. On that occasion, police concluded there was insufficient evidence to pursue prosecution as it was impossible to prove a relationship between the loans and donations and the offer of places in the House of Lords. On this occasion, Fawcett's letter seemed fairly clear: a knighthood appeared to be offered 'in response to' significant donations, donations which weren't simply to a charity, but helped renovate Charles's personal property. It is hard to understand how Fawcett could make such promises without the full knowledge of Charles, and we know Charles was aware of the donation and the honour, which he personally presented to Mahfouz at an undisclosed meeting. There is no suggestion Mahfouz did anything wrong, but there were clear grounds for suspecting Fawcett and Charles had broken the law, so I reported both to the police. In early 2022, the broadcaster Jonathan Dimbleby, who is a close friend of Charles, was invited on to Radio 4's *Today* programme to defend the prince, where he said it 'beggars belief' to think Charles could have been aware of the cash for honours arrangement, although this seems to be a view based entirely on the 'good chap' theory rather than an objective assessment of the facts. Norman Baker, who also wrote to the Metropolitan Police about the matter, said in response:

Arise Sir Jonathan [. . .] When the going gets tough, Jonathan Dimbleby is rolled out to defend the prince. The idea that Dimbleby skates over, is the 'I know nothing', kind of Manuel [from *Fawlty Towers*] response to everything. Fact is, we know

Charles and Fawcett are Tweedledum and Tweedledee. Charles has said he's the one man he cannot do without. So the idea that Fawcett would be doing stuff without Charles knowing, it is inconceivable.

Quite. The police, unfortunately, also appear to be taking a generous approach to the former prince, now King, first dragging their feet and making no discernible headway in investigating the matter for several months, and then announcing in November 2022 that a file was being sent to the Crown Prosecution Service without so much as asking Charles for an interview, let alone conducting one. One person quipped: 'They didn't even send Charles a questionnaire,' a reference to the famously sluggish police response to the Partygate scandal.

If a politician faced half the accusations faced by Charles and his family, whether it's unpalatable views on race, hypocrisy on the environment, boorish and rude treatment of staff or serious 'gaffes' during public engagements, let alone criminal behaviour or suspected abuse of public office or taxpayers' money, they would soon be out of office, whether at the hands of the prime minister or the voters. Accusations of sexual assault against MPs have been surfacing in recent years and the police have taken action, with Charlie Elphicke and Imran Ahmad Khan both being forced to resign and later serving time in prison. That's a stark contrast to the police response to Virginia Giuffre's complaint against Andrew, a complaint made in London to the Metropolitan Police. Labour's Rupa Huq was swiftly suspended by the party after she described Kwasi Kwarteng as 'superficially Black', while other MPs have faced widespread criticism for racist language, including former chief whip Mark Spencer using the phrase 'some little man in China' and James

Gray reportedly mixing up former chancellors Nadhim Zahawi and Sajid Javid while joking that Asian people 'all look the same'. Again, the response is very different to the muted reaction to similar remarks made by Philip who, while facing some criticism, was protected from any serious consequences. A public figure who is accountable and who understands the need for confidence in the office they hold doesn't even need to be found guilty of anything to lose their job. Deputy Speaker Nigel Evans resigned because of criminal charges being brought for sexual assault, charges for which he was later acquitted. In Germany, too, it is understood that the highest office in the land must be seen to be beyond reproach, as we saw with the resignations of presidents Horst Köhler and Christian Wulff. While Köhler's resignation was criticized at the time, he had himself been criticized for making comments that appeared to support the use of the German military to advance the national interest overseas. Failing to receive support from the Bundestag, he felt he had no choice but to resign. Two years later, Wulff resigned after formal corruption investigations were launched, relating to his time as minister president of Lower Saxony. He too was later acquitted. Royalists I debated with at the time saw this as a failure of the republic, that two heads of state would resign in quick succession. Surely the opposite is true. Having heads of state who are accountable, who believe they must be held to the highest standards, is a system that is *working*, not failing. In the UK we simply choose to turn a blind eye and claim it 'beggars belief' to think ill of the King.

## #NotMyKing

The long list of complaints that can be made against Charles, William and others renders them unsuitable for public office. Given the chance, I certainly wouldn't vote for them were there an election for head of state. You may disagree, of course. Perhaps you simply don't believe the charges against the royals, or don't see them as being sufficient to count against the good you believe they bring to the country and the roles they occupy. I suspect, however, that in a free and fair election, in which all the evidence is laid bare, they would struggle to be elected as Britain's head of state. You may point to opinion polls, which tell us the percentage of public support for William and Charles is in the mid- to high sixties. Firstly, there are elected heads of state in Europe who have poll ratings well in excess of 80 per cent. Secondly, the ratings for William and Charles are as much a product of indifference, a largely uncritical and often defensive media, and the nature of pollsters' questioning. They are judged against their own benchmarks, free from real scrutiny beyond tittle-tattle and the occasional scandal.

Imagine for a moment that an election for head of state was declared, that Charles declared himself a candidate and that another three or four eminent people also secured nomination to run for the office of president. Imagine Charles standing in a studio, going head to head with other candidates, being challenged on his environmental hypocrisy, his actions towards Edzard Ernst, his knowledge of cash-for-honours deals allegedly being arranged by his former valet. Do we really imagine he would withstand that kind of scrutiny?

I would welcome the chance to go head to head with Charles,

or William, in a live TV debate. To ask them about the serious questions I have raised above, to ask them, simply, why they believe they should be in their position just because of the family they were born into. Do you believe they would accept that challenge? They wouldn't dare, unless they are as lacking in self-awareness and good judgement – and advisers – as Prince Andrew was when he agreed to that *Newsnight* interview. How would they cope with being directly questioned, with being challenged by someone who treats them as equals, as public figures open to scrutiny and criticism? Not well, I imagine. It's unlikely they'd risk the spectacle of Charles or William storming off the set because I failed to offer them sufficient deference.

Even if he made a good fist of defending himself, for a lot of voters this would be the first time they'd seen Charles challenged so directly. The first time they would have heard of many of these allegations and scandals. He *might* win an election, but I doubt it. That is the fundamental problem with a hereditary head of state. It is very likely that in King Charles we have a head of state we would not elect if the opportunity was available to us. It is an affront to democracy to have a head of state we would never choose in a free and fair election.

And this is the crux of the problem with the monarchy, at least on the limited question of who our head of state should be. The argument here isn't to say, 'These are bad people, get rid of them,' but to point out that they are ordinary. Deeply flawed, raised in strange circumstances, they are not equipped with the judgement and character needed to live up to the highest standards in public life. They are protected by deference, indifference and a well-funded press operation. But these ordinary people, in any other circumstances, would not be the people we would choose to elect. We would instead find any number of more decent, honest, eloquent and accomplished people to serve in the highest office in the land.

You may well disagree with my assessment of Charles's character, or William's. That's fine. But if your response is, 'Well, I like them so we should keep the monarchy,' then what you're really saying is, 'My guy has the job, so I don't want you to get to choose, in case he loses it.' How is that different to a supporter of Rishi Sunak arguing against another general election on the grounds that, in their view, Sunak is a great leader who is honest, decent and who cares deeply about the country he leads? In other words, if you like Charles, vote for him.

To criticize the royals is to highlight the failure of the monarchy in both holding our head of state to the highest standards and in denying a free and fair choice of head of state. To argue that the monarchy itself is popular – or at least retains a majority in favour of retention – and therefore that choice is not needed misses the point. There is no free and fair vote on the future of the monarchy. No regular return to the voters, not just to seek their opinion but to ask them to decide on who the head of state should be.

Support for the monarchy is sustained by a dishonest fairy-tale image, a deferential media and an acquiescent political class too keen on the monarchy or too fearful of speaking against it. It is time to let the daylight in on the magic, to see the family and the institution for what it is, and to have a serious, grown-up conversation about the state of our constitution and the country we want to be.

# 5.

# A Constitution Fit for a King

In his report on the election of a hung parliament in 2010, here in the UK, and the uncertainty it created around the formation of a new government, the American comedian Jon Stewart referred to the Queen as a 'glorified tea-towel seller', a reflection of the common view that the monarchy is little more than a quaint decoration, a harmless hangover from a bygone age. It's not just in the US that the monarchy's place in our constitution is often misunderstood, but here in the UK too. The suggestion that 'it ain't broke', or that it's harmless, reflects the same idea – that the monarchy is decorative, purely ceremonial. Yet the Crown sits at the heart of Britain's constitution as the source of political and legal authority. As terminology is often used interchangeably, it's worth making a distinction between Crown, monarchy and monarch. It is the Crown that is the source of power – power exercised by government through the Privy Council and royal prerogative. The monarch formally signs off on the use of that power, but only on the instruction of the prime minister or ministers, while the monarchy is the whole cast of royals and all the trappings that gives this arrangement an air of regal respectability.

When we answer the 'it ain't broke' argument, we must look at the place of the Crown within our political system and the role it plays in concentrating power in the hands of the few, at the expense of many. The Crown, a source of real power, protected from serious scrutiny by the monarchy, a family and institution steeped in mythology and itself guarded by deference, is key to the failures of Britain's constitution. Constitutional reformers who demand an elected upper house, or electoral reform, are often missing one of the main fault lines in our political system: founded on monarchy, we are still governed using the outdated toolkit of a monarchy, regardless of whether or not it is the King himself who wields power. The demand for a republic isn't just about the job of head of state. It is a demand for a better, more equitable democracy.

## The Sovereignty of Government

During an episode of *Have I Got News For You*, not long after Tony Blair's departure from Downing Street, Ian Hislop quipped that our democracy rested on the principle of one-man, one-vote, and that one man was Gordon Brown. This is not far from the truth. If the Commons is content to pass the government legislation, as it usually is – albeit with a lot of arguing and hot air – the prime minister's authority is almost absolute, because Parliament's authority is absolute. Stig Abell, in his book *How Britain Really Works*, quoted a conversation he had with former Liberal Democrat leader Paddy Ashdown. Abell wrote: '. . . he pointed out with grim relish that a dominant government could "send all the Jews in Britain into a gas chamber", and there would not be a ready constitutional means of stopping it.'

Ashdown's comment recalls Lord Hailsham's phrase 'elective dictatorship', coined in his 1976 Richard Dimbleby Lecture in which he warned of the very limited constraints put on

Parliament, a Parliament increasingly under the control of government. Hailsham explained:

> Not so long ago, influence was fairly evenly balanced between government and opposition, and between front benches and back benches. Today, the centre of gravity has moved decisively towards the government side of the House, and on that side, to the members of the government itself ... The sovereignty of Parliament has increasingly become, in practice, the sovereignty of the Commons, and the sovereignty of the Commons has increasingly become the sovereignty of the government, which, in addition to its influence in Parliament, controls the party whips, the party machine and the civil service.

This control over Parliament comes from a variety of places, including formal procedures, patronage and certain political realities that might temper more independent-minded responses from MPs who sit behind the government front bench. A government, by design, will usually have the support of the majority of MPs and as such will have control over anything that the Commons must decide, particularly the fate of any legislation that is brought in. But the government itself has additional levers of power it can use. Government sets Parliament's agenda, deciding what will be debated and when and for how long. While the opposition can introduce amendments, it's unlikely they'll get too far. If the government has a small majority or faces a large rebellion, a strategically savvy opposition can give a prime minister cause to step back and avoid defeat by withdrawing a bill or accepting the amendment. But by and large the government will get its way. As Abell says: 'Parliament [. . .] is free to do its main job: allow the government of the day to make laws [...] Most parliamentary business is government business.'

What is the point of Parliament, you might wonder, if all it does is agree to the government's laws? On so-called 'opposition days', where the official opposition can put forward motions, it is more theatre than business. They may propose motions that cause political problems for the government, but their proposals have no chance of leading to any kind of binding decision or new law. Again, Abell points out the weakness of this process when he cites the October 2017 opposition proposal to pause the roll-out of the Universal Credit system. Tory MPs were told to abstain, the vote was passed unanimously and 'literally nothing happened'. There are other ways the opposition can raise issues in Parliament, but all of them are equally pointless, save for the potential for causing the government some embarrassment.

A lot of parliamentary time is, according to the 2018 Democratic Audit, 'ritualistic, point-scoring and unproductive in terms of achieving policy improvements'. A private members' bill is one sponsored by a backbench MP. You would think in a free and fair democracy that any MP could propose a new law and have at least some expectation that it would be subject to a binding vote, but the reality is that these bills only get anywhere if the government allows them to. This can be to the government's advantage if the bill is contentious or a low priority, but where allowing it to become law is seen as the right thing to do, whether politically or morally. The Sexual Offences Act 1967, which decriminalized homosexuality, the Murder (Abolition of Death Penalty) Act 1965 and the Abortion Act 1967 all started as private members' bills, but none would have been allowed to pass if the government had opposed them.

A lot of the government's authority in the Commons is

simply a product of their having a majority, one inflated by the disproportionate voting system. While backbench rebellions do happen, and have been more common in recent years, they are somewhat constrained by the large number of MPs who are formally part of the government and therefore bound by collective responsibility. To quote the Democratic Audit: 'The government has created a huge "payroll vote" of ministers and unpaid pseudo-ministers on the first rung of a promotion ladder, simply to help maintain control of these excess numbers by dangling a chance for preferment.'

In recent years, the payroll vote has been as high as 170, according to the Institute for Government. That's almost half the total number of Conservative MPs in the current Parliament, duty-bound by their appointment to a government position to vote with the government or resign. These powers of patronage – and their control of Parliament – can to a large extent be traced back to the Crown and the incomplete evolution from monarchy to democracy.

Opposition MPs are largely reduced to campaigning and seeking to influence, rather than contributing to any serious decision making. Even there they are disadvantaged to some extent by the lack of resources. They are provided with 'Short Money',* which is available to assist opposition parties in carrying out their parliamentary responsibilities. However, as if to advertise the power of the government benches, in 2015 the Chancellor George Osborne cut this fund by 19 per cent with little warning.

The usual pattern of governments commanding comfortable or, as is often the case, very large majorities between 1945 and

---

\* Named after Labour MP Edward Short, Leader of the House of Commons 1974–6, who first proposed the payments.

2010 has, I believe, given rise to the expectation that the Commons is there to do the government's bidding, that the government should be able to command the Commons to pass its legislation and to block everything else. This was apparent during the 2017–19 Parliament and the Brexit debates. For the first time in decades, there was a sense of genuine parliamentary independence and real debate between the two sides of the chamber. Yet there was indignation and outrage from some politicians and commentators that MPs would obstruct the will of the elected government, missing the point that we had elected a parliament and it was to that parliament that government is answerable. As infuriating as that debate may have seemed to many on the outside looking in, particularly to those who supported the government's efforts to 'get Brexit done', this was surely what Parliament is meant to be – a place where our representatives can truly debate issues.

The one feature of the House of Commons that has a little more bite – and in which MPs can enjoy greater independence – is the select committees. Although they had been an ad hoc feature of Parliament for some time, permanent select committees, which will usually have a remit set around a particular department or area of government policy, were introduced in 1979. They can take expert testimony, cross-examine witnesses and produce reports and recommendations. Beyond that, they are largely powerless to do much more than cause the government some embarrassment. Republic has given evidence to these committees on the question of honours and on the matter of the Duchy of Cornwall's refusal to pay corporation tax. The 2013 investigation by the Public Accounts Committee, chaired by Margaret Hodge, criticized the Treasury for failing to properly scrutinize the duchy's accounts, and question the tax avoidance, suggesting (rather politely) that the arrangement 'may give it [the duchy] an unfair advantage over its competitors'. The Treasury's response was, 'The Treasury has a constructive working relationship with the duchy, and challenges decisions where appropriate.' Well, that's that sorted then.

With the abolition of the Fixed-term Parliaments Act (FTPA), the power to dissolve Parliament returned to the government through the use of the royal prerogative. The royal prerogative gives the government a great deal of authority, not just in deciding when to call elections but also when to prorogue Parliament and therefore set the length of parliamentary sessions. The prerogative also grants the government considerable power of patronage, well beyond the appointment of ministers and secretaries of state, including the opportunity to offer or withhold honours, peerages and other sought-after appointments and titles. Norman Baker was appointed to the Privy Council because, as he explained in . . . *And What Do You Do?*, the party had been given a quota of gongs and honours to dole out to their MPs, but the gift was Nick Clegg's to give or withhold. Baker accepted the offer for reasons he explains in his book, not least because it would 'annoy the sort of Establishment figures I had been railing against all through my political career, and especially those who desperately aspired to membership [of the Privy Council] themselves'.

All of these honours and positions are in the gift of the prime minister. Such patronage is a powerful tool for keeping people in line. The party whips, whose job it is to maintain discipline within the ranks of backbenchers, can easily suggest the awarding or withholding of some perk or another to have most people fall into line behind the leadership.

One of the most egregious abuses of patronage is the appointment of loyal acolytes to the House of Lords. They may be ministers who have served their leader well, MPs who have lost their seats or stood down at an election, or party donors who have greased the wheels of the party machine over the years. All and sundry are offered seats in our parliament as a quid pro quo for supporting a party leader or prime minister. That we allow such corrupt practices to continue in the full light of day is as shocking as any royal scandal.

All these roads lead back to the prime minister. The extent of their authority varies from one prime minister to the next, but as the PM determines the shape, size and membership of the Cabinet, it is usually considerable. There is an underlying contradiction between the theory of prime minister as chair of the Cabinet and 'first among equals' and the real power they wield to the extent that accusations of presidentialism are commonplace. Yet presidents are usually far more constrained by their constitution than a prime minister might be. The British PM is, for example, far more powerful in domestic affairs than the US president. It would be more accurate to complain of King Rishi than President Sunak. What president, after all, has a Privy Council?

## The Privy Council

The Privy Council is often talked about as a 'ceremonial body' that has no real purpose, but in truth it is a source of considerable executive authority. Its powers are substantial and wide-ranging, not least because they are poorly defined, little understood and even less scrutinized, outside a small number of parliamentarians and academics who stop to take an interest.

The Council has four 'mechanisms' for exercising power: Orders *in* Council, which include Statutory Orders, Prerogative Orders and Proclamations; and Orders *of* Council. It is through the Privy Council that ministers exercise royal prerogative powers. Some prerogative powers are well known, such as the use of proclamations to dissolve Parliament at election time or declare war, although even here there is uncertainty about the role of constitutional convention in limiting the government's power. Some commentators have suggested Tony Blair's decision to allow a Commons vote on military action in the Middle East, followed by David Cameron's vote on military action in Syria, sets a precedent for parliamentary approval. The fact is that such precedents and conventions are only there so long as the prime minister wishes to follow them.

While a lot of the Privy Council's business is mundane, prerogative Orders in Council have the force of primary legislation, laws passed by Parliament. This is, in the words of Patrick O'Connor QC in his 2009 report for the charity Justice, 'a problem of real substance: well beyond mere harmless and quaint ceremonial. It is surely a loophole in our constitutional safety net.'\*

The Privy Council is one of the oldest institutions in the country, and it is from its earliest iteration that a subset of counsellors was split off to form the Common Council, the precursor to Parliament. As early as 1351, there were complaints that the King was using the Council to circumvent Parliament, a charge still levelled today (although, in the twenty-first century, replace King with prime minister). In a sense, though, it is not that old at all, because the Privy Council of the seventeenth century has long since been replaced by a modern successor. Through the

---

\* If you want to know more about the Privy Council, O'Connor's report is well worth a read: https://files.justice.org.uk/wp-content/uploads/2015/09/06170807/The-Constitutional-Role-of-the-Privy-Council-26-January-2009-.pdf.

evolution of our parliamentary system, the Council has moved from a council of advisers to a monarch, to a council of ministers that instructs the King. To suggest, as is often done, that today the Privy Council 'advises' the monarch is a fiction that hides a very modern constitutional reality: that government uses this ancient and archaic body to wield significant executive power.

There is no good reason why the Privy Council should continue, not least because its functions make no sense when taken as a whole. This 'dysfunctional body', as O'Connor calls it, has 'no consistent rationale' for its wide range of powers, which are a 'rag bag of historical accidents'. Decisions made during one year include proclamations of bank holidays, closure of burial grounds, constitutional matters relating to overseas territories, armed services pay and pensions, appointment of the chair of the BBC, UN sanctions against North Korea and an order relevant only to the Isle of Man. Quite why these matters can't be carried out by government ministers and their departments or presented to Parliament, where they might be properly discussed, is something of a mystery. The Council itself doesn't discuss these matters. Like some bizarre secret society, they meet roughly once a month, standing in a semicircle facing the monarch and read out each order or proclamation, to which the monarch simply says 'approved'. Orders of Council are simply signed off by the relevant minister.

Perhaps the reason commentators and journalists often believe the Council is purely ceremonial is because the ceremonial is all we really see. The membership is vast, as once you are a Privy Counsellor you retain the honour for life, forever being permitted to use *Right Honourable* before your name. The process by which you are given membership is an arcane one, which Richard Crossman, a member of Harold Wilson's cabinet, described as 'dull, pretentious [. . .] and plain silly'. Yet behind closed doors, the Council can make significant decisions, without recourse to Parliament, that can have a profound impact on people's lives. As O'Connor points out, prerogative Orders in Council, which have the effect of law:

> are not laid before Parliament, at any time. One of the import-
> ant checks and balances in the Human Rights Act 1998 is
> therefore also evaded. The responsible minister does not have
> to make a 'statement of compatibility' with rights under the
> European Convention on Human Rights. They are obscurely
> published as annexes to the annual volume of statutory instru-
> ments: it takes a good librarian to find them.

To take one egregious example, it was these Orders in Council that were used to deprive the people of the Chagos Islands of their homeland in the mid-1960s. The islands were part of the British colony of Mauritius in the Indian Ocean. Unfortunately for the islanders, the UK had agreed that the US could build an airbase on Diego Garcia, the largest island of the Chagos Archipelago. With Mauritius heading for independence, the British government used an Order in Council – the British Indian Ocean Territory Order 1965 – to split the Chagos Islands from the rest of the colony and retain possession, before forcibly removing the inhabitants and denying them any chance to return. They have been fighting for that chance ever since. In 2001, it appeared they could be close to forcing the government to allow them to return to their homes, until in 2004 ministers enacted a fresh Order in Council that declared that 'no person has the right of abode in BIOT [British Indian Overseas Territory] nor the right without authorisation to enter and remain there'. To this day, the Chagossians remain dispossessed of their land. Not only did they never have a say, but the people of the UK and even Parliament didn't get a say, either.

Proclamations use regal power to maintain ministerial control over Parliament, not least on the questions of prorogation and dissolution. The dissolution of Parliament, and the subsequent calling of a general election, is entirely in the hands of the prime minister, using the King's power. This wasn't the case for the ten years of the Fixed-term Parliaments Act, a law designed to remove that power and hand it to Parliament. But before and since it has been the prime minister who determines the date of an election and the length of time between dissolution and election day. This gives the governing party significant political advantage over opposition parties, an advantage that cannot be reasonably justified other than on the basis of party interest. By law, elections must be called every five years. Quite often, as in 1983, 1987, 2001 and 2005, a prime minister will go to the polls after four years. However, if things aren't going so well, or if a new prime minister has been appointed and wants more time before risking an election, they will wait the full term, as happened in 1979, 1992, 1997 and 2010. On each occasion the prime minister was able to choose the timing of the polls, within certain constraints, to suit their own interests. The Fixed-term Parliaments Act wasn't a well drafted law and contained a significant flaw, in that MPs could choose to cut short a parliament for any reason, and of course if the government couldn't get the necessary two-thirds vote it could otherwise repeal the law by a simple majority. In 2017, and again in 2019, the government called on MPs to allow an election, and opposition parties felt it politically necessary to agree.

The Privy Council today is not an ancient, ceremonial body, but an annex of government used to quietly and without proper scrutiny make numerous decisions, many of which have the force of law. There is no clear limit to its powers, save for those powers prescribed elsewhere by statute. When, in 2004, the House of Commons Public Administration and Constitutional Affairs Select Committee called on the government to identify the prerogative powers, the government provided two lists, one for domestic affairs and one for foreign affairs. These included the power to make treaties, deploy armed forces, regulate the Civil Service and grant honours. Yet the government added a note which, in summary, said, 'These are the powers we can identify now, there may be others we identify as and when the need arises.' In other words, if there is no law to say a prerogative power does *not* exist, then it does. That leaves a lot of room for the executive use of law-making powers that circumvent Parliament.

There is really no reason for the Privy Council. It is part and parcel of our constitutional monarchy. It survives simply because, like the monarchy, it serves the interests of the government at the expense of proper parliamentary scrutiny and democratic decision-making. Its survival is helped by its association with the monarch, as proposals to reform or scrap the Council or its powers are met with accusations of an attack on the Crown itself. It is, like the Crown and the Lords, a relic of feudal times when kings governed the country by whim. And, like the Lords, it has no place in a modern democracy.

## The Other Place

The problem of excessive government power is exacerbated by the weaknesses of the House of Lords. Those who defend the Lords often do so on the grounds it can challenge and frustrate government legislation. Ostentatiously referred to by MPs as 'the other place', its unelected status, according to its supporters, can be a benefit to parliamentary debate. While no party in the Lords has a majority, and peers often defeat the government, those defeats can be overturned in the Commons, and any real power to block legislation is limited. The Lords tend only to succeed in stopping laws being introduced by making their passage through Parliament too much of a headache for ministers. If ministers are so minded, however, they can ultimately get their legislation through as originally drafted, leaving the Lords largely powerless to further obstruct their efforts. The Lords caused a stir in 2020 during the passage of the EU (Withdrawal) Bill, when five amendments were passed by peers, one of which sought to protect unaccompanied child refugees. Despite these government defeats in the Lords, all five amendments were overturned and the bill became law later that month.

Aside from these practical limitations, there is a serious question of legitimacy. Should a hereditary peer or a Lord appointed by the prime minister be determining which laws to challenge and which to allow through? If the upper house is going to challenge and frustrate the government, surely they need to be accountable in some way to the public?

As with the monarchy, the Lords is sustained by mythology and wishful thinking. Just as the monarch is celebrated for their longevity, wisdom and independence, so too are the Lords. For the Lords, another virtue is added to the list: expertise. The argument goes that by appointing the Lords we get people who wouldn't necessarily wish to stand for election or, if they did, wouldn't be elected, but who nevertheless provide expertise in the subject matter of the bills that pass through the house. Such experts include scientists, economists, educationalists, retired judges and former senior police officers.

This is one of the most common points put up against Lords reform, often together with the refrain 'we don't need more politicians!' It's an odd argument for several reasons, not least because the Lords are politicians, they just aren't elected or accountable. With over eight hundred Lords currently in the house and most proposals for an elected alternative setting the size at between two hundred and three hundred, an elected upper house would give us fewer politicians. Yet, the refrain is really about setting apart 'experts' – people it is assumed would approach the role from a point of detachment and authority – from 'politicians' – people assumed to make decisions on the basis of party loyalty or career advancement. The cynicism aside, the House of Lords doesn't live up to the promise.

It's important to remember that Parliament is there to make laws we must all be bound by, and so on a matter of principle and in the interests of good government it must reflect and represent the whole society it is legislating for. It is often said that the Lords is a 'house of review', or 'revising chamber', but it is in every sense a parliamentary house that makes decisions on the law of the land. It can and does instigate, amend and pass legislation, so the democratic principles that apply to the Commons should also apply to the Lords. In representing wider society, Parliament isn't there to make 'expert' decisions. Its primary purpose is not to answer technical questions but those of values, principles and priorities. There are already experts in a parliamentary system: they belong in the Civil Service and in committee rooms, giving evidence to elected representatives.

Take Robert Winston, an expert in fertility and IVF and one example I've heard cited many times before as the sort of expertise the Lords provides. Winston, who was made a Labour peer in 1995, can tell the Lords what is possible in the field of IVF and other fertility procedures, but a decision on what will be done is a moral, financial and political one. In other words, Winston can say what services the NHS *could* deliver, but decisions on what the NHS *should* deliver must be made by accountable representatives, people who represent the diverse views and values of our wider society.

And Lord Winston is not a representative example. Of the eight hundred or so lords, about three hundred account for the bulk of the parliamentary work and regularly attend debates and participate in votes. Those who do are far more likely to be political appointees with a party background and allegiance, including former MPs and party staff. Of all lords, 34 per cent had 'representational politics' as their main profession in 2017, by far the largest single bloc. Another 27 per cent list business, commerce or banking and finance as their profession. Fewer than 1 per cent have backgrounds in transport or manual labour. There are more former employees of the palace (two) than manual labourers (one). On the notion of professional expertise, the Electoral Reform Society said in its 2015 Lords report: 'While health debates in the Lords can boast doctors, medical research fellows and surgeons, the Commons can also draw on the experience of GPs, NHS managers and medical professionals from across the NHS.'

A more obvious point, if you were to take a moment to watch a sitting of the House of Lords, is how woefully unrepresentative it is. Only about a quarter of peers are women and fewer than 6 per cent are Black or Asian. More than half are over seventy years old, with 74 per cent being over sixty-five. Hereditary peerages exacerbate the problem of a lack of diversity, with these ninety-two peers overwhelmingly being men, as is also the case with the twenty-six bishops who make up around 14 per cent of the House.*

We continue to guarantee seats in our parliament to church leaders, something we share with theocratic Iran. This isn't a comment against religion so much as to say it is fundamentally wrong, in a democratic society, to elevate not just one faith, but one church, above all others. More so given the great chasm that exists between the values of the church leadership and the wider public on issues such as LGBTQ+ rights. As recently as August 2022, the Archbishop of Canterbury, Justin Welby, affirmed the 'validity' of the Church's 1998 declaration that gay sex is a sin, and in doing so gave credence and legitimacy to every homophobe in the country. If that is genuinely Welby's view then so be it, but if he wants a seat in our parliament, perhaps he can put that view to the public and seek election.

In 1997, Tony Blair stripped away most of the hereditary peers, leaving ninety-two in place, a move better described as a change than a reform, and one which enhanced the power of political patronage at the expense of hereditary privilege. Blair felt compelled to allow Parliament to debate further reform in 2007, yet nothing came of it. Promises by Nick Clegg three years later faced significant opposition from Labour and the Conservative backbench. (During the 2007 debates, one Conservative MP voiced an interesting but pertinent defence of maintaining the status quo, that to be rid of the remaining hereditary peers would leave the Queen exposed as the last remaining hereditary

---

\* I use approximations because there is no fixed number of lords, and the number continually changes each time someone dies, retires or is appointed. The number is currently somewhere around 850 and has continued to grow in recent years.

figure in the British state, raising questions about the legitimacy of the monarchy.) However, it is perhaps the power of patronage – which serves the interests of Labour and Conservative parties alike – that best explains the Lords' survival.

Accusations of cash-for-peerages are nothing new, yet neither Labour nor the Conservatives have shown much willingness to address the issue head on. During the final days of the last Labour government, a joke went around Parliament: 'Q: How do you address a Labour donor? A: M'lud' – a reference to the correlation between those who had given the party large donations and new appointments to the upper house. In December 2022, the *Guardian* reported that twenty-seven Conservative peers had each donated more than £100,000 to their party. To read the detail of how the Lords works, it is shocking it hasn't become a bigger scandal, and there is no wonder that until now government parties have been content to keep this tawdry show on the road.

It is interesting that Keir Starmer has returned to this issue, and I'm inclined to believe he is sincere when he talks about the need for reform. Whether he believes in it enough to see it through we shall have to wait and see, although already some are fighting back.

In December 2022, the Speaker of the Commons, Lindsay Hoyle, gave an interview with Andrew Marr in which he spoke out against Labour's plans for an elected upper house. It was an extraordinary thing for a Speaker to do, because he is required to remain impartial on matters that will come before the House. I can only assume and hope that, when it comes to debating Labour's proposals, Hoyle will recuse himself from the Speaker's chair. His comments, however, were nothing new in that they reflected a deeply conservative view of the Commons. In the interview he said: 'At the moment, it's very clear the House of Commons, the elected house, has supremacy; once you have a second house that's elected, then you're into an arm wrestle about who has the power [. . .] We don't need the competition. Supremacy is going to remain with the Commons.'

Part of the argument against an elected upper house, which was repeated by quite a few otherwise democratically minded people in response to Labour's latest proposals, was the notion that it would cause gridlock, a stalemate between the new house and the House of Commons. Some pointed directly to the US, where the Senate can block legislation and budgets, as an example of such gridlock. Yet the US system is a far cry from Britain's parliamentary model and an upper house in the UK would not be like their Senate. It is possible to have a strong upper house and have simple mechanisms for overcoming deadlock. In Australia, where usually a third of the Senate is up for re-election when the lower house faces the polls, a deadlock can potentially be broken by calling a 'double dissolution' election, which means all senators and MPs in the lower house go to the polls at the same time. That gives voters the opportunity to reconstitute the Senate so that it will pass government legislation. If voters choose a new Senate that continues to block that legislation, then they have effectively acted as a check on government power. Moreover, unlike in the binary world of US politics, in Australia and the UK we have multi-party politics, and a government with a minority in the upper house can negotiate different majorities for different bills, drawing on support from different parties each time. If they cannot get a majority to support a bill, that's the upper house doing its job.

The Lords fails the test of democratic principle as much as the monarchy, which is hardly surprising as they both originate from the same wellspring of powerful landowners defending their power and wealth at the expense of everyone else. When we talk about abolishing the monarchy in favour of a republic, we need to think big. We are bound to a constitutional monarchy when we could have a true parliamentary democracy. These undemocratic, antiquated institutions have no place in a modern nation. Unelected patronage corrupts our politics and only further centralizes authority in the office of the prime minister.

## Writing it Down

When I was at school, constitutional reform was a marginal issue, considered by most to be of little interest outside A-level politics classes or meetings of the Liberal Democrats. Over the last thirty years that has changed. In December 2022, the Labour Party launched *A New Britain: Renewing our Democracy and Rebuilding our Economy*, a report drafted by former prime minister Gordon Brown, which set out a range of measures to 'put power and resources in the hands of communities, towns, cities, regions and nations', including an elected upper house and greater power for local government. Keir Starmer also promised new 'constitutionally protected social rights – like the right to health care for all based on need, not ability to pay', which, he claimed, would be 'entrenched'. It's unfortunate that Starmer didn't commit to a written constitution, because without one it is impossible to entrench anything in British law.

It has been claimed by critics of written constitutions that they are unnecessary, because all the reforms we may want can be introduced by Parliament without the extra bother of writing it all down in one document. However, this misses some important points, not least that anything Parliament does Parliament can undo. If Labour introduces new rights in the next parliament, a future government can take them away. If the Lib Dems managed to introduce proportional representation for Westminster elections, a future government could revert to first past the post. If Parliament introduced an elected upper house, a future government could reform it to suit its needs or simply abolish it. Nothing is entrenched and nothing is protected from the danger of partisan attacks. Yes, we could scrap the monarchy without introducing a written constitution. But while restoration of the Crown would be unlikely, details of how the republic works would be subject to the whim of each government.

Perhaps the closest thing we have to an entrenched law is the Human Rights Act, but this is only entrenched in a political sense, not a constitutional one. If Parliament wished to, it could scrap the HRA with a majority of one. The difficulty it has is that we would remain a party to the European Convention on Human Rights, which mirrors the provisions of the HRA. Our government could remove us from that convention, but that would put the UK in the company of Putin's Russia and Belarus. It is also a complicated process to devise an alternative rights law that would be materially different to what we have, and moreover the HRA forms part of the Good Friday Agreement, which brought an end to thirty years of violence in Northern Ireland. All that said, if the government was unconcerned about these matters, the HRA could be repealed tomorrow and there is nothing any of us could do about it.

The same is true of devolution, which is assumed by many to be a permanent feature of British life since its introduction in Scotland and Wales in 1999. Yet, as has been the experience in Northern Ireland, such devolved powers are the gift of Westminster, and what the government in Westminster gives, so they can take away. While it is unlikely that the Scottish parliament would be abolished, it is hardly beyond imagination that a future government might curtail its powers. It is also not impossible that a scandal or crisis may give a future UK government cause or cover to abolish both Welsh and Scottish parliaments and return us to a unitary state. As is made clear in a House of Commons Library briefing note: 'Under the UK constitutional tradition of "parliamentary sovereignty" devolution is, in theory, reversible, and the devolved institutions products of UK statute.'

As with the monarchy and the Lords, it appears some commentators make a virtue of Britain's uncodified constitution simply because that's what we have. The reason given is often the much-vaunted flexibility of our constitution, a flexibility that is as much a fallacy as the independent monarchy. Or, as legal commentator Adam Wagner tweeted in July 2022: 'Flexibility just means "can be manipulated by the smoothest or most dastardly operator". Just write the thing down, because the next charlatan won't be as incompetent and sloppy as Johnson.'

On a range of issues, such as the Fixed-term Parliaments Act, constituency boundaries, the number of MPs in the Commons and so on, the prime minister can introduce changes that may or may not serve their party's interests. Yet on the big-ticket issues, such as Lords reform, the lack of clarity or structure in our constitution can act as an obstacle to reform, making change more, not less, difficult. That's largely because there is no mechanism for reform other than legislation passed by Parliament and, as I said above, what one parliament gives another can take away.

Of course, it is often claimed that written constitutions are inflexible – the US Second Amendment, the right to bear arms, is often cited as a case in point. Yet this is simply not the case. Since the ratification of the US Bill of Rights, which is made up

of the first ten amendments to the Constitution, a further seventeen amendments have been passed, the most recent in 1992.
That's an average of one amendment every thirteen years. A further six have been proposed by the United States Congress
during that time but have not been ratified by the states. The
constitution is designed to ensure both the federal and state governments are largely in agreement, but there is a clear process for
proposing and ratifying amendments, which allows definitive
decision-making. The reason the US has retained the Second
Amendment isn't because it's difficult to remove, but because, as
yet, they have chosen not to remove it for cultural and political
reasons. In Ireland, too, the written constitution has changed a
number of times. Since the original constitution came into force
in 1937, there have been thirty-two amendments, a rate of more
than one every three years, although in practice there have been
years when a number of changes have been approved in one go.
The German constitution has been amended fifty times since its
inception in the late 1940s, including a number of amendments
to accommodate the reunification of East and West Germany.
Written constitutions can also be revised wholesale, as in France
in the 1950s and in Switzerland, which introduced a new constitution on 1 January 2000. It has since been amended ten times.

The Irish constitution can only be changed by way of a referendum, so Irish citizens can know that their system of government
is one of their choosing and decided at every stage by democratic
means.* Some constitutions don't require referendums to be

---

\* Contrast that with arguments over the use of referendums
that rumbled on between the Brexit vote in 2016 and the UK's
departure from the EU in 2021. Previously, the House of
Lords Select Committee had looked at the role of referendums
to determine whether they were constitutionally necessary in

changed, but instead allow Parliament to introduce and agree amendments. However, they almost all require either a super-majority of two-thirds or more, meaning it's unlikely to pass with just one party in favour, or, as in Iceland, the same amendment must get through Parliament twice, either side of a general election. My view is that referendums ought to be used, and probably only used, for constitutional amendments, as this is how we make the people sovereign while maintaining the fundamentals of a representative parliamentary democracy. We elect representatives to make laws and to govern, but we all ought to have the opportunity to determine the rules by which they govern. Some time ago I contacted a number of constitutional experts to ask their view on the need for a referendum to achieve the abolition of the monarchy. The consensus was that it wasn't strictly necessary, but it would likely be politically essential. Or, as it was put by Matt Qvortrup, professor of political science and international relations at Coventry University, 'a very democratic thing should be done in a very democratic way', a sentiment I wholeheartedly agree with.

Again, defenders of our constitution will often say, 'Well, it works.' But, again, we must ask ourselves, 'Works for whom?' And how long do we leave ourselves with so few checks and balances in the hope that the 'good chap' theory of government holds true? I'm not suggesting we're heading for state tyranny, but governments can do many things that fall well short of dictatorship that nonetheless diminish our democracy, freedom and quality of life. We saw with the Johnson government a casual disregard for constitutional convention. The government is

---

certain areas of reform. The answer they came up with could be summarized as 'We're not sure.'

now introducing voter ID laws, which are likely to suppress voter turnout to the benefit of the Conservative Party, while in September 2022 Jacob Rees-Mogg introduced a bill to scrap all EU laws that remain on the British statute book in one fell swoop, giving ministers the power to determine the fate of individual laws with limited reference back to Parliament. As George Peretz KC warned in an article in the *Guardian*, the bill 'gives ministers huge powers to replace those rules with new rules, without any need to consult those affected and usually without any vote in parliament – and when there is a vote it will be a yes/no vote, after one short debate, and under the threat that the rules will vanish completely if parliament says "no"'. In other words, the royal prerogative has come back to haunt us.

The British constitution works for the government. It fails the rest of us. Even if we make reforms, unless we codify key parts of our constitution they can easily be undone. Beyond the theatrics that promote the myth of the Crown, the state opening of Parliament, the weekly audiences with the PM and the Accession Council that meets at the start of each reign, the throne sits empty, its power and purpose transposed to Downing Street.

To underscore the point, a fascinating account of the final hours before Boris Johnson's resignation as party leader, written for the *Financial Times* by Sebastian Payne, tells of growing concern that Johnson might ask the Queen for a snap election, a request that, by convention – it is claimed – the monarch would be bound to refuse. Johnson was unlikely to make such a request, not least because it would have been politically disastrous for the Conservative Party. Nevertheless, the men in grey suits, including Cabinet secretary Simon Case and Edward Young, the Queen's private secretary, discussed how this might be avoided. According to Payne, 'it would be politely communicated to Downing

Street that Her Majesty "couldn't come to the phone" had Johnson requested a call with the intention of dissolving parliament'.

It is extraordinary that our constitutional checks and balances have deteriorated to a game of hide-and-seek, but the fundamental point is that the head of state felt powerless to refuse any request made by the prime minister.

The answer cannot be to formalize or reinvigorate the monarch's power, because that would quickly prove untenable. Their hereditary status has been the primary reason for their loss of power in the first place. As with the Lords, a virtue is made of the monarch's independence, while at the same time their lack of democratic credentials is why they are expected to obey the prime minister in all matters. Any effort by a king to exercise power independently, to frustrate the government or Parliament, would cause a crisis the monarchy would be unlikely to survive. But the upshot of that is an impotent head of state and a prime minister with unrivalled power, subject only to the limitations of politics. If our next prime minister were to pull off an unprecedented majority, his or her authority would be unassailable.

## Our Elective Dictatorship

Step back for a moment and take a look at the shape of our supposed parliamentary democracy and we can see how power is funnelled, from the moment election results are declared, from Parliament to Cabinet to prime minister, whose own power is enhanced by the use of the royal prerogative and Privy Council. That power is left unchecked by the absence of a codified constitution, effective upper house or independent head of state. I say *supposed* parliamentary democracy because the centralization of power, which has for decades prompted concerns of an 'elective dictatorship', is what marks out the difference between a parliamentary democracy and a constitutional monarchy. That we are the latter and not the former is the source of a lot of the weaknesses in the UK's constitution.

There are many calls for constitutional reform, whether changing the electoral system, abolition of the Lords or greater devolution. But unless we grasp the central importance of the Crown, such reforms will not deal with the root of the issue. That's not to say other reforms aren't necessary; they are. But they should all be seen in the context of a broader ambition. Just as the Crown is the centrepiece of our constitution, so it must be at the centre of debates on reform. While the institution of monarchy should be abolished for all the reasons set out in this book, the task is more than replacing one head of state with another – it's about rebalancing power between government, Parliament and people.

Some argue piecemeal reform is more realistic, more achievable, but to date that reform has been offered up in very small pieces indeed. In the meantime, the power of the state remains highly centralized and almost unlimited in scope. Written constitutions are there for one fundamental reason: to constrain power. Those constraints are born of experience, of centuries of corrupt, violent and oppressive regimes. As democracy began to flourish, most countries sought to guard against abuses of power or a return to tyranny, knowing that those in power should not be trusted to be 'good chaps'. In the famous words of Lord Acton, power tends to corrupt and absolute power corrupts absolutely. Perhaps the UK's historical distance from the worst tyranny has made us complacent. I'm not suggesting we're one election away from disaster, but that complacency has left us exposed to abuses of power, an overbearing government and the impotence of second-rate institutions.

There are those, including on the left, who argue in favour of a powerful government, as otherwise there would be too many compromises to make on delivering an elected agenda. Just as some Labour figures argue against proportional representation because it will, they argue, work against party interests, others believe a strong Labour government is good for the country and therefore so is our centralized constitution. But seeing 'good of the party' as synonymous with 'good of the country' is hardly a democratic or ethical position, not least because it is surely up to voters to determine what they believe to be in their best interests.

Anyone proposing a written constitution knows that codifying the rules by which our politicians can govern is no panacea, but a written constitution would provide guard-rails to protect our democracy, allowing us to hope for good government while being prepared for bad. While a public intolerant of abuses of power is important, at times of populism or simply when people of limited integrity are in office, limitations on power protect our democracy for us and future generations. In the UK those limitations, checks and balances are almost completely absent in a constitution that rests on very different, outmoded values and assumptions. This is why more fundamental change is needed, to a parliamentary democracy founded on the principles of equality of citizenship and popular sovereignty. That change doesn't need to be revolutionary. We already have the core building blocks in place: a non-partisan, if ineffective, head of state, two Houses of Parliament with the prime minister in the House of Commons and a set of constitutional statutes that provide for elections, rights and devolution. The challenge is to take what we have and make it democratic, top to bottom. And where better to start than at the top?

## PART THREE

# ABOLISH THE
# MONARCHY

# 6.

# The Imagination to Change

In early 1999, researchers at Hamilton College in New York State conducted an extensive survey of racial attitudes among young adults between the ages of eighteen and twenty-nine. They were, as the authors pointed out, the first generation of Americans who had been born after the major civil rights battles of the 1960s and in a country 'without formal barriers to racial equality'. The results were mixed. While most respondents gave positive responses to questions on their personal attitudes, such as whether they would date someone of a different race, just over half supported a 'separate but equal' philosophy, allowing some kind of segregation so long as everyone has equal opportunities. Even more shockingly, the survey found that by 'small but consistent margins, respondents were less likely to describe blacks as equally intelligent, peaceful, and hard-working as whites'.

On the question of whether the US would elect a Black president, 54.5 per cent of these young people said it was unlikely to happen soon. Just ten years later, those same Americans witnessed the inauguration of President Barack Obama.

In the 1990s, acceptance of same-sex relationships in the UK was below 30 per cent, while same-sex marriage was barely discussed, even among rights campaigners. LGBTQ+ people could legally face discrimination, including a formal ban from serving in the military. As recently as 2012, same-sex relationships were accepted by fewer than 50 per cent, according to the British Social Attitudes survey of that year. By 2019, 85 per cent of UK respondents supported not just same-sex relationships but same-sex marriage. Since the 1990s, LGBTQ+ people have gone from very few protections to, more or less, full equality, at least in law.

Change happens. It happens not just because new generations replace old, but because action is taken to raise awareness of an issue, challenge old assumptions and win support for a new way of thinking. Of course, plenty of prejudice and discrimination continues, as witnessed by rising anti-LGBT hate crimes in the UK in recent years, and the right-wing backlash in the US against critical race theory, an academic discipline that tries to understand ongoing discrimination long after formal barriers to equality have been removed. While progress rarely goes unchallenged, we nevertheless have witnessed significant changes in attitudes on a wide range of issues over the past two or three decades.

I mention this because in the first few years that I spent campaigning for the abolition of the monarchy, a common response from my own side was, 'I agree, but it won't happen in my lifetime.' My reply was always, 'Why not? It must happen in someone's lifetime; why not ours?' Recently I've seen much more optimism among Republic's most active supporters. Few people say, 'Not in my lifetime,' not because they believe it's imminent, or inevitable, but because they believe it can be done. So while, from where we stand today at the start of the 2020s, abolition of the monarchy still seems unlikely to happen anytime soon, history tells us that big shifts in attitudes, and big moments of change, can happen quickly and unexpectedly.

## Let's Start at the End

Sit back and imagine, for a moment, you just got home from work, you're sitting on your sofa watching the evening news, or scrolling through the day's headlines on your phone, and you watch extraordinary scenes from Parliament. A debate has concluded, and MPs have headed for the division lobbies to vote on the Monarchy Referendum Bill. The vote is passed with great excitement from MPs and the millions of people around the country who have been telling pollsters that it's time for a republic. The starting gun has now been fired on a national debate and a referendum on the future of the British monarchy.

Fast-forward six months and you're staying up one Thursday evening to watch the results come in. By midnight it's clear: Britain has voted to ditch the monarchy, adopt a new constitution and choose their next head of state by popular vote. That vote will be held within a few months and again, for the third time, you are witness to history being made as our first president is declared. The inauguration would be a moment to celebrate our best values and traditions, to welcome leaders and dignitaries, plus the huge numbers of our friends and well-wishers from around the world. At the centre of a global media sensation, the people of these islands will have stood up and proudly declared ourselves to be citizens, not subjects, to be free to govern ourselves in every sense, to tear down no-entry barriers that have kept us out of some of the key parts of our constitution, to abolish archaic institutions, building on our best traditions and making history that future generations will come to celebrate.

It might seem fantastical. But all this can happen, sooner than many would believe possible, if we have the imagination to change, the determination to persuade and the belief that we are all better than the outmoded values represented by the monarchy. The ground has never been more fertile for change, and change is already happening. Not only are attitudes towards the monarchy shifting, but so too are underlying attitudes on issues of equality, democracy and social and historical justice. As the world continues to move on, the monarchy, unable and unwilling to adapt, will be left behind, the outgoing tide of changing values leaving it washed up against the rocks of its own choosing. And it's not just in the UK where change is shifting the sands beneath the foundations of monarchy. Across the Commonwealth and Europe, too, people are questioning why we put up with strange and archaic institutions, institutions that have historical connections not to society's best endeavours and most noble ideas, but to empire, slavery, elitism and subjugation.

From 2018 to 2022, support for the monarchy in the UK fell sharply, from highs of 75 per cent to 60 per cent, while support for abolition reached 27 per cent. In January 2023, one Savanta poll showed opposition to the monarchy at 32 per cent, while support was down to 55 per cent. Among those under 45, support had dropped below 50 per cent. A YouGov poll in early 2023 showed the number of people 'proud' of the monarchy had fallen further, from 55 per cent to 43 per cent, while net favourability had fallen 24 points, with 55 per cent broadly positive to 35 per cent broadly negative. Enthusiasm for celebrating major royal events has always been much lower than support for retention of the institution, with just 14 per cent excited about the recent jubilee or the birth of Prince George nine years earlier. There is a distinct difference between telling pollsters you are content with the status quo and being enthusiastic about the monarchy. That enthusiasm is lacking, while the status quo is losing support.

In the Netherlands, support for the monarchy has dropped sharply in recent years, from a high of 80 per cent just a few years ago to 50 per cent today. In an echo of what happened after Queen Elizabeth's death, at the accession of Dutch King Willem-Alexander in 2013, Hans Maessen, a businessman – not at all typical of radical protesters – was arrested for doing nothing more than holding up a sign calling for the monarchy's abolition. Unlike Charles, Willem-Alexander apologized for the arrests, but it was a sign of growing uncertainty about the monarchy's place in Dutch society. Maessen used the opportunity to re-energize the Dutch republican movement. Since then, journalist Floris Müller has led the charge as chair of Republiek, including a high-profile court case against the government that brings into question the King's legal privileges and the impact they may have on the Dutch justice system. The Spanish monarchy has also seen a collapse in support, with more people wanting it abolished than retained and around half supporting a referendum on the question.

In Canada, support for the monarchy has fallen below 50 per cent. In Australia, a republican prime minister, Anthony Albanese, has appointed a minister for the republic. In New Zealand, too, there is cause for optimism. But it is the Caribbean that is likely to provide the touchpaper that will ignite republican sentiment throughout the Commonwealth. Barbados ditched the Crown in 2021, sparking renewed debate across the region. As discussed earlier, Jamaica, Antigua and Barbuda, the Bahamas and Belize are all actively pursuing republicanism.

In the UK, with constitutional reform high on the agenda, the monarchy lurches from crisis to crisis. Questions are being raised about cash for honours, the truth of allegations against Prince Andrew and a culture within the royal household that appears to tolerate petty jealousies, bullying and racism. The questionable behaviour of the royals is not new. But what is new is a public less tolerant and more critical of that behaviour, and the family's loss of their trump card, the Queen. The Queen was their heat shield, able to deflect even the most serious questions and accusations, unable to do wrong in the eyes of much of the media and political class and, if she did, not someone many dared criticize publicly. With Charles on the throne, that first line of defence is gone, in her place a man few would hesitate to criticize if they felt it was warranted. Ahead of us isn't the extended family of old, the princes, princesses, dukes and earls able to pack the balcony at weddings and jubilees. Instead, we are left with the King, the prickly and unremarkable William, Kate and Camilla. Beyond that two other men will continue to remind people – for very different reasons – what's wrong with the royals. Prince Harry, seemingly on the run from his own family, and Andrew on the run from serious allegations of sexual assault. As daylight gets through, behind the curtains of deference and secrecy, we increasingly see an institution that is ripe for challenge and criticism.

A perfect storm threatens to break. Shifting attitudes, falling support for monarchies here and in Europe, moves to ditch the Crown under way across the Commonwealth and a King who has not inherited the deference enjoyed by his mother, all conspiring to threaten the monarchy. Added to all that is a growing and active republican movement, something that has never existed until recently. The royal ship is holed and listing, with the public increasingly uninterested in rescuing it. But it isn't going to sink beneath the waves without a concerted effort from those who want it gone. And while this is achievable, it won't be easy. So the question we need to address is simple: how do we go about abolishing the monarchy?

## Lessons Learnt

On 4 July 2000, the Hon. Justice Michael Kirby of Australia's High Court delivered the Menzies Memorial Lecture at the Great Hall, King's College, London. The theme of Kirby's lecture was the Australian referendum on a republic, which had been held on 6 November the previous year. Having come down clearly on the side of constitutional monarchy, Kirby nevertheless gave an authoritative and detailed assessment of why republicans lost that vote, setting out 'ten lessons' Australians could take from the experience.

One important lesson, which the Australian Republic Movement (ARM) has since sought to learn from, was the perception that the republican cause was closely associated with the Australian Labor Party (ALP). Kirby also pointed out that republicans were to some extent outmanoeuvred by the prime minister, John Howard, a staunch monarchist who had promised a referendum during the 1996 election but who vociferously opposed ditching the monarchy:

> . . . the republicans were probably outflanked by the strategy of the Prime Minister, Mr. Howard whose unwavering support for the present constitutional arrangements was never in doubt. His offer locked republican supporters into a time frame and then a model which it was difficult or impossible to change in any material respect. Ideally, from a republican point of view,

there should have been an in principle plebiscite, followed by a less hasty procedure and a more intense period of public education and debate.

Perhaps, ultimately, the biggest problem the ARM faced was one of perception. Their campaign was seen as 'elitist', centred around the political and cultural 'great and good' of Sydney and Melbourne while failing to reflect the variety of views and experiences from across this vast continent. The issue was brought to a vote too soon, with insufficient effort to build consensus and in a manner that aroused the suspicions of a public already sceptical of their politicians: a 'politicians' republic' in which MPs would choose the head of state pushed for what appeared to some to be partisan political advantage.

It is often said here in the UK that it wouldn't be possible to get a republic because no party would make it part of their manifesto, and no government would want to lose the power the Crown gives them. However, while Kirby makes the point that in Australia it is near impossible to win a constitutional referendum without bipartisan support, that referendum was nonetheless granted by John Howard, one of the most conservative prime ministers in a generation. The hurdle in Australia is particularly high, as those wanting change need to win a double majority: a majority across the whole population and a majority vote in a majority of the six states. It's this high bar for change that makes bipartisan support necessary. As it happened, in 1999 the republic fell short of a majority in all states and nationally, where it was defeated 45 per cent to 55 per cent.

In the UK, referendums only need a simple national majority and here, as elsewhere, there are other interesting lessons to learn. Australia, the UK and New Zealand all show us that you don't need the governing parties, or any of the major parties, on side in order to get a referendum. A few years before the monarchist John Howard gave Australia a vote on a republic, New Zealand's government granted a vote on electoral reform, despite over-whelming opposition to reform from Parliament. Here in the UK, David Cameron, who opposed electoral reform, wanted to keep Scotland part of the United Kingdom and supported British membership of the European Union, granted referendums on switching to the Alternative Vote for Westminster elections, Scot-tish independence and Brexit, winning two and losing one.

In New Zealand there had been growing unhappiness with the status quo, unease exacerbated by two consecutive elec-tions, in 1978 and 1981, in which Labour won the popular vote but lost the election. The main parties, including Labour, were not particularly interested in reform. While the issue received some high-profile support, notably from Geoffrey Palmer, who briefly served as Labour prime minister from 1989 to 1990, most MPs on both sides remained opposed to change, includ-ing Jim Bolger, the National Party prime minister who succeeded Palmer. Bolger, like Howard, made political capital from agreeing to a vote despite little political support for change. Labour had previously reneged on a promise of a ref-erendum on the question of voting reform, and so it made sense for him to promise what Labour had failed to deliver. Neither party wanted to ditch first past the post, but both ended up agreeing to a referendum. A non-binding plebiscite was held in 1992, which supported reform with a majority of 85 per cent. A second question, on the preferred voting system, gave a majority for the Mixed Member Proportional system (MMP). A year later, a binding referendum was passed with a majority of 54 per cent on a turnout of 83 per cent.

With both the New Zealand and Australian campaigns there was a sense of elites being rebuffed. In New Zealand, according to Rod Donald MP, co-leader of the New Zealand Green Party (1995 to 2005), speaking a decade later, there was a 'David and Goliath battle' that ensued between the plebiscite in 1992 and the referendum a year later. Opponents of reform launched the Campaign for Better Government, which had the support of big business, senior politicians and, 'more importantly, big money'. However, a big spend on TV advertising appeared to backfire, reinforcing the image 'that the referendum was about FPP backed by big money versus MMP backed by the little people'. Donald quotes a cartoon in a national newspaper the week of the referendum, which asks simply: 'Want a good reason to vote MMP? Look at the people who are telling you not to.'

It has been argued that a factor in the Brexit vote was a perception of the EU being supported by elites, whereas Brexit was backed by people who felt abandoned by those in Westminster and Brussels. The 2011 UK vote on electoral reform, which was heavily defeated, was also, to some extent, lost on the perception of reform being the concern of politicians, particularly the unpopular Nick Clegg, and a distraction from what mattered to ordinary voters. Whatever the reality, the perception is powerful. The lesson here is twofold. Firstly, as Labour MP Clive Lewis said at a meeting of Labour for a Republic in late 2022, change will not come from Parliament. Nor should it.* While Parliament will have to get involved at

---

* All that said, it is a poor reflection on our MPs that so few of them acknowledge the growing list of scandals and outrages associated with the monarchy. It's as if Parliament and monarchy exist on parallel tracks, rarely crossing paths unless it's to their mutual advantage. MPs will troop in for the grand

some point, to give us a referendum and enact the necessary constitutional changes, impetus for change must come from the ground up. Public opinion is key, as politicians will, when pushed, follow public opinion more readily than the public will get behind a political project. Secondly, while high-profile support is necessary, change isn't won by big names. It is won by force of argument, smart campaigning and lots of hard work.

## Republic

Campaigning for big change always has to overcome the inherent advantage of the status quo. Even in electoral politics, incumbency gives governments an advantage over opposition. With constitutional change, the opportunity to ask voters is not readily granted every four or five years, and most constitutional change boils down to one thing: taking power from those who have it. So, before any such vote is put to the people, it's a good idea to have some idea that the people might say yes.

Popular support is no guarantee of success, however, as House of Lords reform has shown. With as few as 10 per cent supporting the status quo, the Lords should have gone a long time ago. But the status quo suits governments of whichever party is in power. What's needed is political impetus; the force of voters that pressure groups galvanize. Time and resources help, but again are not enough. Just ask the Electoral Reform

---

opening of Parliament and will be obsequious at the time of royal birthdays, weddings or jubilees, just as the royals will do what they must within their limited constitutional responsibilities. Beyond that the two institutions seem keen to look the other way.

Society, first established in 1884 and now sitting on a war-chest in excess of £50 million. With Starmer's recent dismissal of electoral reform, that goal looks no closer now than thirty or forty years ago, despite progress being made in winning support from unions and grassroots members. The two biggest factors that determine the success of a campaign or social movement, according to those who study these things, are political opportunity and resources, combined with good strategy, hard work and a dose of luck. In other words, a well-resourced campaign will still struggle if there aren't opportunities already there to capitalize on. At the same time, opportunities will be missed if organized movements lack the resources to project their voice and create momentum through public debate. For Republic, until recently, opportunities and resources have both been in short supply.

It was on the Queen's birthday, 21 April 1983, that a small band of republicans met in London in response to a letter in the *Freethinker* magazine from librarian Albert Standley. The letter proposed the formation of a society that would advocate republican ideals and promote the alternative to the monarchy. This was the pre-internet era, a time of greater deference and fewer opportunities to bypass the dominant media narratives or political interests. Although it received some notable support during the 1990s, in large part due to the work of Professor Stephen Haseler, who was chair of Republic from 1990 to 2004, the group remained small and inconspicuous for much of the next twenty years. It has largely been in the last decade or so that those of us involved in Republic have been able to make some headway, with progress quickening since 2019.

Our focus has been on creating what opportunities we can through proactive campaigns, making use of major royal events, scandal and political moments to press our case, raise funds and get more people involved. Over the last ten years, campaigns have been run, stories broken in the press and work done on fleshing out and testing a strong case for change. Ironically, we gained a lot of momentum on 16 November 2010, the day Kate and William announced their engagement and intention to get married on 29 April the following year. From that point on, through to the day of the wedding, we were inundated with media requests, received tens of thousands of pounds in donations and had countless opportunities to debate the issue on air and at various events around the country. 2012 brought similar attention to the issue with our response to the jubilee. Having held a 'Not the Royal Wedding' street party the year before, this time Republic organized a protest on the South Bank of the Thames at the time of the royal pageant.

Beyond big royal events, Republic's researchers have presented a clearer picture of royal finances, generated press coverage through freedom of information requests and raised questions around royal secrecy. One of our earliest FOI requests was in 2008, following reports of Prince William borrowing an RAF Chinook helicopter to fly down to the Isle of Wight for a friend's stag do. The RAF at the time made excuses for William and said senior officers were aware of the purpose of the flight, so my colleague William Summers wrote to the RAF requesting details of their promised investigation into the incident. What emerged was that officers hadn't known about the purpose of the flight and that William had 'misled his superiors over trips in military helicopters costing £50,000 – while allowing officers to take the blame'. On more than one occasion I have reported royals to the police, including Prince Andrew, whom I reported on suspicion of criminal damage after it was revealed in the press that he had deliberately rammed his Range Rover into the gates at Great Windsor Park, a scandal I dubbed Gategate. The police weren't interested, but the story ran for two days. The letter to the Queen that I organized in early 2022, signed by 150 ex-services personnel, calling for Andrew to be stripped of his military titles was reported around the world.

These are all small steps aimed at raising awareness of the issue and the campaign, and to get people thinking critically about the monarchy. Each action has merit, but they are not nearly enough to win the longer-term objective of abolition. For that we need to scale up our actions, find ways to reach more people and increase the impact of what we do. There are of course campaigns, such as Extinction Rebellion, that rely on limited resources and gain attention through drastic action. But those actions are taken on the back of decades of work promoting the environmental message and in the context of widespread concern about climate change. Extinction Rebellion is an interesting case that raises another useful point, which is the extent to which people need to be won over, and how, for a campaign to reach its end goal.

Most campaigns are predicated on the idea that public opinion must be mobilized in order to get those with the power to effect change to do so. With Extinction Rebellion, the public are broadly sympathetic to their end goal, while with Republic we have more work to do to win over a clear majority of public opinion. What campaigns won't do, however, is sign up a majority to the level of commitment and enthusiasm shared by campaigners. This might be why some recent environmental activism has been met with hostility. People who are sympathetic to the goals of climate activists see their actions as disproportionate or counterproductive. Whether that's a fair assessment or not is neither here nor there, but the point is that all campaigners can really hope for is that enough people feel strongly enough to make a difference when it matters. Take party politics as an example. In the last few months of 2022, Labour were reaching poll ratings of 45 to 50 per cent, sometimes higher, but it would be a mistake for any Labour activist to assume half the country shares their enthusiasm for the party.

Likewise with Republic, we know that our job is to reach several different audiences, to persuade them to agree with the simple proposition that the monarchy should be abolished, and to hold on to that view until we get to referendum day. That proposition comes in three parts: that the monarchy is a problem, that a republic is the solution and that this matters enough to take a view, or support change. Each of our audiences will react differently to how we talk about the issue, too, because people who have always been republicans don't need much convincing, while people I would call 'soft republicans' – those who say, 'Okay, I agree in principle, but . . . ', or, 'Yes, I agree, but does it matter?' – need to be persuaded that the problem matters enough to warrant committing to supporting the monarchy's abolition. With 'soft monarchists' – those who support the monarchy, whether because of tourism or some sense of its constitutional value, but who are open to persuasion and debate – we need to show them what we believe the problem is, and reassure them the solution is both attractive and viable, before we have a chance of moving them into our camp. Committed monarchists, I'm afraid, aren't on our radar, other than as foils with whom to debate the issue. Many of them will no doubt support the new status quo once the monarchy is gone, but many will simply have to accept the majority view that it had to be abolished.

Whichever audience campaigners speak to, each campaign must find its own strategies. What is always the case, however, is that things don't simply change because of shifting opinion, but through concerted, deliberate effort.

Quite often I read analysis of public attitudes to the monarchy, or of the republican cause, that takes a very passive view of cultural and political change. The suggestion seems to be either that the flow of public opinion one way or the other is driven by forces we have no influence over, or conversely there is an assumption that the movement is at full tilt, getting a fair crack of the whip, and yet failing. The latter appears to believe that voters have given due consideration to the question of the monarchy and made up their minds, thereby explaining the opinion polling. The former suggests that we simply must bide our time until a moment when the public mood turns in our favour. One commentator wrote, not long after the Queen's funeral, that republicans were 'defeated', yet this is ahistorical and lacking a serious understanding of political and social movements. As with all movements, this is a process, a journey that requires certain steps to be taken and hurdles overcome before we have a chance of seeing success in the near distance. It makes no more sense to suggest republicans are defeated than it would have done to declare Edmund Hillary had failed in his bid to conquer Everest on the day he reached base camp – particularly now, with polling showing support for the monarchy fracturing and declining, serious questions being asked of the institution and a growing republican campaign. As a measure of that growth, Republic's income more than doubled from 2020 to 2022, to more than a quarter of a million pounds.

This is not to explain away failures or mistakes, or to suggest we are now set on a path of inevitable victory. We could have done more, just as previous generations could have fought harder and smarter. Yet we are where we are. Today there are many causes for optimism and everything to play for in this fight for a better democracy. Not least, I am increasingly confident that we have the arguments to win people over. On many occasions, at live debates, I have seen audiences switch from voting for the monarchy at the start of the evening to supporting a republic ninety minutes later. Several years ago, I debated the issue at the Oxford Union and we lost by a mile. We won the debate in 2021 by a similarly comfortable margin. The same happened in January 2023, when I debated with Professor Robert Hazell. Within the space of one hour, support for a republic went from around 25 per cent to 52 per cent. This is anecdotal, of course, and polling shows we have a lot more work to do, but our challenge is less about what arguments we use and more about getting ever-increasing audiences to stop and listen.

It is telling that recent polls asking whether the monarchy should be abolished show as many as 15 per cent saying 'don't know'. This can only mean that they have doubts about the institution – otherwise they'd answer 'don't abolish'. But they are yet to hear enough about the alternative to get them firmly into the republican camp. It is by finding ways to reach millions more people and engaging with them more frequently on the issue that we will get Parliament to sit up and take notice, and to then get and win that referendum. The most effective way to get that mass audience is, of course, through mass media. Therein lies one of our first challenges.

## The BBC

There are plenty of criticisms levelled at Britain's press, but one criticism that is misplaced is their lack of impartiality. That's not because the *Mail*, *Sun* or *Guardian* are balanced, or politically neutral in their coverage of the news, but because they aren't required to be, and nor should they be. A free press is a fundamental part of a democratic society, and while there are legitimate questions about press ownership and the ethics of some journalists and columnists, it is necessary for papers to be free to take an editorial line, to choose what to report and how (just as it's reasonable to expect certain standards of decency and honesty). The same cannot be said of the BBC and other national broadcasters, who are legally bound to provide impartial news coverage.

While questions can be asked about the royal coverage of ITN, Sky News and Channel 5, it is the BBC that produces the most news content, has the greatest resources to bring to bear on national events and political coverage, is the most trusted news source and is, unfortunately, the worst culprit when it comes to failing to report on the monarchy in a fair or balanced manner. It is the BBC, too, in my view, that should be setting the standard for independent, fearless journalism, something it does on so many other issues, particularly, although not only, foreign affairs. Yet, when it comes to coverage of the monarchy, the BBC's failure is wholesale and comprehensive, almost completely abandoning journalistic standards or any pretence of balance or independence. The scale of the corporation's failure on royal reporting is something to behold, and is only compounded by their refusal to see that failure for what it is or to engage meaningfully with these criticisms.

The BBC is legally required to achieve balance and cover subjects with 'due accuracy and impartiality'. The word 'due' is important here, as the BBC recognizes that not every issue requires impartiality:

> It does not require absolute neutrality on every issue or detachment from fundamental democratic principles, such as the right to vote, freedom of expression and the rule of law. We are committed to reflecting a wide range of subject matter and perspectives across our output as a whole and over an appropriate timeframe so that no significant strand of thought is under-represented or omitted.*

Despite this apparent commitment to reflect 'a wide range of perspectives' and to 'always scrutinise arguments, question consensus and hold power to account with consistency and due impartiality', on the issue of monarchy these noble undertakings are simply set aside in favour of coverage that is, to say the least, sycophantic and deferential.

I first raised this issue with the BBC in 2011 in response to their coverage of the royal wedding, then again a year later for the jubilee and a third time in 2013 in reaction to the somewhat bizarre way they reported the birth of Prince George. In March 2011 senior BBC directors David Jordan and Helen Boaden agreed to meet with us. We were, to put it politely, brushed off with all the usual defences, including the claim that balance would be achieved 'over time'. In early 2023, as we approached Charles's coronation, I wrote again pointing out that they had

---

\* https://www.bbc.co.uk/editorialguidelines/guidelines/impartiality.

now had twelve years and we were still waiting for this balance to materialize.

I should be clear about what I mean by lack of balance. Firstly, this isn't simply a demand for campaigners like me to be given more airtime or to be invited more often on to the BBC's flagship news programmes, although that should happen much more than it does. It is primarily about the BBC's own content, their editorial choices about what they cover and don't cover, the tone and manner of reporting and their collusion with the palace in covering major set-piece events. Perhaps their most egregious failure is in presenting the monarchy as almost universally loved and royal events as attracting national interest and attention. Opinion polling prior to the Queen's 2022 jubilee showed just 14 per cent were committed to celebrating the event, the same number that, in 2013, said they were 'very interested' in the royal birth, while almost two-thirds were not interested. Just 11 per cent said they were 'very interested' in the jubilee. Likewise, in 2011, 79 per cent said they were either 'largely indifferent' to the wedding or 'couldn't care less'. As I've said previously, polling shows a complex picture and a diverse range of views on the monarchy, with both republicans and monarchists in a minority* and support for retaining the institution in decline. In 2018, in the run-up to the Harry and Meghan wedding, Republic commissioned a YouGov poll that sought to get a more nuanced picture of how people felt about the royals. As with other big events, a sizeable majority (66 per cent) were not interested in the wedding,

---

\* When I cite these polls, I'm not suggesting we're a country of republicans, but that we are also not a country of royalists. The polling paints a complex picture.

while feelings towards the individual members of the royal family were mixed. Yet if you watch the BBC's coverage you would be forgiven for believing we are a nation of staunch royalists. The effort to promote the royals seems quite deliberate, as this paragraph from my 2013 letter to James Harding, then director of news, makes clear:

> Perhaps sensing it had misjudged public interest in the birth, the BBC resolved to manufacture a mood of celebration. Reporters told us that the 'world was waiting' and that the country was gripped by 'royal baby fever' despite all evidence to the contrary. A somewhat embarrassed reporter in Bucklebury assured us that, while the town's inhabitants showed every sign of being oblivious to the birth, he could 'almost hear champagne corks popping behind closed doors'. Outside Buckingham Palace, Luisa Baldini described a 'huge crowd' before the camera panned to show around 200 people, no more than would be found on any other warm summer evening.

It was perhaps journalist Simon McCoy, standing outside the Lindo Wing of St Mary's Hospital that same year, who reported back to the studio the most honest assessment of their own coverage when he said, 'Plenty more to come from here of course, none of it news ...' When my colleague James Gray trawled through the BBC's website in 2011, he identified four hundred royal wedding stories, only seven of which made any mention of republicans and most of those were 'highly disparaging in tone'. Republicans, numbered in the millions and making up approximately a quarter of the population (higher, according to some recent polls), were dismissed as 'a tiny group of "refuseniks" and "naysayers" who were "frustrated" by the wedding'. An online article entitled 'Republicans' Royal Wedding Frustration' made the baseless claim that 'real, die-hard republicans are pretty difficult to come by' – a statement that was demonstrably untrue. A few days before the 2022 jubilee, I repeated the exercise, finding two hundred stories on the BBC News website, but just one that mentioned republicans or offered any serious, critical analysis.

You may say this is our failure, that republicans haven't said or done enough to attract news coverage. While we certainly need to do more, such an assessment misunderstands the problem. Of those hundreds of news stories, most are trivial. Royal press officers are busy offering up soft-soap stories that carry headlines such as 'Royal Baby: Prince Charles thrilled at news of birth', or 'Corgis: How the Queen fell in love and started a phenomenon'. A lot of it is the result of commercial PR companies, pushing products and brands (such as Brand Finance and Ma'amite) by associating them with the monarchy. BBC journalists also go looking for this content, giving us reports such as 'Platinum Jubilee: Queen's solid, gentle leadership – Archbishop of Wales', and 'Platinum Jubilee: People who met the Queen talk of their memories'. But they steer clear of anything that reflects the diverse range of public opinion, challenges the monarchy or talks about the organized opposition.

It isn't a complete blackout. I have been invited on to *BBC Breakfast*, as have some other critics of the monarchy. There have been discussions on some radio programmes and on occasion the BBC presents a balanced article on their website. But the overwhelming picture celebrates and promotes the monarchy, putting a positive spin on even the most egregious royal scandals – the standout exception being the *Newsnight* interview with Prince Andrew – all while diminishing dissenting voices. In the run-up to the 2011 wedding, Radio 4's *Today* programme called to ask if I would appear to discuss 'how this is a bad time for republicans'. After I pointed out that republicans were having a very good time as a consequence of the raised media profile, energized supporters and increased income, the invitation was withdrawn.

A year later, producers contacted republicans in Australia, looking for commentators to take part in a jubilee documentary featuring Gary Barlow, which wanted to focus on the Commonwealth. In their email they explicitly told the Australians they were 'hoping to speak with people ... who have a respect for the Queen' and that they were 'not interested in hearing a personal bad word against the Queen'. The email exchange went on to say that the documentary is 'to celebrate her reign'.

For the 2022 jubilee, the BBC were again spending hour upon hour talking to royal commentators, celebrities and members of the public, conversations that rarely moved away from vapid speculation and overblown tributes, telling the viewers at home, with all the hushed tones of experts sharing profound truths about our mystical monarch, how marvellous the Queen and the royals are, and how lucky we are to have a monarchy. Once or twice a presenter would patronize the audience with the observation that, 'Of course, not everyone supports the monarchy and it's important we reflect those views', before agreeing that most people do and reverting back to endless chatter about duty, dresses and how many prime ministers the Queen has had. Three months later, the UK had a new monarch, a major constitutional moment that raised serious questions about democratic values, Charles's record and character and British politics. I am not aware of a single dissenting voice being allowed on the BBC during the ten days after the accession of the new King, save for one or two invited on to discuss empire and the Commonwealth. Of course, the royalist reply will be that this was ten days after the death of a monarch and not the time to start questioning the institution, but that's a dishonest and unworthy response. If you support a hereditary monarchy you must accept that death and inheritance become political and constitutional moments – as daft as that may sound – and that it was the accession of the King, not the death of the Queen, that warranted serious discussion, open challenge and forensic reporting. Yet, aside from reports of protesters being arrested, there was little debate or coverage of the complexities of the issue or the diversity of public opinion. Once more the BBC subordinated itself to the palace press office.

I don't see this as a conspiracy. It is more a case of a well-entrenched culture that on one hand is fearful of a tabloid backlash should they offer more critical coverage, and on the other hand can't recognize what's wrong with what they're doing. Royal events, even weddings, are used to promote and prop up a contested institution. BBC journalists must step back and report these events, not simply join in.

Even BBC stalwart David Dimbleby questioned the extent of BBC collusion with the palace, just weeks after presenting the coverage of the Queen's funeral. Speaking at the Henley Literature Festival, Dimbleby reportedly said the BBC will 'not go near' controversial topics such as the duchy's refusal to pay corporation tax or royal demands for a host of legal exemptions, saying: '. . . all those issues are never touched by the BBC because I think they feel their viewers will not like it – a visceral feeling. I think it is wrong and these things should be properly examined.'

The veteran broadcaster also said that during the coverage of the funeral they received a continual stream of emails from the palace 'dictating which clips of footage could not be shown in future broadcasts'. The collusion between broadcaster and palace is very real, and should be deeply concerning for anyone who believes in the most basic of democratic principles and the importance of independent journalism.

There's been a great deal of debate about the BBC's impartiality over recent years, not least around Brexit, the environment and a perceived pro-government bias. David Elstein, former chief executive of Channel 5, in responding to a lecture by Emily Maitlis in August 2022, put his finger on a key issue:

> ... whole areas of public discussion – for instance, stories of racism – are exempt from the concept of 'balance' because society is overwhelmingly of one point of view. Much trickier is an issue like Brexit, where decades of uncritical coverage of the EU left the BBC with few news employees who could even understand the desire to leave, and equally left many amongst the viewing public highly dubious about the BBC's trustworthiness on the subject.

In my view, this neatly encapsulates the problem the BBC has with the monarchy. BBC journalists are professional, well trained and on most issues do a fantastic job. But if there is a culture that makes assumptions about the monarchy, coupled with a senior leadership that on one hand is cautious of backlash and on the other is close to the social circles that are offered gongs and invited to royal lunches and garden parties, then unconscious – as well as deliberate – bias is inevitable.

The BBC needs to change its ways because, as things stand,

they are projecting a dishonest view of the monarchy and public attitudes towards it. Whether it's inviting on so-called royal experts, colluding with the palace PRs or ignoring a huge body of opposition, the picture you get from our national broadcaster is grossly distorted. Just imagine if it wasn't. Imagine for a moment if the BBC ceased all collusion, stepped back and made a determined effort to be entirely neutral and detached in their royal coverage. Imagine if they applied the same editorial standards to covering William or Charles as they apply to coverage of Labour, the Conservatives or Liberal Democrats. Imagine if the BBC were forensic and fearless in their analysis and reporting of royal scandals, not just reporting what has been uncovered but seeking to apply its resources to uncovering whatever it is the royals are hiding, not accepting at face value the statements of palace press officers but insisting on interviews with the royals themselves. Imagine if they gave fair, proportionate and serious coverage to the issue and to republican opinion. Imagine if they hosted serious and informed debates about the institution and its future, and the democratic alternatives. That would be when millions more hear those debates for the first time, learn about the scandals for the first time and engage with the republican argument for the first time.

One final word on the BBC. I'm not saying that without the corporation changing its ways the republican cause is lost. In the age of social media, a more diverse mainstream media, and with imaginative and engaging strategies, we will overcome the BBC's bias. But that lets the BBC off the hook too easily, and their coverage does a disservice not only to republicans, but also to the whole country. If our national broadcaster set a higher standard of free, independent and fearless coverage of the monarchy, others would follow. The debate would take hold and the country could then genuinely engage in an intelligent, informed conversation about what kind of constitution we want. How could monarchists oppose such an approach? If the monarchy is as good as they say it is, such scrutiny will play in their favour. If not, then how is dishonesty or self-censorship the answer?

## Changing Our Constitution

In 2015 I was invited to give a talk to students at Eton College. It was an interesting evening and, contrary to common expectations, students – who ranged from ages eleven to eighteen – were open to a serious discussion on the subject with plenty of support in the room for a republic. Halfway through the evening, one of the younger boys stood up and asked how much it would cost to make the switch from monarchy to republic, suggesting that changing all the coins and stamps alone would cost a fortune. It used to be a common question, although less so now, but my answer was simple: 'What do you think will happen when Charles becomes king?' We now know the answer to that, of course, which is that designs change but cash and stamps with the Queen's head remain in circulation and are phased out in the usual way. It's a trivial issue, but reflects a common assumption that such a transition would be complex, time-consuming and costly. Curiously, one legal commentator who is usually known for his astute and insightful analysis, writing in early 2022, suggested the transition to a republic would make Brexit seem like a walk in the park, although he didn't elaborate on why that would be. Thankfully that isn't the case.

Barbados won its independence from the UK on 30 November 1966. At the time the country opted to retain the Queen as head of state. In doing so it inherited Britain's constitutional conventions and many of our laws, save for any that were superseded by their new constitution or subsequent statutes. Laws passed by Parliament would be signed by the governor-general on behalf of the Queen. In essence, the Bajan political and legal infrastructure was not a whole lot different to that of the UK, except for the lack of a House of Lords and the monarch not being resident on the island. Then, on 30 November 2021, the country became a republic. The constitution was amended by Parliament, the sitting governor-general, Sandra Mason, was elected unopposed as president, an inauguration ceremony took place, royal standards were lowered and officials who had sworn an allegiance to the Queen took new oaths to the republic. The following day, life carried on.

There is a fallacy I've heard repeated many times over the years: that changing the British constitution to become a republic, and writing that constitution down, would involve rewriting every law that makes reference to the Crown, unpicking every rule and convention that makes mention of the monarch, royal prerogatives or the Privy Council and embarking on a lengthy process of reviewing and revising every piece of legislation so that it fits the new constitutional order. Yet, as Barbados and many other countries have shown, that's not how constitutional change works.

In Barbados, the Constitution (Amendment) (No. 2) Bill, 2021 was no more complicated than any other legislation. A substantial proportion of the Bill asserts the continuation of various offices of state and government, ensuring existing arrangements carry on uninterrupted, while chapter four establishes the office of president. A brief section under the heading 'Existing Law' includes the following four points:

(a) any reference to Her Majesty the Queen, whether or not that expression is used, or to the Crown or to the Sovereign shall be read and construed as if it were a reference to the State;

(b) any reference to the Governor-General shall be read and construed as if it were a reference to the President;

(c) any reference to Crown lands shall be read and construed as a reference to State lands; and

(d) any reference to Her Majesty's dominions shall be read and construed as a reference to the Commonwealth.

Barbados is hardly unique in making a transition to a republic. Ireland completed its transition in 1949, when a simple Act of Parliament, the Republic of Ireland Act, 1948, came into force. The Act is short and simply removes all remaining links to the British Crown. Iceland made a similar transition to that of many Commonwealth countries in 1944. They had gained independence from Denmark in 1918 but had retained the Danish monarch as head of state, subject to review in 1940. The German occupation of Denmark at the time of that review no doubt focused minds, but the transition was nevertheless straightforward. As with Barbados, their governor, or regent, Sveinn Björnsson, was elected to serve as the first president. Mauritius, too, took a similar path in 1992 when it ditched the British Crown and chose Veerasamy Ringadoo, their outgoing governor-general, as president. It is likely, as I've mentioned earlier, that half a dozen Commonwealth countries across the Caribbean will follow suit and adopt republican constitutions in the coming years. While the UK will have to deal with the dissolution of the monarchy, rather than simply separate from it, the constitutional changes are no more complex than elsewhere. Indeed, other countries made much more dramatic transitions throughout the 1990s.

In March 1990, Lithuania became the first state within the USSR to declare its independence. Initially the government adapted its Soviet-era constitution to ensure a smooth transition to an independent state, but within two years a whole new constitution had been devised and approved by referendum in October 1992. During the first few years of the 1990s, numerous countries made similar moves from dictatorship to democracy, including Czechia and Slovakia, both of which had to adapt first to democracy and then contend with the dissolution of Czechoslovakia on 31 December 1992.

In South Africa, a wholly new constitution was agreed in 1996, replacing the 1993 interim constitution that paved the way for the end of apartheid. Here, as in Eastern Europe, such a drastic change in political and constitutional arrangements was managed relatively quickly and without tearing up every piece of legislation passed by the previous regimes. Where a pre-democracy law was later found to contradict the new constitution, the constitution would win out, making the law either void or unenforceable. This would particularly be the case in the area of human rights, where social or political restrictions might remain on the statute books until challenged in court or repealed by Parliament. Such is the force of a written constitution that it isn't necessary to proactively identify every such piece of legislation and repeal it, as it is already overridden.

In the UK, this issue of laws conflicting with a new constitution is unlikely to arise, as we have had a framework for human rights for seventy years, first under the European Convention on Human Rights and then, additionally, since 2000, the Human Rights Act. Any new constitution adopted as part of the move to a republic would assume the continuation of these rights while remaining silent on most matters of domestic civil or criminal law. Its primary focus would be on the structure of the state and the powers of each of its constituent parts.

The idea that any of this is beyond the wit of the British public is fanciful. Parliament frequently passes more complex legislation and has recently had to contend with the complications of extricating the UK from the EU. Brexit has an impact on complex trade and economic regulation and international treaties, not least the Good Friday Agreement and the position of Northern Ireland. Reforming the British constitution, by contrast, simply improves and alters domestic arrangements for choosing and granting powers to our parliament, government and head of state, while further empowering voters. It would not be difficult.

## One Giant Leap for Britain

In looking at the detail of constitutional change, it is important to take a step back and remember what this is all about and why it's so important. The debate won't be won on technicalities and clauses. It will be won on values, principles and the imagination of a fairer, more democratic Britain. We know the British people share those values of equality, democracy and a basic sense of fairness. We also know the British public, while as committed as ever to the ideals of democracy, are increasingly disenchanted with the UK variant. As the More in Common study I mentioned in chapter three tells us, there is widespread unease with the way our politics is conducted, and there is an awareness that power is highly centralized and too often unresponsive to the needs of communities around the country, particularly those furthest from Britain's political centres. Public attitudes towards the monarchy are also shifting and, with King Charles, the royals will find it much harder to maintain the fiction of a noble institution committed to public service.

The good news is that there is a viable, achievable democratic alternative. It doesn't require revolution or the tearing up of the core tenets of our parliamentary system. What needs to be done is relatively simple – a set of reforms that would have far-reaching consequences for the quality of our democracy. We take what we have – two Houses of Parliament, prime minister and Cabinet, and a head of state with a limited constitutional role – and we make it democratic, top to bottom. A small step for our parliament, a giant leap for our country.

I don't wish to oversimplify or trivialize the transition to a republic, but as other countries have shown, it is a well-worn path, relatively easy to navigate, and certainly worth the effort. Parliament, with the input of civil society, unions, other parties and perhaps a series of consultative conventions, would draw up a draft constitution. That constitution could be made law by Parliament, with the proviso that amendments to abolish the monarchy are put to a referendum, or the whole document could be put to a public vote. If the public are already in favour of a republic and the drafting process has been sufficiently inclusive, this ought to pass. However that is achieved, once a republic has been approved by the voters, the transition is no more complex than it was in Barbados. A date is set for the new constitution to come into force, an election is held for our first president and on the day of promulgation we witness the public inauguration of our elected head of state. The president takes office and Charles Philip Arthur George Mountbatten-Windsor retires to a quiet life as a private citizen and a place in the history books as Britain's last monarch.

Some journalists describe royal events as historic, including the birth of Prince George. But what would be more historic than the British people stepping up to the ballot box and declaring, 'No more monarchy, today we embrace democracy – today we are citizens, not subjects'? The world really will be watching as the most famous monarchy is abolished, our democratic friends and allies cheering us on, while people living in monarchies around the world may watch and wonder if this presages their own monarchy's demise. We may give hope to those who have fought oppressive monarchs, monarchs who have sought legitimacy by befriending Britain's royals. We like to see ourselves as a beacon of democracy, but how much brighter will that beacon shine when we abandon a monarchy founded on elitist, outmoded values and put equality and citizenship at the heart of our new constitution? How much stronger will be the cause of democracy around the world when Britain signs up to those principles without hesitation, when we take a loud and powerful stand against corruption, nepotism and hereditary privilege?

Imagine that day when we gather in squares around the country to celebrate the inauguration of our new constitution. Imagine the global coverage, the palpable sense of excitement as we collectively adopt a constitution of our choosing, which represents our values and gives us firm control over who governs and who represents us. The day of the referendum, when the results come in, announcing to the world our intentions;

the day of the election when we show the world we can step up and choose a head of state who represents the best of us; the day of the inauguration when we witness the fruits of our democratic endeavours become a reality. These days will be historic. The contrast with major royal events couldn't be greater, reminding us that with monarchy we are mere spectators. But as citizens of a republic we are active participants in a system of our own devising. These moments will define Britain and these milestones will be celebrated by future generations. And then on the day after the inauguration, life will continue as before but for an essential point of difference. We would live in a society that believes whoever we are, in whatever circumstances we are born into, we are citizens who can not only choose our president, but also aspire to one day be chosen to serve as Britain's elected head of state.

# 7.

## A Democracy We Can Be Proud Of

It was a mild but overcast day in Reykjavik on 29 June 1980. Although voting was slow to begin with, by close of polls at eleven p.m., more than 90 per cent of voters had turned out to choose Iceland's fourth president. There were four candidates on the ballot: three men and one woman. Early counting showed it was a two-horse race, with the leading candidates too close for anyone to predict the outcome. At around six the next morning, the final district, East Iceland, declared its results, confirming what many had hoped: that they had elected Vigdís Finnbogadóttir president. Vigdís* became the first woman in the world to be freely and fairly elected as head of state, and the first female head of state in Europe who wasn't a monarch.

Vigdís's election was spurred on by a powerful women's rights movement. Five years earlier, they had staged the Women's Day Off, when 90 per cent of women took the day off from their jobs, housework and childcare for twenty-four hours. The moment brought large parts of the country to a standstill and led to new equal pay legislation being introduced in

---

\* Iceland uses patronymic last names, rather than inherited family surnames. It is usual to refer to people by their first name, even formally, something I'll do here.

Iceland's parliament within months. Vigdís was relatively well known as a lecturer and theatre director who had presented French lessons on national television. She hadn't planned to run for president and denied all interest up until the last minute, but was persuaded by an unofficial, grassroots campaign that saw countless people from all walks of life encourage her to stand. There wasn't any expectation of victory, either, as Vigdís told a reporter after declaring her candidacy – people simply wanted 'at least one female face among the candidates'. In a BBC radio interview thirty-five years later, the then former president recalled the moment that 'tipped the scales': a long and 'beautiful' telegram sent from the crew of the fishing boat *Gudbjartur*, encouraging her to run.

To put the election into context, from 1971 to 1983 only three women had been elected to Parliament in Iceland, and in 1980 there were no women in Cabinet. Men made up 96 per cent of local government representatives. The presidential election result was close to the end, with Vigdís winning 33.79 per cent to 32.31 per cent for Guðlaugar Þorvaldsson, an economics professor and former finance minister. As Vigdís told the BBC years later, she was pleased it wasn't a landslide, saying she was 'so happy that it was very narrow ... that was a great thing, because it proves that it was something that was very important ... it was proving that you have to work [to persuade women to support women in office]'.

Contrary to the view that such elections are divisive, the opposite proved to be true. Shortly after the result came in, Guðlaugar said, 'I wish her well ... and call upon the nation to unite behind her.' The press also hailed their new head of state and the historic significance of the moment. The *Dagblaðið* described Vigdís as 'everybody's president', adding, 'Icelanders saluted this morning a new Head of State, elected yesterday, Vigdís Finnbogadóttir. They will unite behind her when she takes office as the country's President on August 1.' The news even made it to the other side of the world, with the Australian newspaper *The Age* referring to Vigdís as a 'leftist' opposed to NATO's presence in Iceland and noting she was 'a divorcee who lives alone with her adoptive daughter'. The 'issue' of Vigdís's marital status was raised by reporters during the election, with some questioning whether she would be able to cope with the demands of public office. Yet not only did Vigdís cope, she excelled and went on to be re-elected three times, serving four consecutive terms in office, finally stepping down in 1996.

The president of Iceland has limited power, and yet the impact of Vigdís's election was in many ways immeasurable. She became a role model for girls and women in Iceland and abroad, and she helped usher in a more egalitarian ethos to a country that had, like most, been dominated by men for centuries. Two decades after she'd left office, girls would still tell her how she inspired them. 'I have given them some confidence in themselves,' she told the BBC. 'And that's what I have given to the girls of this country. If she can, I can.' Vigdís also advocated environmentalism, arguing for reforestation of swathes of Iceland. Today, now in her nineties, Vigdís remains an advocate of causes close to her heart. As recently as late 2022, she condemned the Afghan government's ban on girls and women receiving education, saying, 'That shows very clearly the insecurity of men who do not want to liberate the women because they're afraid.' Today Iceland is 'the world's most gender-equal country'. Forty-seven per cent of MPs are women, as is the prime minister, Katrín Jakobsdóttir, in office since 2017 and the second woman to hold the post. Katrín has spoken of the inspiration she has taken from the former president.

Vigdís Finnbogadóttir shows us what a head of state can be, how someone chosen from the people, by the people, can rise above the political fray and represent their nation eloquently, intelligently and in a way that is meaningful and inspiring. To quote Svanhildur Halldórsdóttir, the president's campaign manager in 1980:

> She proved that we have what it takes to be leaders, it is not the prerogative of men. She proved that women are not inferior to men, something that we, her supporters, already knew. She stressed our roots – our cultural heritage – and led us out to the fields. Brought the position of President closer to the people and treated everyone as equals – women, men and children.

The office of president in a parliamentary republic can have a real impact on a society, both in the democratic process of choosing our head of state and in choosing people who represent change or who can eloquently communicate our values or highlight important issues. Ten years after the historic Icelandic vote, Ireland too elected their first female president, Mary Robinson. Robinson had previously served in the Senate but stood and won the presidency as an independent candidate, the first person to do so. As a senator and lawyer, Robinson had already made a huge impact on life in Ireland, campaigning successfully on gay rights, contraception, divorce and legal aid. As president her popularity topped 93 per cent. She ended her term a few months early to take up the post of United Nations high commissioner for human rights in 1997 and has since been a tireless campaigner on a range of issues, including climate justice. Robinson was succeeded by Mary McAleese, the first president from Northern Ireland, who sought to help bridge sectarian divides at a time when British and Irish governments were pursuing peace through what became the Good Friday Agreement.

Richard von Weizsäcker, born to German aristocracy and who served in the German army during the Second World War, went on to become, in the words of one obituary, 'guardian of his nation's moral conscience'. He remains one of only two German presidents to serve two terms in office and his time spanned the reunification of his country in 1990. Five years earlier, on the fortieth anniversary of the end of the war, von Weizsäcker made a historic speech to the Bundestag in which he confronted Germany's horrific legacy. Saying that those born after the war could not be blamed for the crimes of their parents and grandparents, he added: 'Every single German was in a position to witness what Jewish citizens had to suffer ... Anyone ... who cared to inform himself could not escape the fact that the deportation trains were rolling.'

Strikingly he was the first leader to recognize 8 May, the day Germany surrendered to the Allies, as 'a day of liberation'. The speech, in the words of Deutsche Welle's Felix Steiner, writing in 2015, established a 'new collective norm of historical remembrance': 'Not with the kind of distance we have now of 70 years, but at a time when millions of those involved in the events – whether as oppressor or victim – were still alive. And, in the face of much resistance from his own party, he gave Germans the task of never forgetting what happened in the years leading up to and during the war.'

In 2012, Germany chose Joachim Gauck to serve as president. Gauck, like Chancellor Angela Merkel, had grown up in East Germany. In the late 1980s he became a prominent pro-democracy campaigner and, after the reunion of Germany, served as the first federal commissioner for the Stasi Records. He was elected with widespread political support, backed by half a dozen parties, including the CDU and SPD. Public support was as high as 69 per cent. His term came to an end in 2017, the same year Austria elected Alexander Van der Bellen as head of state. Van der Bellen was the son of refugees and a professor of economics. He is also the first Green head of state in Europe to be elected by popular vote.* In 2011, Ireland elected a new president, Michael D. Higgins, a poet and politician who had been a Labour MP (a minority party in Ireland) and has campaigned vociferously on issues such as poverty and social justice. He has remained hugely popular and widely respected in Ireland and abroad.

The formal function of a president in parliamentary democracies varies from country to country, although typically they hold limited reserve powers. Finland's presidency made a transition during the 1990s from a position with some executive power, particularly in foreign affairs, to a more typical and limited role, while also moving from being a post chosen by MPs to one directly elected by the people. Martti Ahtisaari was the last president to hold real authority under the old constitution and the first directly elected president. Ahtisaari was a diplomat who rose to prominence as a UN special envoy to Kosovo and helped negotiate the subsequent peace process. In 2008 he won the Nobel Peace Prize for 'his important efforts, on several continents and over more than three decades, to resolve international conflicts'. His successor was Tarja Halonen, Finland's first female president who, like her Irish counterparts, had championed social and economic rights.

---

\* Raimonds Vējonis, president of Latvia from 2015 to 2019, was the first Green president in Europe, although Latvian presidents are elected by their parliament, not directly by the voters.

None of these men and women are perfect, of course, and all have faced criticisms, as you would expect in democratic societies. And there are others who have served as president who have fallen short of the standards their citizens might hope for. But the point I'm making here is simple – electing a head of state does not guarantee faultless, virtuous leaders, but it does allow us to choose men and women who are interesting, engaging, eloquent and inspirational. To believe that someone in public office is beyond reproach, that they are uniquely gifted, wise or dignified simply isn't credible. Yet as elected heads of state, while their power is largely circumscribed, they can nevertheless speak up on issues of justice, good government and the big challenges their nation faces. The contrast with Britain's monarchs couldn't be starker.

From time to time, people demand I name my choice of head of state in a British republic. Of course, that's not possible, any more than Germans or Icelanders can tell us who their next president will be before votes are cast. But what other countries show us is that electing our heads of state gives us a unique opportunity to choose people who can do the job with integrity and independence. We have seen how problematic the monarchy is, how it fails to live up to the standards we expect in public life, uphold our most cherished values or perform any meaningful constitutional role. We have seen that, while there are challenges ahead, the abolition of the monarchy is well within our grasp, should we choose it. Now we answer that other perennial question of the monarchy debate: what would we replace it with? And the answer is not only a different way of choosing our head of state, but a reformed constitution that completes the historical journey from monarchy to democracy: a parliamentary system rooted in democratic values and the idea that we are citizens, not subjects.

## A Better Constitution

It has been said that one of the strengths of Britain's constitution is that the head of government, the prime minister, must face the bear pit of the House of Commons and survive the weekly scrutiny of prime minister's questions. I agree. And while that strength shouldn't be over-egged – for all the hot air, the prime minister is usually safe until the next election – the Commons offers a means of challenging, stress-testing and, on occasion, defeating the prime minister and the government. This need to go directly head to head with two hundred or more of your political opponents, we hope, puts pressure on parties to choose effective leaders – ineffective leaders are soon found out. It would certainly have been interesting to have seen George W. Bush or Donald Trump face up to such a challenge.

For all the problems of Britain's constitution, the fundamentals of parliamentary democracy are strong. It provides the potential for greater government scrutiny, challenge and defeat at the hands of opposition parties. The problems we face aren't the fault of representative parliamentary democracy, but the faults within the British variant: a constitutional monarchy. The solution is not to throw the constitutional baby out with the bathwater, but to take what we have and make it fundamentally democratic, with the rights and sovereignty of the people being at the heart of a new way of doing politics.

No constitution is simple. But the British one is, for most people, impenetrable. If even the experts struggle with elementary questions, such as whether a referendum is required to scrap the House of Lords or change the voting system for Westminster elections, what chance does the wider electorate have?

A good constitution should set out a clear framework for exercising power, stating what institutions there are, what power they have and how those who occupy them are chosen and removed. Here in the UK, the pieces are there, so we can, with relative ease, put together a draft written constitution by pulling those strands together in a single document. It would begin with stipulating that we are a sovereign people, a nation of citizens and a union of nations – assuming the Union is still intact – and that each nation may* govern itself through a devolved parliament. It isn't necessary to set out every detail of devolution in the new constitution. Instead, the constitution can state that devolved powers and those reserved to Westminster are provided for in current law, and that those powers, and the constitutions of the devolved parliaments, cannot be amended without a referendum of the people of the relevant devolved nation.

## Great Britain and Northern Ireland

Here my focus is on the national, UK-wide constitution and the means by which we become a republic, so I won't go into any more detail on how devolved nations are governed. While I will refer to the Union and the UK, I don't dismiss the possibility of the Union coming to an end. Assuming we're likely to stay together for a good few years yet, this leads neatly on to a rarely discussed question, which is the name of our country, our nation

---

* I say 'may' rather than 'will' as England doesn't have a devolved assembly. I don't know if it's likely to in the future, but surely the constitution should make that option available should voters want to go down that path.

of nations. The United Kingdom of Great Britain and Northern Ireland has just passed its one hundredth birthday, created by default as a consequence of the partition of Ireland in 1922. Before then, the United Kingdom of Great Britain *and Ireland* had lasted a little longer, since its creation in 1801 with the full union of the Kingdom of Great Britain and the Kingdom of Ireland (who already had the same king). The Kingdom of Great Britain had been around for just ninety-four years since 1707 and the Acts of Union, which brought England and Scotland together in political union.* The Kingdom of England, of course, had a longer history, albeit one interrupted by the ill-fated Commonwealth. Yet as far as modern Britain is concerned, one of our defining traditions (I'm being a little facetious here) is the changing of our name approximately every one hundred years. It seems we're due another change some time soon. And what better reason than the need to remove 'kingdom'?

I appreciate that these names, and the place of each nation within the Union, can provoke strong emotions, but assuming we become a republic before Scotland, Wales or Northern Ireland break away, it would be simple enough to drop the Kingdom and become the Union of Great Britain and Northern Ireland, or simply Great Britain and Northern Ireland. This name could survive Scottish independence, and if Northern Ireland was reunited with Ireland we would become Great Britain.† In everyday life, of course, we would continue to be

---

\* In a legal and constitutional sense Wales was, at this point, considered to be part of the Kingdom of England, and therefore part of the Union between England and Scotland.

† The 'Great' in Great Britain comes from the French 'la Grande Bretagne', which distinguishes Britain from Brittany, which the

Britain, call ourselves British or refer to whichever constituent nation or identity we prefer.

## The Fundamentals

The constitution of the Union of Great Britain and Northern Ireland would first establish that the people are sovereign and that we are, for now at least, a union of nations. It would also establish that our system of government is a republican parliamentary democracy, codified in a single document, our contract with each other and those we choose to govern us amendable by referendum.

In writing down our constitution, not everything needs to be included, as I've said before. The objective is to set down fundamentals, to provide clarity where it's most important and to set limits on power. A written constitution would also provide explicit and accessible means for change and reform. Just as importantly, our new constitution could set out the principled basis of our democracy. The most famous example is, of course, the opening line of the US Constitution: 'We the people of the United States.' But there are many other examples from which to draw inspiration. Article 1 of the Irish constitution says: 'The Irish nation hereby affirms its inalienable, indefeasible, and sovereign right to choose its own form of Government, to determine its relations with other nations, and to develop its life, political, economic and cultural, in accordance with its own genius and traditions.'

The sentiment is clear, stated explicitly in terms of popular

French also call Bretagne. So I suppose we have the French to thank for calling us great.

sovereignty and democracy. The Swiss constitution invokes noble sentiments 'in the name of Almighty God', including 'the knowledge that only those who use their freedom remain free, and that the strength of a people is measured by the well-being of its weakest members'.

Iceland's constitution, which unlike those of Ireland and Switzerland, makes no mention of God or religion, begins with 'Iceland is a Republic with a parliamentary government', while Finland's constitution is similarly short and direct in its opening statement – 'Finland is a sovereign republic' – and quickly goes on to add, 'The constitution shall guarantee the inviolability of human dignity and the freedom and rights of the individual and promote justice in society.'

In a country such as ours, with a rich literary tradition that includes contemporary poets like Benjamin Zephaniah, John Cooper Clarke and Carol Ann Duffy, not to mention a plethora of exceptional novelists and songwriters, it must be a simple task to write something similar for our own sovereign republic. I make no claim to literary greatness, but a new British constitution could open with the following declaration: 'Great Britain and Northern Ireland is a republic with a parliamentary government. The people of England, Northern Ireland, Scotland and Wales are sovereign, with an inalienable right to choose our form of government and to shape our nation in accordance with our most cherished values and traditions.'

However we choose to say it, the sentiment ought to be the same: that 'we the people' are sovereign, we're in charge of our own destiny and no power sits above us, beyond accountability and scrutiny, save for the law of the land, which we will determine through our own democratic process and under which all citizens are equal.

## Popular Sovereignty

In the UK, a virtue is made of parliamentary sovereignty which, as we know, in practice means the sovereignty of government. The idea of popular sovereignty was met with alarm from some commentators when the efforts of the May and Johnson governments to implement Brexit faced fierce opposition from those concerned about the manner of the planned exit. Yet popular sovereignty is not the same as majoritarianism or the 'tyranny of the majority'. It is the notion that, while we 'the people' delegate power to Parliament and government, we retain the last word in how we are governed. This can be done in practice through requiring referendums to change the constitution. The sovereignty is personal and individual, as well as collective. As citizens we must all be free to live our lives as we see fit, within limits set in law only to protect others; limits agreed through open and democratic processes. That's why it's important to respect people's individual rights while also enabling society at large to come together to determine the shape of our democracy. By guaranteeing rights, while also putting our constitution in the hands of the people, we make both the citizen and the citizenry sovereign, leaving the hard slog of governing and legislating to those we elect to do the job, while ensuring each of us can contribute to that process in a meaningful way.

In recognizing the rights and equality of citizenship, it's also necessary to say something about the Church. While it's not a central pillar of the republican argument, not least because the importance of the Church has faded considerably in recent decades, it should be a given that a republican constitution is a secular one. This isn't the case in every republic, but if a new constitution is being written in the first half of the twenty-first century, it makes no sense to have a state religion. Of course, with the abolition of monarchy and the Lords, the Church would no longer have a claim to the role of head of state or guaranteed seats in our parliament. But the established church – which is only established in England – enjoys considerable privileges from being recognized as the state church. It cannot be right that in a society of equal citizens, each of whom is free to determine their own beliefs, there is one faith that is privileged over the others.

## A Parliamentary Republic

Having set out these fundamental principles – principles that leave no room for hereditary power, monarchy or the Lords – we can now lay down the core building blocks of our republic. The structure will be familiar to you: a parliament, both houses elected by the people, will be the centrepiece of our constitution. This is where we establish the departure from constitutional monarchy and embrace the principle of parliamentary democracy. Parliament should be freely and fairly elected, able to engage in debates and propose legislation without the assumption they are there to do the government's bidding. It must be clear that Parliament's job is to make the best decisions based on the values and interests they represent. I'm not suggesting an end to political parties or the whips – far from it – and I'm not naive enough to believe there would be an end to the hard-nosed business of politics. Parties are a natural by-product of a free society in which people can act collectively to achieve their aims. And where most MPs are elected not on the basis of their personal character or record but on the back of the public's views of their party, whips can at the very least ensure their MPs live up to their voters' expectations. However, we can reduce the control government has over Parliament and encourage free and meaningful debate.

The House of Lords would be gone, titles abolished and former peers free to stand for election. In its place an elected Senate, with the power to block and challenge the Commons, which would enhance the power of Parliament as a whole, making it easier to hold the government to account and demand a greater consensus and care in the passing of legislation. It would be easy to devise mechanisms that would break any deadlock, but the most effective method would be for parties to discuss, negotiate and develop laws that have broad support in the wider community, enhancing Parliament's claim to be representative of the people who elect them.

This notion of the supremacy of the Commons only serves the government. In a parliamentary democracy, Parliament should be central. Its power would be defined by the constitution, and it would have supremacy over the government. It's the body through which we express our sovereignty on matters other than constitutional reform, which would be reserved for the people to decide by direct vote. We would, as best we can, aim to reimagine our parliament as a forum for meaningful debate and decision-making, not grandstanding and rubber-stamping. A fully elected parliament with two chambers, one of which is far more independent than the other but which nevertheless has just as strong a claim to represent the interests of the people, will shift power from government to Parliament and from Parliament to people.

The abolition of aristocratic titles, along with the honours system, and the introduction of a new system of honours – one that does not allow politicians either to nominate or to award any honour or title – would further loosen government's control of Parliament. Honours could be awarded on behalf of the people in the name of Parliament, but Parliament's role would be limited to a cross-party committee that appointed and monitored a constitutionally independent honours commission, a commission that would not include any current or former politician or party official. A new set of honours would be reserved for those who had performed exemplary service above and beyond the call of duty, or who had committed significant acts of bravery. In an instant, government – and opposition leaders – would see their power of patronage significantly weakened, as they lost the opportunity to keep backbenchers in line with the promise of a knighthood or OBE, or the threat of being denied baubles and titles. Similarly, any other appointment made by government, whether to head up a new agency, serve as chair of the BBC Board or take a role on the board of the Charity Commission, should be made with greater scrutiny and be accountable directly to Parliament – preferably the Senate, who would have greater independence – and so reduce the scope of cronyism and patronage.

Another innovation, which is by no means an original proposal, is a stricter limitation on the payroll vote within the Commons. A limit of 10 or 20 per cent would provide a streamlined government and a freer parliament.

It is necessary for government to be able to govern efficiently and effectively, perhaps more so today than at any time in history. Yet there is a distinction, one that is often lost, between governing and legislating. It is a distinction lost in large part by the subservience of Parliament and the tendency to focus on party leaders, giving the impression that a prime minister is chosen to make all the decisions, like some latter-day monarch.

Rediscovering this distinction and empowering Parliament to act as an effective check on the government would greatly improve both governing and law-making. While law-making wouldn't simply be done at the insistence of ministers, government would also benefit from a greater focus on policy and delivery within the existing framework of laws, rather than the modern habit of responding to every crisis and headline with new legislation. On the other hand, while a government with the support of a majority in the Commons would continue to have a good chance of getting its legislation through, Parliament would have a meaningful say on whether or not it did, and to what extent it could be amended. It would also be reasonable and desirable to allow opposition and private members' bills a fair chance of becoming law. Still, with a Commons majority in support of the government, this would be a challenge, but if that majority were small, or rested on a coalition of parties, it would not be impossible. This would require a structural and cultural change to the way the Commons works, with MPs and the Speaker having control of the agenda and the power to recall Parliament or decide on the timing of recess, and an explicit recognition that a loss in the Commons is not a cause for a government to fall, something that should only happen, outside of an election, by the failure to pass a budget or survive a vote of confidence. Coupled with fixed terms that MPs cannot simply choose to cut short, this would empower Parliament and enhance the independence of MPs on both sides of the House.

Just as Parliament should be subordinate to the people, a relationship enshrined in the constitution, so government should be subordinate to Parliament. As a CEO of a major corporation is subordinate to its board, as the board is to their shareholders, the PM and ministers are tasked with the job of running the government and ensuring the effective delivery of public services and economic management, accountable to Parliament. If Parliament persisted in supporting a government the people were dissatisfied with, voters will take the matter into their own hands at the next election, in the meantime lobbying a stronger opposition and the elected upper house to challenge the governing parties as best they could.

None of this is a far cry from where we are, but the checks and balances, and the power of Parliament in the face of government, would be greater and more meaningful. And the business of governing and legislating would be done within the limitations of the constitution – the people's contract with those we appoint to govern and legislate. Of course, as with any contract or constitution, there is a presumption that attention would be paid to the rules and that everyone would act in good faith. While a good constitution assumes that we cannot trust those in power, we do assume that those in power will follow the rules we have laid down. Yet someone still needs to enforce those rules when they are either inadvertently broken or deliberately ignored.

## An Elected Head of State

For all the checks and balances within Parliament, the elected upper house, greater independence of MPs in the Commons and greater scrutiny and accountability of executive powers, it is quite possible Parliament might agree to laws that conflict with the constitution. These may be laws that seek to interfere with the power or independence of the judiciary, grant the government new powers, conflict with the authority of devolved parliaments or reduce the rights of certain sections of society. It may be that the government uses its legitimate powers to introduce measures that conflict with the constitution. In these circumstances the constitution is not a barrier to legitimate decision-making, but a shield, protecting the people from an abuse of power by politicians. The question is who, how and at what point does someone enforce the constitution and stop such laws and policies taking effect? The answer is that it can be the courts, after decisions are made or laws enforced, ruling in response to a case being brought by citizens and campaigners. Or it can be the head of state, before decisions are signed off or laws passed. We have seen that as things stand the head of state cannot and will not protect us from abuses of power or 'unconstitutional' new laws. Firstly, because the monarch no longer has any power to intervene, and trying to claw back such powers might jeopardize the monarchy itself. Secondly, because by definition a new law passed by Parliament cannot be in conflict with the constitution. Parliament is sovereign, no codified constitution exists and statute trumps all.

The courts are similarly powerless, save for rare examples such as the 2019 ruling on the use of the prorogation. A court might conclude a law to conflict with the Human Rights Act, but they cannot strike the law down, or overrule Parliament. In a parliamentary republic the president and courts could – and in my view should – be able to strike down legislation, but solely on the grounds that any such law contradicts the constitution. In the process of making new laws, the role of the head of state in a republic would, ordinarily, be to grant assent to a bill, the final step – as now – that makes it law. Unlike a monarch, an effective, elected head of state could decline to grant assent if, in their considered opinion, the law is unconstitutional. The president of our new republic, like the presidents of other parliamentary republics, would not be able to oppose a law because they disagree with it, but only if and when they believe it contradicts the constitution.

Here, the constitution represents the rules set down by the people, boundaries set by all of us to determine what powers politicians have. The president is the guardian of our constitution and would be expected to ensure those rules are followed, and to step in if politicians seek to exercise powers we have not granted them. As with laws passed by Parliament, so with decisions made by government. Overall the authority of government would be considerable and only clearly demarcated on issues of constitutional reform, human rights and their relationship with other institutions of state, such as Parliament and the courts. But that leaves a fair amount of room for stepping over the line. For instance, if government defunded the Electoral Commission and introduced regulations that would indirectly disenfranchise certain voters, this could be considered unconstitutional by the president or the courts, with the president able to step in quicker and earlier to protect the integrity of elections until such time as the courts can reach a view. If government appointments continue to be signed off by the head of state, as many are now, a president could challenge appointments that appear to be corrupt, or conflict with the rules voters require government to abide by.

There are those who recoil in horror at the thought of the government's will – or that of Parliament – being thwarted, often on the grounds that both represent the will of the people. But a constitution sets down limits that provide longer-term protections against short-term, knee-jerk policies or the tyranny of the majority. In agreeing our constitution we will have established, as a nation, that we are all equal in rights, regardless of race, gender, sexuality, disability and so on. So it remains democratic and legitimate for a president, or the courts, to strike down attacks on those rights, or on our constitution, even if – in that immediate moment – a clear majority of the people support the government's position.

Of course, if there is a very clear view in the country that the government or Parliament should have certain powers they currently lack, it is quite possible to identify the relevant clause in the constitution, draft an amendment and ask the people if they agree to change the rules we had previously set down. The role of the president, as guardian of our constitution, is to stand in the way of politicians who wish to overstep their power, not to stand in the way of the democratic will of the people. However, a written, codified constitution and a clear set of rights recognizes more fundamental cross-generational values that in the long term represent the people's view of the kind of society we wish to be, and the need to respect the rights of everyone regardless of whether they fit neatly into the prevailing public mood or are part of a majority. So to revisit and redefine those fundamental values that underpin our society should be harder to do than simply passing legislation through Parliament.

Some of this sounds rather dramatic, conjuring up images of great political and constitutional battles, but the experience of republics is that by and large the existence of these structures means governments and parliaments operate within the checks and balances. The president and courts provide an occasional corrective where decisions or laws drift across the line. Political life goes on, but with the safety net to protect us from those who might wish to act in bad faith, threaten our rights or undermine our democracy.

A president in a parliamentary republic has three main duties. Firstly, they are chief ambassador, representing the people and the state at home and abroad, away from the day-to-day fray of parliamentary politics. Secondly, as discussed, the president guards the constitution, ensuring where necessary that the boundaries and limits it sets are respected. Finally, the president acts as referee at times of political crisis or stalemate. As ambassadors of their nations, presidents such as Vigdís Finnbogadóttir and Michael D. Higgins have done exceptionally well. Vigdís was praised for her role as host of the Reykjavik Summit in 1986 in which US President Ronald Reagan and Soviet leader Mikhail Gorbachev met to discuss nuclear proliferation, and again as a national leader in the aftermath of the Flateyri and Súðavík avalanches in January and October 1995, which killed a total of thirty-four people. Higgins speaks not just for Ireland but for the whole of the Irish people, including the vast diaspora spread around the world, as he did in his 2022 Christmas message:

> At this time of year we recall with pride not only the contribution our diaspora make to the culture and life of their new homes, but also we remember those Irish who may be experiencing a sense of loss of belonging, away from their origins, loved ones, and who are hurting at this time. It is right that we think of them, and not only at Christmas.

I have mentioned the great esteem President Weizsäcker was held in as the voice and conscience of Germany, as the country grappled with the appalling legacy of Nazism. This ambassadorial role doesn't get the attention of political leaders, but it is a role worth playing, one which can be done with an eloquence, insight and independence King Charles is incapable of or unwilling to emulate.

A British president would be non-partisan, expected, upon

inauguration, to resign any party membership or other associations that might compromise their independence. They would be free to speak on national issues and represent shared values, short of interfering in party politics, while championing a plethora of good causes, celebrating national milestones, seeking to build bridges, to represent all the people of our nation. They would also lead the way in speaking to and for our nation at times of national tragedy or celebration, not having to resort to cut-and-paste statements issued by press officers, but able to connect with people meaningfully and sincerely.

As we see a continuing trend towards a more splintered politics and greater chances of hung parliaments, our president would have the independence and authority to play that third, important role at times of political crisis or stalemate: that of chief adviser, referee and facilitator, who can ensure governments can be formed under the most challenging circumstances. Rather than Schrödinger's monarch, we would have a head of state who is very much present and involved, not protected by faceless bureaucrats or fearful of embarrassment. We would have a head of state above politics but involved in ensuring the constitution works in delivering stable government. This might include clarifying the rules, so political claims and counter-claims on who has the right to be prime minister didn't undermine confidence in the system. It could also be a role of negotiator, bringing party leaders together and ensuring discussions and decisions were conducted in good faith and in a way that was as transparent and accountable as possible. While the party leaders vied for power and advantage, the president could put the good of the country front and centre.

For the most part, our president would be our cheerleader and representative, chosen by us from among us, someone we believed represented our values and who had demonstrated the integrity, skill and eloquence to perform the role well. No one is able to represent every view, community or perspective, and we shouldn't fall into the royalist trap of expecting our head of state to act as some kind of messiah. But rather than dismiss the good sense of the British public, we could instead embrace the prospect of choosing people who represented the best of us, who inspired us to do well by others, to have ambition and hope, and to have confidence in our democracy.

## Down with the Crown

As we transition to a republic it's worth pausing briefly to consider what would happen to the Crown and its assets, and what would become of the royals. That last question is easy enough, as the extended Mountbatten-Windsor family would simply be free to live their lives as they wished. Their titles would all be gone, as would their legal privileges and state funding. They privately own considerable wealth and land, so while they may have to downsize from the opulence they currently enjoy at our expense, they would continue to live in great comfort and without the need to work for a living. They would, of course, no longer enjoy the income of the Duchies of Lancaster and Cornwall, but as Harry and Meghan have shown, there are other ways for ex-royal celebrities to make a fortune, at least for now. Should they find themselves on hard times, then of course they would be free to find jobs and knuckle down, earning their own salary like the rest of us.

Charles would no longer get to choose whether he paid income tax or the rate at which he would pay it and, when he died, his estate would be liable for inheritance tax. Most of the homes the family occupy either belong to the duchies, the Crown or directly to the state, so these would need to be vacated – just as the prime minister vacates the flat in Downing Street and Chequers once they leave office. Homes of historic or cultural importance could become museums or galleries, while the less notable properties could be left to the Crown Estate to manage as they see fit, to raise funds for the government.

The Crown Estate would remain largely unchanged aside from its name, which could be the National Estate or Historical Estate or similar, with all its surplus income continuing to flow to the Treasury. The two duchies could easily be merged into that portfolio of land, the final 'surrender' of Crown lands to Parliament, swelling the Estate profits by more than £50 million a year.

Buckingham Palace, as well as Kensington and St James's Palaces and Windsor Castle, should rightly become museums and galleries, open in full, all year round. It would be a wonderful thing if the Mall and Constitution Hill, the road that runs between Buckingham Palace and Green Park, were pedestrianized, the grand gates at the front of the palace left open, the ceremonial guard kept in place and the whole area from the doors of the palace up the Mall to Trafalgar Square turned into a public space free of traffic and dedicated to celebrating our culture and history in all its colourful complexity. Buckingham Palace already houses one of the world's largest collections of art, so this would be a great opportunity to see more of it on display all year round, alongside museum displays that, while reflecting the historic role of the monarchy, celebrated our long tradition of struggling for democracy, freedom and equality.

Currency and stamps adorned with the face of Charles III would continue to circulate until natural wastage saw them replaced with designs featuring national heroes, explorers, scientists and champions of our most cherished shared values. King's Counsel, until recently Queen's Counsel, would become Senior Counsel, while other institutions bearing 'Royal' in their name could each decide how best to transition – if at all – to a name that better reflected our democratic ethos. Then of course we would choose a new national anthem, one for the Union as a whole, to complement those anthems enjoyed by the constituent nations. As with the preamble of our constitution, it is hard to imagine a country with such rich cultural and musical traditions struggling to find a thumping, rousing score that would have all of us raising the roof at the next Olympics.

In all of this, the transition would simply feel right, as we reallocated funds and national assets towards a shared, public purpose and reshaped the symbols and language of state and nation to reflect all of us and our contemporary values, rather than the authoritarian values of feudal kings and eighteenth-century aristocrats. Just as we adjusted to the change of monarch, so too would we adjust to a change to our new, more democratic institutions and the symbols that represented them and the nation they served.

## There is No Panacea

A common straw-man argument put up by royalists is to suggest that republicans see a republic as a solution to all our problems. We don't. I've never met anyone who believes that. But there's something pernicious in the charge. It appears to dash all hope of change or progress, suggesting that if a reform or proposed solution to one set of problems isn't going to solve *all* our problems then why bother? The answer, of course, is we should bother because a transition to a republic will solve several political and constitutional issues while making it easier to tackle others. Ten, twenty, one hundred years after that transition, we will continue to face political, social, economic and environmental problems, which a new constitution will not and cannot solve. But we will have given ourselves the political tools and national institutions to make facing those challenges easier and hopefully make our responses to them more equitable.

A republic would rid us of an institution that is mired in corruption, that demands secrecy, seeks to avoid accountability and fails to account for its awful legacy of slavery and empire. A republic would put on a pedestal our best instincts and most cherished traditions, ridding us of the need to compromise our values to make room for nepotism and hereditary power. And a republic would fundamentally shift power from government to Parliament and to the people, enshrining our sovereignty, establishing stronger checks and balances, empowering people to determine the shape of our politics and empowering a revitalized and more democratic parliament to realize its promise as the centre of national debate and a place where the interests of all can be fairly represented. Finally, a republic would allow us to choose effective, independent heads of state – men and women chosen by us to do a clearly defined and important job, not claiming greatness through birth, or feigning faultlessness through secrecy and deference, but to serve as best they can with a seriousness of purpose and an understanding that they represent and are accountable to the British people.

In our republic we could have a more honest and straightforward relationship with the state, with all of us taking shared ownership of it and its institutions. With a more democratic division of power, more interests could be represented, making it more likely – although never guaranteed – that decisions would be made in the interests of everyone, not just the few. And where the few – the rich, the powerful, those born to hereditary privilege – seek to subvert the rules or ignore the constitution, clear boundaries would have been established. In our president we would have someone to guard the perimeter.

At present the system is geared to benefit a few, not by design or conspiracy, but as the result of an incomplete evolution from monarchy to democracy. The result is declining trust in our institutions, a population that remains committed to democratic values, but which is increasingly dismayed by the way our democracy functions, convinced that the system is 'rigged to serve the rich and powerful' and that politicians are largely uninterested in what they think. The loudest defenders of the status quo are the greatest beneficiaries, and so it will be up to the rest of us to become loud proponents for change, not on the promise of a panacea, but on the promise of a fairer, more democratic Britain.

## Our Republic

One claim about the monarchy saddens me. It is the suggestion that it is the monarchy that makes our country special, unique or colourful. That without it, Britain would be colourless, uninteresting and unable to play an influential role in the world. It's a view that is, to say the least, unpatriotic. I use the term patriotism quite deliberately, to give it renewed meaning: a sense of belonging and a concern for our society that is positive and creative, which isn't to the exclusion of others, doesn't denigrate others and doesn't put us on a pedestal. Patriotism should allow us to celebrate what's good about our country while having honest, serious debates about where things have gone wrong, where people have been let down. Surely anybody who understands our country, who cares about the people, the places and the history and who revels in our culture, must know how much more we are than one state institution.

Britain faces many social, economic and environmental challenges. But in facing up to those challenges we must draw on our own individual and communal strengths, not cling to an institution that does not, cannot and will not help. And whether it's tourism, industry, culture or tackling climate change, those strengths are abundant. We are a nation rich in political and cultural traditions, as well as a country spoilt for its natural beauty. From the magnificence of the Scottish Highlands and Islands, the poetic beauty of the Lake District and Yorkshire moors, the breathtaking scenery of Eryri and the Welsh coastline, to the Giant's Causeway in County Antrim, and the lush green of the English countryside from Cornwall to Kent – this is truly a 'green and pleasant land'. Our culture continues to reach all parts of the globe, from the music of Holst and Elgar, through the poetry of Burns and Byron, and the literature of Emily Brontë, Jane Austen and Dickens, not to mention the popular music, literature, art and cinema of the twenty-first century. Our scientists have shaped – and helped save – the modern world. It was Alexander Fleming who discovered penicillin, Alan Turing who invented the world's first computer and helped shorten the Second World War by breaking the Enigma code, and Tim Berners-Lee who invented the World Wide Web. Francis Crick, Rosalind Franklin and Maurice Wilkins, along with the American James Watson, discovered the double-helix structure of DNA, and Alec Jeffreys pioneered genetic fingerprinting three decades later. From Charles

Darwin to Stephen Hawking, we have produced scientists who have transformed the way we understand our world.

This isn't about saying we're the greatest nation on earth, but about recognizing what greatness we have and where it comes from. Like other nations, we also have plenty to apologize for, particularly on the question of empire and slavery – from the early conquests of the Americas to the violent crushing of the Mau Mau uprising in the 1950s. But still, our future is bright, and our country is a place worthy of celebration. Not because of the monarchy, but because of us. Because of the ordinary women and men who every day strive to do extraordinary things, whether they are composers or teachers, global stars or nurses. A republic, if anything, is a recognition of the wonderful courage, resourcefulness, brilliance and creativity of all of us. A republic means we recognize that we are quite capable of stepping up to the challenges we face as a nation. And we can make facing those challenges so much easier by equipping ourselves with institutions that are founded on solid, noble principles and which work for the common good.

I have no doubt in my mind that we will get there. Sooner than any of us might imagine, we will set off to polling stations around the country, from Truro to Thurso, Brighton to Bangor and in every village, town and city, and we will freely choose to vote for the abolition of the monarchy. It will be a historic moment, and one we can all be proud of in years to come, not just because so many will take part in that vote, but because of the hard work that will have got us there. We will have persuaded millions of people to take another look at the issue, to reassess the myths and the false claims perpetuated about the monarchy – the tourism, the global appeal and the fictional strengths of having a puppet King and a powerful PM. We will have done the hard slog to tell a great story, to set out the next chapter in our nation's history, to engage effectively with broadcasters and politicians, to ensure the country can have a fair, intelligent, public debate about the monarchy and the way we're governed.

A study of history can offer us wonderful insights into how we arrived at this moment, what forces shaped our nation and the world we live in, and can tell us great stories about the heroes and the villains who have shaped those forces. Yet history hasn't stopped. We don't learn history so as to be trapped by it. Just as generations before us pursued change, whether in curtailing the power of kings or extending voting rights to every adult in the country, recognizing and protecting the rights of racial minorities, women, people with disabilities and LGBT communities, so our generation can continue to shape the course of history.

History is for ever being made but is never lost. The legacies of our ancestors – for good or bad – will always be with us, as will their palaces and monuments that remind us of our past. And when we do take that step and become a republic, we will be making history all over again. It will be a moment witnessed by the world and never forgotten by this country. A republic is a legacy that we leave to future generations, something entirely achievable, profoundly democratic and that will make Britain a fairer and better place for all of us.

# Acknowledgements

In a sense, this book is a product of many years' work and so my thanks must extend beyond those who have helped directly with writing it. I would particularly like to thank my mum and dad, and brother and sister Paul and Clare, for all their support and encouragement over the years. Campaigning for the abolition of the monarchy can be challenging and having my family support what I do has been hugely important. For their support, advice and encouragement during the writing process, I am grateful to Tim Sharp, Alex Runswick, Jonah Bloch-Johnson, Norman Baker, Matt Turnbull, Anna Britten and Phillip Hall.

I also feel indebted to the many incredible people whom I have had the pleasure to work with at Republic. Professor Stephen Haseler, who first encouraged me to get involved and later to take on a central role in the campaign. John and Suzanne Campbell were also hugely supportive in the early years and became good friends along the way. Sadly Stephen, John and Suzanne are no longer with us, but each was instrumental in guiding Republic towards a more successful future.

My thanks also to Jon Temple, a key member of the team at the time I first joined Republic, and Leo Boyes, who offered me wise counsel and support while I found my feet in the campaign. Most people involved in Republic are volunteers, but I've also been privileged to work with some fantastic colleagues who helped Republic step up to the challenges of campaigning during the major royal events of 2011 and 2012. William Summers and

James Gray were instrumental in shaping the campaign before and during this period and have contributed to Republic in more ways than I have space to mention. Cathy Elliot, Pia de Keyser and Mic Dixon also deserve thanks for their significant contributions, the latter in producing the documentary *The Man Who Shouldn't Be King*.

Andrew Child, Ken Ritchie, Kes Evoy, Austin Wellbelove and Robbie Parkin all helped keep the show on the road over recent years. Emily Robinson, Jen Gingell, Paula Feehan, Peter Cafferkey, Gareth Robson, Jayde Bradley, Loretta Caughlin, Pauline Godfrey, Ed Halsted, Scott Reeve, Peter Jenkins, Paul Francis and Matthew Hulbert also deserve a thank-you for their support. I should make a special mention of John Cross, who has produced some excellent research and pursued important freedom of information requests, as well as our current team of directors, volunteers and staff.

Over the years I have had the opportunity to collaborate with and learn from colleagues from across Europe and the Commonwealth who deserve my thanks. They include Floris Müller, Hans Maessen and Bram van Montfoort from the Dutch campaign Republiek; Magnus Simonsson, Olle Nykvist and Maria Backman from the Swedish campaign Republikanska föreningen; Per Hanson and Jon Leren from the Norwegian campaign Republikk; Lewis Holden from New Zealand Republic; Sandy Biar from the Australian Republican Movement; and Tom Freda from Citizens for a Canadian Republic.

I would like to thank and acknowledge those who have worked to challenge the status quo, whether with a view to reform or abolition, including Dr John Kirkhope, Professor Jenny Hocking, Andrew Lownie, the late David McClure and the indomitable *Guardian* and *Sunday Times* journalists, particularly Rob Evans and Gabriel Pogrund respectively, who have thrown a spotlight on some of the royal household's most egregious failings. Finally I wish to thank Alex Christofi and the team at Penguin Random House for giving me the opportunity to write this book.

Graham Smith is CEO of the campaign organization Republic, which aims to abolish the monarchy and replace it with an elected head of state.

# Index

Abbey, Nels 127
Abell, Stig 154, 155–6
*Abolish the Monarchy* 24
abolition
  abolition test 21, 33
  principle of 67, 69–70
  process of 176, 198
  raising awareness 195–6
  risk of 58
  support for, rising 186
  *see also* Republic; republic (UK)
Abortion Act (1967) 156
access and consent, royal family 102–7
Act of Settlement (1701) 36, 83
Acton, Lord 179
Acts of Union 226
Afghanistan 219
Africa 127
*The Age* 219
Agnew, Rosemary 95
Ahtisaari, Martti 222
Air Ambulance charities 25
al-Assad, Hafez 124
Al Thani, Sheikh Hamad bin Jassim
    bin Jaber 106–7, 123
Albanese, Anthony 187
Alexandra, Princess 79
Alliance of European Republican
    Movements (AERM) 109
ambassadors (royal family) 22, 128–34
  Caribbean tours 22, 31, 133
    Edward and Sophie 133–4
    embarrassment of 133–4
    protests 133
    William and Kate 133, 134
  Commonwealth countries
    royal exploitation of 129–30
    royal reporting 128–9
    royalist mythology in relation to 130–1

  ineptitude of 22–3
  phony sanctimony insult 134
  William's lecturing of African
      people 128–9
Amess, David 77
Anderson, Christopher 120
Andrew, Prince, Duke of York 111, 188
  acquaintances 22–3
  character of 144
  criminal damage 195–6
  government role 144
  reputation 22–3
  security, request for 77
  sexual offences accusations 144–5
    interview with *Newsnight* 145, 204
    maintains innocence 145
    out-of-court settlement 145
    police response to 148
  stripped of honorary titles and
      patronages 145–6
  letter from ex-services personnel
      115–16
  UK trade ambassador 22
  wedding to Sarah 15, 17
Anne, Princess Royal 78
  'hardest-working royal' 28–9, 31–2
Antigua and Barbuda Reparations
    Support Commission 133–4
Anzac Day 31
apartheid regime 140, 141
Arnold, Jacques 39–40
Ashdown, Paddy 154
Association of Leading Visitor
    Attractions 12
Augusta of Cambridge, Princess 98
Australia 56, 57
  defeat for elites 192
  'double dissolution' election 171
  referendum on a republic 189–90

Australian Labor Party (ALP) 189
Australian Republic Movement (ARM)
    189, 190

Bagehot, Walter 107
Baker, Norman 40, 77, 88, 147–8, 159
Baldini, Luisa 203
Balmoral 78, 92, 127
Barbados 125, 129, 187, 210
    constitutional change 210–11
Barlow, Gary 205
Bath 14
BBC 200–9
    accession of Charles 205–6
    balance, lack of 201–2
    Brexit coverage 207
    funeral coverage of Elizabeth 207
    impartiality 200, 207
        legal requirement 201
    promoting royalty 202, 203–8
    republicans, lack of coverage about
        203–4
    royal reporting
        bias 201–2, 205–7, 208
        honest and fair approach 208
        lacking balance and independence
            200
        sycophancy and deference 201
Beatrice, Princess 77
Bercow, John 49
Berners-Lee, Tim 245
Best, George Percival 82–3
bicycling monarchy 109
Bill of Rights (US) 174–5
BIOT (British Indian Overseas
        Territory) 163
Björnsson, Sveinn 211
Black Lives Matter movement 139
Blair, Tony 161, 169
Blenheim Palace 61
Bluebell Railway 79
Boaden, Helen 201
Bolger, Jim 191
Bolland, Mark 29
Booth, Cherie 49
Botha, P. W. 140
Brand Finance report (2012) 20–2, 23, 25
brand value 19–23

Braverman, Suella 115
Brexit (2016) 43, 192, 207, 213
    debate 158
    EU elites 192
British constitution see constitutions (UK)
British Indian Ocean Territory Order
        (1965) 163
British people
    culture and achievements of 245–6
    dissatisfaction with British democracy
        67, 68
    support for democratic values 67
    untrustworthiness of 70–1
British Social Attitudes survey (2012) 184
Brooke, Heather 73–4, 93
Brooke, Peter 17
Brown, Gordon 154, 172
Browne, Gaston 134
Bruce, Fiona 26–7
Buckingham Palace 9–10, 61, 78, 92, 241
    1844 Room 11
    art collection 10–11
    Bow Room 11
    crowds 14
    history 10–12
    opened to tourists 17
    Picture Gallery 10, 11
    publication of annual accounts 17–18
    Throne Group 10
    tour guides 10–13
Burrell, Paul 121

Cabinet 102–3, 160
Callaghan, James 41–2, 105
Cambodia 54
Cambridge Emeralds 98
Cameron, David 161, 191
Camilla, Queen Consort 188
campaigning 195–9
Canada 56, 132
carbon emissions 124–5
carbon offsetting 126
Caribbean
    embarrassment for royals 133–4
    protests against royal visits 22, 31, 133
    reparations, calls for 132, 134, 143
    republicanism 132, 187
    resentment towards the monarchy 132

Carl XVI Gustaf, King 109
Carlos, King Juan 109
Case, Simon 177
cash-for-peerages accusations 170
Catherine, Princess of Wales 188
  engagement to William 195
  public engagements 32
  wedding to William 14
  see also William, Prince of Wales:
    Kate and
Chagos Islands 163–4
change 184, 186, 192–3
Changing of the Guard 60
character, in politics and private 117–18
charities 23–7
Charlemagne 69
Charles I, King 82
Charles III, King 72, 123
  access to Cabinet papers 103
  accession 205–6
  belief in natural order 119–20
  cash gift from Sheikh 106–7, 123
  character of 118–19
    personal behaviour 120–1
    petulance 121
    sensitive to criticism 118–19, 125–6
    snobbery 119–20
    temper 120–1
  claims to the duchies 85
  donation from Qatar 123
  environment and
    carbon footprint of 124–5
    carbon offsetting 126
    defensiveness 125–6
    travel arrangements 91–2, 124–5
  honours for cash accusations 146–8
  influencing public policy 50
  letters 50, 94
  meetings with Middle
    Eastern royals 124
  paying and avoiding taxes 85–6, 90
  politics of
    criticises human rights abuses 124
    defence of human rights 122
    hypocrisy 123, 124–5
    interventions 123
  popularity, lack of 188
  as Prince of Wales 25, 29–30, 31

private income 85, 86, 87
public support 150
'spider memos' 105–6
views 50
  alternative medicine 118–19
  challenges to 118–19
  environmental matters 125–6
  scientific matters 118
visit to Cambridge (2020) 91
wedding to Diana 14, 17
Chequers 92
Chester Zoo 14
Chesterton, G. K. 59
China 55, 124
Chinese government 66
Church of England 139
Churchill, Winston 51, 53
Civil List 16, 17
Clarence House 78
Clegg, Nick 159, 169, 192
Cleverly, James 115
climate change 124–5, 126
collective responsibility 157
Common Council 161
Commonwealth Heads of Government
    Meeting (CHOGM)
    (2018) 130
Commonwealth of Nations 128–30
  Caribbean republicanism 132
  as Empire 2.0 130
  free association 131
  membership 131
  monarchies and republics 131–2
  origins of 130, 131
  royal family and 128–30
  royalist mythology 130–1
  titular head of 130–1
Commonwealth People's Forum 137–8
Commonwealth realms 56
consent see access and consent, royal
    family; royal consent rule
Conservative Party 115, 177
Constance, Ellen 97–8
Constantine II, King 54
Constitution (Amendment) (No. 2) Act
    (Barbados) (2021) 210–11
Constitution Hill 241
constitutional monarchy 36, 43

constitutions
  amendments 175, 176
  constitutional change 210–13
  Finland 228
  framework 225
  France 172
  Germany 172
  Iceland 228
  Ireland 175
  referendums 175, 176
  Switzerland 172, 228
  UK 36–7
    Act of Settlement (1701) 36
    codifying 177, 180
    crisis 44, 46–7
    defence of 176
    failure of 154
    flexibility of 174
    governmental power 177
    impenetrability of 224
    monarchy as defender of 38–42,
      46, 47
    process of change 210, 213
    reform 172, 179
    for a republic 214–15
    strength of 224
    unwritten 172
    virtue of 174
    written 172–3, 180, 225
  Union of Great Britain and Northern
    Ireland 227–8
    declaration for 228
    rules 236–7
    state church and 229–30
    written 227–8, 236–7
  unwritten 172
  US 174–5
    amendments 175
    Bill of Rights 174–5
    Second Amendment 174, 175
    written 172–3, 175, 179, 180, 212
Cooper Clarke, John 228
coronations 60–1
corporation tax 85–7
corruption 108–10
Corruption Index 57
Court Circular 28, 29–30
courts 235

Cousins, Robin 26
Cox, Jo 77
Crick, Francis 245
critical race theory 184
Cromwell, Richard 36
Crossman, Richard 162
*The Crown* 23
Crown
  checks and balances, lack of
    41, 42
  definition 153
  power of 40
  reform 179
  state institution 84
  under a republic 240–1
*The Crown and The Establishment*
  (Martin) 16
Crown Estate 21, 22, 76, 81, 84
  land and property of 82
  purpose of 81–2
  under a republic 241
Crown Estate Act (1961) 82
Crown Jewels 21
culture 245
Czechia 212

*Dagbladid* 218
*Daily Mail* 29
*Daily Mirror* 17
Darwin, Charles 245–6
Davies, Alan 54
Davies, Dai 77
Dawe, Sandie 15
Dawkins, Richard 118
Day, Elaine 119–20
debates
  Bath (2012) 2
  Oxford Union (2021) 2
Declassified UK 123
democracies 67–8
  accountability 68–9
  British, dissatisfaction with 67, 68
  elections 68–9
  equality 69
  undemocratic institutions 70
  values, support for 67–8
Democracy Index 56–7
Democratic Audit 157

Democratic Unionist Party
    (DUP) 43
Denmark 55, 56, 57, 211
devolution 173–4
Diamond Jubilee 2, 20
Diana, Princess of Wales 121
    wedding to Charles 14, 17
Dimbleby, David 206–7
Dimbleby, Jonathan 147–8
Disasters Emergency Committee 31
diversity 115–16
divine right 18, 69, 70
Donald, Rod 192
Downing Street 41
Duchy of Cornwall 30
    corporation tax 85, 86–7
    Crown property 76, 81, 83–4
    freedom of information requests
        101–2
    income tax 85–6
    legal status 86
    as a property company 21, 85
    royal revenue from 21, 76, 81, 85
    state ownership of 76, 81, 83–4
    statute 84
    surrender of lands to Parliament
        240, 241
    tax affairs and accounts 158–9
Duchy of Lancaster
    Crown property 76, 81, 83–4, 85
    private property, Charles's claim 85
    as a property company 21, 85
    royal revenue from 21, 76, 81, 85
    state ownership of 76, 81, 83–4
    statute 84
    surrender of lands to Parliament
        240, 241
Duffy, Carol Ann 228
Duke of Edinburgh's Award 26–7
Dumfries House 146
Dunt, Ian 2–3, 4, 55, 62

Earthshot 127–8
    Earthshot Prize 26, 30, 127, 128
The Economist 56–7
Eden, Anthony 51
Edinburgh Castle 14
Edward IV, King 83

Edward, Prince, Duke of Edinburgh
    22, 133–4
Edward VII, King 40, 88, 97–8
Edwards, David 14–15
elections
    in democracies 68–9
    legal requirement for 164
    prime minister's decision 164
elective dictatorship 42, 154–5, 178–80
Electoral Reform Society 168, 193–4
Elizabeth I, Queen 69–70
Elizabeth II, Queen 40–1, 70
    agreement to pay income tax 88–9
    birthday (1983) 194
    inheritance 89
    long reign 51–2
    popularity of 188
    speech to CHOGM (2018) 130
    visit to Leicester 79–80
    visit to Romsey 80
Elizabeth, Queen Mother
    see Queen Mother
Elphicke, Charlie 148
Elstein, David 207
embrace of convenience 37
The Empire's New Clothes (Murphy)
    128–9
The English Constitution (Bagehot) 107
English Reformation 69
environment 124–8
Epstein, Jeffrey 22, 144
Ernst, Professor Edzard 118–19
Eryri (Snowdonia) 14
Eswatini 54
Eton College 209
EU (Withdrawal) Bill (2018) 166
Eugenie, Princess 77, 78
    gap year 78–9
European Convention on
        Human Rights 173, 213
Evans, Nigel 149
Extinction Rebellion 125, 196

Fawcett, Michael 146–8
Ferguson, Sarah see Sarah,
        Duchess of York
Fiennes, Caroline 24
Finland 5, 56, 57, 222, 228

Finnbogadóttir, Vigdís 116, 217–20, 238
Fitzwilliams, Richard 19–20, 39
Fixed-term Parliaments Act (FTPA, 2011) 159, 164, 174
Fleming, Alexander 245
Flynn, Paul 35–6
Francis of Teck, Prince 98
Franklin, Rosalind 245
free press 200
free speech 71–2
Freedom of Information Act (2005) 93–4
  historic documents 98–9
  royal exemption from 93–6, 99–100
Freeman, Edward 83
*Freethinker* 194
Fry, Stephen 54–5, 56
Fulani, Ngozi 136–7

Gaddafi, Saif 22
Gategate 196
Gauck, Joachim 221–2
gay monarchs 114
Gender Equality Index 57
George I, King 37, 40
George II, King (Greece) 53–4
George III, King 82
George, Prince 101, 113–14, 186
George V, King 60, 88
George VI, King 101, 131
Germany 5, 56, 172
  horrific legacy 221
  liberation 221
Giuffre, Virginia 144, 145, 148
Giving Evidence report 23–5, 79
Glorious Revolution 36, 82, 83
Gloucester, Duke and Duchess of 92
Golden Jubilee 79
Good Friday Agreement 173, 213, 221
Gorbachev, Mikhail 238
Gordonstoun 27
government records 98
governments, sovereignty of *see* sovereignty of government
Gray, James 148–9, 203
Greece
  monarchy
    abolition 53–4
    restoration 53–4

  republic 54
Greenpeace 126
Grieve, Dominic 50, 96, 117
*Guardian* 15, 18, 45–6
  Charles's access to Cabinet papers 103
  financial scrutiny of monarchy 105
  legal battles
    Prince Charles's letters 50, 94
    secrecy of Prince Philip's will 96
  royal consent rule 104, 105
*Gudbjartur* 218
Gudlaugar Thorvaldsson 218

Hague, William 30
Hahn, Kurt 27
Hailsham, Lord 41–2, 154–5
Hale, Lord 43
Halldórsdóttir, Svanhildur 220
Halonen, Tarja 222
Hamilton College 183
Hamilton, Willie 16
Hampton Court 61
'hard-working royal' 28–32
  league table 28–9
  trophy 28–9
Harding, James 203
harmless argument 2, 4, 66, 67–73, 153
  access and consent 102–7
  corruption 107–10
  'it ain't broke' 62, 153
  lobbying and secrecy 93–102
  royal expenses 73–87
  tax avoidance 87–92
*Harry & Meghan* 130
Harry, Prince, Duke of Sussex 188
  Meghan and
    criticisms of the monarchy 132
    departure from the UK 132, 135
    interview with Oprah Winfrey 135
    lack of public interest in 202
    wedding 18, 135
  paying for police protection 77–8
  *Spare* 122, 127
  suing the British government 77–8
Haseler, Professor Stephen 194
Hattersley, Roy 2, 18
*Have I Got News For You* 154
Hawking, Stephen 246

Hazell, Professor Robert 198
head of state (UK)
    accountability 107, 152
    choice, lack of 3
    chosen on merit 150–2
    convention 43
    elected 3, 45–6, 52, 69–70, 70, 116, 150,
        150–1, 151, 234–40
    hereditary 51, 62, 114–15, 151
    intervention 45–6
    obsolete and redundant 44, 46, 178
    see also presidents: in the UK (future)
Heath, Edward 16
Henry VIII, King 69
hereditary lineage 114–15
hereditary monarchy 112
heritage tourism 19
Higgins, President Michael D. 222, 238
Highgrove 78, 91
Hill, Symon 71, 72
Hirsch, Afua 130, 142
Hislop, Ian 154
history
    books 61
    for future generations 61–2
    making of 247
    palaces, castles and museums 61
Hitchens, Peter 1, 53
Hitler, Adolf 53
Hodge, Margaret 158
Holden, Lewis 129
Holness, Andrew 133
homelessness 87
Hong Kong 56
honours for cash exchange 146–8
honours system 60, 61, 147, 159, 231–2
House of Commons 9, 38
    select committees 158
    supremacy of 38, 170–1
House of Commons Public
        Administration Select
        Committee 165
House of Lords 9, 69, 70
    abolition of 231
    appointments to 159–60
    defence of hereditary peers 169–70
    democratic principle, failure of 171–2
    elected, proposals for 170, 171

    expertise 166–7, 168
    legitimacy of 166
    'the other place' 165–6
    patronage 170
    political appointees 167, 168
    practical limitations 166
    professions of members 168
    reform, proposals for 169, 170
    religious appointments 169
    unelected status 167, 168
    unrepresentative 168–9
House of Windsor 60
Houses of Parliament 9, 14
How Britain Really Works (Abell) 154
Howard, John 189, 190, 191
Hoyle, Lyndsay 170–1
Human Freedom Index 57
Human Rights Act (HRA, 1998)
        163, 173, 213
Hunt, John 27
Hunt, Peter 137
Huq, Rupa 148
Hussey, Susan 136–7, 138, 141

Iceland 5, 56, 57, 211, 228
    egalitarianism 219
    as a gender equal country 219, 220
    influence of Vigdís 219
    presidential election (1980) 217–19
    women's rights movement 217
impartiality 47–51, 52
income tax 85–6, 88
Index on Censorship report (2023) 101
India 129, 131
innovators 65
Institute for Government 157
interests 49
Ireland 5, 56, 57, 131, 211, 222
    female president 220
    partition 226
    reunification of 59
    written constitution 172

Jakobsdóttir, Katrín 219
James II, King 36, 82
Javid, Sajid 45, 115, 149
Jeffreys, Alec 245
Jobson, Rob 121

Johnson, Boris 176
  breaches of Covid rules 72
  character, criticisms of 117
  forced to resign as prime minister
    44–5, 46, 177
  plans to dissolve parliament 177–8
  threat to rule of law 42–3
  unlawful prorogation of Parliament 43–4
Johnson, Lyndon B. 140
Jordan, David 201
judges 49

Kaituni, Tarek 22
Katrín Jakobsdóttir 219
Kennedy, John F. 140
Kensington Palace 12, 92, 241
Kent, Duke and Duchess of 92
Kenya 126–7
Khan, Imran Ahmad 148
Kingdom of Great Britain 226
Kingdom of Ireland 226
Kings Counsel 242
Kingsmill 20
Kirby, Hon. Justice Michael 189, 190
Kirkhope, Dr John 101–2
Köhler, Horst 149
Kwarteng, Kwasi 115, 148

Labour Party 41–2, 172
laggards 65
law-making 233
Leakey, Lieutenant General David 1
legislation 233
leverage 104
Lewis, Clive 192
LGBTQ+ people 183–4
LGBTQ+ politicians 115
Lithuania 212
lobbying 95, 97, 105–6
London Declaration (1949) 131
London Pride 14
long habit 3, 4
longevity 51–2
Lownie, Andrew 100–1

Maessen, Hans 187
Mahfouz, Marei Mubarak bin
    Mahfouz 146–8

Maitlis, Emily 207
Major, John 89
Mall 14, 241
The Man Who Shouldn't Be King 101
Marmite 20
Martin, Kingsley 16
Martin, Michael 73–4
Mary, Queen 98
Mason, Sandra 210
Mauritius 163, 211
McAleese, Mary 116, 220–1
McClure, David 97
McCoy, Simon 203
McFarlane, Sir Andrew 95–6, 97
Meghan, Duchess of Sussex 78
  accused of bullying 135
  fitting in with royal family 135
  wedding to Harry 18, 135
  see also Harry, Prince, Duke of
    Sussex: Meghan and
Meghan Markle: An American Princess 135
Menzies Memorial Lecture 189
Metaxas, Ioannis 54
Metropolitan Police 77, 78
Mey, Castle of 146
Michael of Kent, Princess 136
Middleton, Kate see Catherine,
    Princess of Wales
Mitchell, Austin 86
monarch, definition of 153
monarchies
  arguments for 54–5
  in Australia
  in Barbados 187
  in Canada 187
  falling support for 186–7, 188
  in the Netherlands 187
  in New Zealand 187
monarchists 2, 32, 36, 197–8, 202
  see also royalists
monarchs
  powers of 37
  Roman Catholicism and 36–7
monarchy (UK)
  abolition see abolition
  constitutional impotence 42, 43–6
  continuity 51
  corrupt institution 108–10

crises of 187–8
defender of the constitution 38–42, 46
definition 153
divine right 18, 69, 70
expenses *see* royal expenses
harmless argument *see* harmless
    argument
historic power of 36
income generation 21–2, 33–4
independence of 40–1, 178
intangible benefits 20, 21, 33–4
'it works' defence 66, 71, 108
lack of public interest in 202–3
overseas anger and resentment
    towards 132
Parliament and 36–7
popularity argument 4, 66, 129, 152
positives of 3–4
profitability argument *see* profitability
    of monarchy
relationship with the Church 69
standards of public life 4
support for 152
    falling 186–7
tangible assets 21–2
taxes 85–92
tourism and *see* tourism; tourism myth
travel arrangements *see* royal travel
unrepresentative of British people
    113–14, 116
values 69–70
*see also* Crown; royal family
Montfoort, Bram van 109
More in Common study (2020) 67,
    68, 214
Morgan, Piers 135, 136
Mos-Shogbamimu, Dr Shola 138
Mountbatten, Lord 100–1
MPs 49
    parliamentary expenses 73–5
    racist language 148
    security 77
    sexual assault cases 148
Müller, Floris 187
Murder (Abolition of Death Penalty)
    Act (1965) 156
Murphy, Philip 99, 128–9
Mussolini, Benito 53

*My Queen and I* (Hamilton) 16
*The Myth of British Monarchy* (Wilson)
    16, 29

Nash, John 11
national anthem 242
National Archives 98
nationalism 58
Netherlands 55, 56, 60, 187
    monarchy 109–10
Neville, Gary 123
*A New Britain: Renewing our Democracy
    and Rebuilding our Economy*
    (2022) 172
New Zealand 57, 132
    defeat for elites 192
    discontent with electoral system 191
    referendum (1992) 191, 192
        Campaign for Better
            Government 192
        electoral reform 191
        Mixed Member Proportional
            system (MMP) 191, 192
    vote on electoral reform 191
New Zealand Green Party 192
*Newsnight* 145, 204
*No Time to Die* 91–2
Nolan Principles 73, 89–90
Northern Ireland 59, 173, 220–1, 226
    *see also* Good Friday Agreement
Norway 53–7
    monarchy 109–10
Nottingham Carnival 14
Nye, William 86

Obama, President Barack 183
O'Connor, Patrick 161, 162, 163
O'Donnell, Gus 47
O'Donovan, Tim 28–9
Ogada, Dr Mordecai 126
opinions *see* views
Orders in Council 160, 163
Orders of Council 160, 162
Osborne, George 80, 81, 157
Otto the Great 69
Outward Bound scheme 27
Oxford Union 198
    debating society (2021) 1, 198

Paine, Thomas 3
Palace of Westminster 9
palatial homes 92
Palmer, Geoffrey 191
Parliament 14
    checks and balances, lack of 41
    debates 158
    democratic legitimacy 68
    dissolution of 164
    elective dictatorship 154–5
    monarchy and 36–7
    opposition days 156
    power shift to 37
    prorogation of 43–4
    purpose of 167
    see also sovereignty of government
parliamentary democracy 38, 44, 176,
        178–9, 180, 224
parliamentary republic 230–4
    centrality of Parliament 231
    duties of president 237–8
    elected Senate 231
    honours 231–2
    legislation 233
    payroll vote 232
    structure 230
    subordination of government 233–4
parliamentary sovereignty 229
party whips 159
Partygate 72
Patel, Priti 115
patriotism 57–62, 244–5
patronage 157, 159, 170
    abuses of 159–60, 170
Payne, Sebastian 177–8
payroll vote 157, 232
Peat, Michael 119
Peppa Pig 20
Peretz, George, KC 177
personal technology 65
philanthropy 28
Philip, Prince, Duke of Edinburgh 16, 26
    Duke of Edinburgh's Award 26–7
    excuses made for 140–1
    interview with Fiona Bruce 26–7
    racist comments 138
    sealing of will, secrecy of 95–7
Plant Heritage 25

Platinum Jubilee 2, 14, 202, 204
    lack of public interest in 202
poaching 127
political parties 230–1
political scandals 72–3, 73–5
Political Stability Index 57
popular sovereignty 229–30
popularity argument 4, 66, 129, 152
Powlesland, Paul 71
Precedent Book 102–3
Prerogative Orders 160, 161, 163
prerogative powers 165
presidents 160
    accountability 223
    in Barbados 210–11
    constraints on 160
    duties 237–8
    in Finland 222
    in Germany 221–2
    in Iceland 217–20
    in Ireland 116, 220
    in Northern Ireland 116, 220–1
    partisan and political 39
    in the UK (future)
        role of 236, 237, 238–40
    see also head of state (UK)
prime ministers 37
    absolute authority 154, 160
    determining election dates 164
    facing the House of Commons 224
    patronage 159
    powers of 41, 160
Prince of Wales's Charitable Fund 106
Prince's Foundation 123
Prince's Trust 25, 26
principles 33–4, 71, 72–3
private members' bills 156
Privy Council 11, 153, 159, 160–5
    as an annex of government 164–5
    'ceremonial body' 160, 162
    decision-making process 162, 163
    'dysfunctional body' 162
    executive power of government 162
    mechanisms for exercising power 160–1
    membership 162–3
    origins and evolution of 161–2
    powers 160
    royal prerogative powers 160–1

secrecy of 162, 164–5
survival of 165
Prochaska, Frank 28
Proclamations 160, 164
profitability of monarchy 4, 16, 18
  brand value 19–23
  profit above principles 33–4
  royal patronage of charities 23–7
  tourism 9–13
  tourism myth 13–19
proportional representation 180
Public Accounts Committee 86, 158–9
public interest test 94–5
public opinion 193, 196, 198
Public Records Act (1958) 99

Queen Mother 99, 100, 138–9, 140
  racist comments 139
Qvortrup, Matt 176

race discrimination laws 105, 140
racism 135–42
  of Charles 137–8
  excuses for 138, 139–40, 140–1
  historic and institutional 139
  against Meghan Markle 135–6
  of Prince Philip 138
  of Princess Michael of Kent 136
  of the Queen Mother 139
  race discrimination law 140
  racial micro-aggression 138
  royal family history of 136–7
  royals' implications in slavery
    139–40, 142
  of Susan Hussey 136–7, 138, 141
RAF Voyager aircraft 125
Reagan, Ronald 238
Rees-Mogg, Jacob 35–6, 38, 177
referendums 172–3, 176
  in Australia 190–1
  support for 190–1
  in the UK 190
The Reluctant Monarch (Sjöberg) 109
reparations 132, 134, 143
Republic 15, 67, 158
  freedom of information requests 195
  income, doubling of 198
  'Not the Royal Wedding' street party 195

opportunities and resources 194
proactive campaigning 194–5
reporting royal misdemeanours 195–6
see also abolition
Republic of Ireland Act (1948) 211
republic (UK) 2
  benefits of 242–4
  case for 4, 5
  Crown's assets 61, 84
  equality and rights 143
  history and tradition under 61
  political support 190
  popular/public support 193, 199
  transition to 84, 209, 214
  see also parliamentary republic
republicans 3, 73, 111, 194, 198, 202, 205
  disparaging comments about 203–4
republics 55
  Australian referendum 189–90
  Barbados 125, 129, 187, 210, 210–11
  Caribbean countries 132
  Commonwealth countries 131,
    187, 212
  Iceland 211
  India 129, 131
  Ireland 131, 211
  Mauritius 211
  worldwide 131–2
Republikanska föreningen (Swedish
    Republican Association) 109
Reykjavik Summit (1986) 238
Riddell, Peter 41
rights 122, 143, 172, 217, 229
Ringadoo, Veerasamy 211
Robinson, Mary 116, 220
Rodrigues, Christopher 15, 16
Roman Catholic Church 69
Royal Archives 99–100
royal charity work 28
Royal Collection 10–11, 21
royal consent rule 102, 106
  exemptions 104–5
    legal 106
    race discrimination laws 105, 140
  protection of private interests 104–5
  vetting future laws 105
    capital and income 105
    inheritance and trustees' powers 105

royal expenses 73–87
  cost to taxpayer 75, 76
  frugality 75–6
  land ownership 81–4, 85
  publication of 75
  security 76–8, 92
    local costs of royal visits 79–80
    Princess Alexandra's visit to
      Bluebell 79
    Princess Eugenie's gap year 78–9
  unchallenged 75
royal family
  as ambassadors *see* ambassadors
    (royal family)
  apologies for historic crimes, calls for
    141–3
  bullying culture 120–2
  character 117–18
  charity work 23–7
  connections with Middle Eastern
    royals 123–4
  frugality of 75–6
  'hard working' 28–32
  inheritance 141–2
  lawbreaking accusations
    King Charles 146–8
    Prince Andrew 144–6
    turning a blind eye to 144–9
  private estates of 83–7
  private interests of 100–6
  private lifestyles of 90–2
  racism and *see* racism
  security for 76–8, 78–80, 92
  treatment and judgement of 117–18
  wrongdoings and misdemeanours
    excused 111, 112
  *see also individual royals*
*Royal Family* 39, 91
Royal Foundation 26
royal household
  extravagance and costs 18
  published accounts 75
  secrecy, corruption and abuse of office 3
  standards 4
royal houses 53
royal land 81–4, 85
*Royal Legacy* (McClure) 97
royal patronages 23–7

royal prerogative 153, 159, 160–1, 177
royal travel
  carbon footprint 124–5
  by chartered flight 91–2
  by helicopter 90, 91, 124
  pollution 124
  by RAF jets 90, 124, 125
  royal train 90–1
royal wills 95–8
royalists 3, 4
  discrediting of Ngozi Fulani 137
  impartiality argument 47–8, 116
  monarchy as self-financing argument
    81
  profitability of monarchy argument
    *see* profitability of monarchy
  rejects criticisms of royals 111
  strawman argument 242–3
  tourism income argument 75
  tradition and history argument 58,
    114–15
  virtue and sacrifice argument 112
  *see also* monarchists
royals *see* royal family
Rubin, Dave 54
*The Rubin Report* 54
Russia 55

same-sex relationships 183–4
Sandringham 78, 92
Sarah, Duchess of York
  wedding to Andrew 15, 17
Savanta poll (2022) 186
Schrödinger, Erwin 46
  Schrödinger's monarch 47
  thought experiment 46
Scotland 226
  independence 59
secrecy (royal family) 93–102, 109
  dignity and 96–7
  historic documents 98
  public interest test 94–5
  royal exemption from FOIA 93–6,
    99–100
    lobbying 95, 97
  royal family documents 99–102
  royal wills 95–8
    Edward VII 97, 98

Prince Francis of Teck 98
Prince Philip 95–7
security 76–8, 78–80, 92
select committees 158
sensitive information 103
Sethi, Anita 137–8
Sexual Offences Act (1967) 156
shared values 59
Sharp, Victoria 96
Shawcross, William 139
Short Money 157
Silver Jubilee 17
Simonsson, Magnus 109
Sjöberg, Thomas 109
slavery 139–40, 142
Slovakia 212
SNP (Scottish National Party) 95
social rights 172
social utopianism 120
soft monarchists 197
soft republicans 197
Sophia, Electress of Hanover 36–7
Sophie, Duchess of Edinburgh 22, 133–4
South Africa 212
South Bank 14, 195
Sovereign Grant 75, 78, 81
sovereignty of government 154–60
    control over Parliament 155–6
    majorities 157, 157–8
    opposition MPs 156, 157
    parliamentary time 156
    payroll vote 157
    private members' bills 156
    royal prerogative 159
Spain 187
Spare 122, 127
Speaker of the Commons 49
Spencer, Mark 148
St James's Palace 10, 26, 92, 241
St Paul's Cathedral 15
standards of behaviour 72–3
Standley, Albert 194
Starmer, Keir 170, 172
state church 229–30
Statutory Orders 160
Steiner, Felix 221
Stephenson, Paul 77
Stewart, Jon 153

Strong, Roy 139
Succession to the Crown Act (2013) 114
Sumption, Jonathan 44
Sun 115
Sunak, Rishi 45, 115, 152
Sunday Times 106, 146
Supreme Court 43, 44
Svanhildur Halldórsdóttir 220
Sweden 55, 56, 57, 60
Switzerland 56, 57, 172, 228

T-Mobile 20
Taiwan 57
Tatchell, Peter 25
tax avoidance 87–92
    cost to Treasury 90
    income tax 88–9, 90
    inheritance tax 88, 89
    royal exemptions 87, 88, 89
Thailand 54
Thatcher, Margaret 51–2
Thompson, Damian 121
Thorvaldsson, Gudlaugar 218
Titchmarsh, Alan 2
Today 205
tourism 13
    brand value 19–23
    history and monuments 9–13
    income generation 19
    royal patronage of charities 23–7
    royals and contemporary monarchy 13
tourism myth 13–19
    income generation 14–17, 18–19
    ticket sales from heritage sites 15
    visitors 14
    weddings
        Andrew and Sarah 15
        Charles and Diana 14
        William and Kate 14
Tower of London 12
trade 22
tradition 57–62
Trafalgar Square 14
Truss, Liz 115, 117
Tudor monarchs 69–70
Tunzelmann, Alexandra von 100
Turing, Alan 245
Twain, Mark 58

Union of Great Britain and Northern
    Ireland 226
    constitution of 227–8
United Kingdom of Great Britain and
    Ireland 226
United Kingdom of Great Britain and
    Northern Ireland 59, 226
United Kingdom (UK) 55, 56, 57
    attitude to the monarchy 58–9
    Brexit (2016) 43, 158, 192, 207, 213
    constitution *see*
        constitutions: UK
    same-sex relationships 183–4
    vote on electoral reform (2011) 192
United Nations Human Development
    Index (2021) 56
United States of America (USA) 55, 58
    constitution 174–5
    racial attitudes survey (1999) 183
unity 59
Universal Credit system 156
University of Exeter 119
University of Southampton 100

Van der Bellen, Alexander 222
Victoria, Queen 88
Vigdís Finnbogadóttir 217–20, 238
VisitBritain 14–16, 18–19
Vos, Geoffrey 96
voter ID laws 177

Wagner, Adam 174
Wales 226
Wallace, Ben 31
Walpole, Robert 37
Walpole, Spencer 83
Watson, James 245
Weizsäcker, President Richard von
    221, 238
Welby, Justin, Archbishop of
    Canterbury 169
Whittle Institute 91
Wilde, Oscar 58
Wilhelm II, Kaiser 53, 60
Wilkins, Maurice 245
Willem-Alexander, King 187
William III, King 83
William IV, King 60, 139, 140, 142

William of Orange 82
William, Prince of Wales
    borrows RAF military helicopter 195
    character of 188
        petulance and arrogance 121
        temper 122
    Earthshot prize 127–8
    Kate and
        anger at Jamaican debacle 134
        Caribbean tour 22, 31, 133
        engagement 195
        lack of public interest in 202
        protests against 22, 31, 133
        wedding to 14
    lifestyle 113
    politics of 122
        hypocrisy 123
        interventions 123
    private income 85, 86, 87
    public engagements 29–31
    public support 150
    shooting wildlife 127
    views 50
        attitude towards Africa 126–7
        criticisms of 126–7
        environmental debate 126–7
    visit to Kenya (2018) 126–7
    wealth of 113
Wilson, Edgar 16, 29
Wilson, Harold 41–2
Windsor Castle 12–13, 17, 61, 78,
    88, 241
    archive 99–100
Windsor Legoland 13
Winfrey, Oprah 135
Winston, Robert 167–8
Women's Day Off 217–18
World Economic Forum 144
Wulff, Christian 149
Wyatt, Woodrow 17, 139

xenophobia 58

YouGov poll (2023) 186
Young, Edward 177

Zahawi, Nadhim 115, 149
Zephaniah, Benjamin 228